Praise for

A CLASS APART

"[Captures] the distinctive and endearing atmosphere of a place 'where the brainiacs prevail.'"

—Ben Wildavsky, *The Washington Post Book World*

"Alec Klein, a masterful reporter and writer, weaves a spellbinding, sympathetic narrative about one of America's best high schools and how its remarkable students and teachers change each other's lives. *A Class Apart* also teaches an important lesson: that even the brightest youngsters—whom other schools often take for granted—need guidance and nurturing from caring adults."

—Dan Golden, Pulitzer Prize–winning reporter for *The Wall Street Journal* and author of *The Price of Admission*

"A vivid portrait of a school where learning is prized by all . . . a gripping view of a school where 'nerd' is considered, by the majority of students, an honored title."

—Adam Goldstein, *Rocky Mountain News*

"A brilliant, joyful, and important story—one of the most revelatory books in years about what's right and wrong in our education system. *A Class Apart* is filled with dramatic surprises, terrific writing, and insights about education in America. As a parent of a school-age child, it got my attention. As a reader, I couldn't put it down."

—Gary Cohn, Pulitzer Prize–winning investigative reporter

"*A Class Apart* is a breath of fresh air and a reminder that children with high IQs and test scores still are thriving in a rigorous academic environment.. . . The depth, quality, and compassion of [Klein's] narrative show his journalistic chops."

—Sophia Rodriguez, *The Post and Courier* (Charleston, SC)

"An honest and interesting book."

—Bob Blaisdell, *Chicago Tribune*

"The vast majority of *A Class Apart* is a bit like a version of *Ripley's Believe It or Not*. You read with jaw at half-mast, encountering one awe-inspiring student after another. . . . Klein doesn't just focus on the kids, though, who are only part of the mystery of Stuyvesant. We also meet quirky teachers and overworked parents who lovingly push their children to achieve the American dream. It is these characters who keep the pages turning at breakneck speed—that and Klein's snappy, journalistic prose."

—Caitlin Carpenter, *Christian Science Monitor*

"If Stuyvesant High School's students can embrace learning so enthusiastically, why can't everyone? Alec Klein, a young Stuyvesant alum familiar with the culture, devotes a year to diving back into the school's daily life in search of answers to that question. Klein's conclusions are surprising and have meaning for public schools everywhere."

—Jay Mathews, education reporter and columnist at *The Washington Post*

A Class Apart

Prodigies, Pressure, and Passion Inside
One of America's Best High Schools

Alec Klein

Simon & Schuster Paperbacks
NEW YORK LONDON TORONTO SYDNEY

For Ryan Isabella

SIMON & SCHUSTER PAPERBACKS
A Division of Simon & Schuster, Inc.
1230 Avenue of the Americas
New York, NY 10020

Designed by Paul Dippolito

Manufactured in the United States of America

1 3 5 7 9 10 8 6 4 2

Library of Congress Cataloging-in-Publication Data
Klein, Alec.
A class apart : prodigies, pressure and passion inside
one of America's best high schools / by Alec Klein.
p.   cm.
Includes bibliographical references and index.
1. Stuyvesant High School (New York, N.Y.) 2. Gifted
children—Education—New York (State)—New York.
I. Title.
LC3995.N5K54 2007
373.747'1—dc22   2007017058

ISBN-13: 978-0-7432-9944-2
ISBN-10:   0-7432-9944-2
ISBN-13: 978-0-7432-9945-9 (pbk)
ISBN-10:   0-7432-9945-0 (pbk)

Gatsby believed in the green light, the orgiastic future that year by year recedes before us. It eluded us then, but that's no matter—tomorrow we will run faster, stretch out our arms farther. . . . And one fine morning—

So we beat on, boats against the current, borne back ceaselessly into the past.

—F. SCOTT FITZGERALD, *THE GREAT GATSBY*

Contents

PART THREE: SENIORITIS
LATE APRIL–LATE JUNE

Prologue: Back to School

April 13, 2006, was like any other Thursday—except for this: I bought a pair of jeans riddled with shrapnel-sized holes. They call it the distressed look. But the only thing distressing about it was the price tag. Two rips by the zipper. One puncture of the left knee. Three gashes in the right shin. The backside shredded with four pockmarks. More than enough ventilation to produce an uncomfortable breeze. The jeans were brand-new but designed to look beat-up, as if I'd worn them in the most rugged of urban circumstances, like rappelling off the side of the Empire State Building. I could almost imagine the factory worker hunched over a worktable, whacking the jeans with a sturdy pickax to induce just the right number of fashionable holes. *So this is what it's come to*, I thought to myself, as I slipped on the torn jeans. *No. Check that. This is what* I've *come to. It's finally happened: I've become a teenager.*

Again.

Which is a strange thing for a middle-aged man like me who can barely remember puberty. When I graduated from Stuyvesant High School in 1985—was it that long ago?—I couldn't wait to get out, get on with the rest of my life, never thinking there was anything remarkable about this New York City school, never thinking I'd come back. But

1

then, more than two decades later, I returned to high school. And the strangest thing of all, I stayed for a while.

In January of 2006, I took a leave of absence from the *Washington Post*, where I am a staff writer, to document the life and times of students and teachers at what is widely considered to be one of the best—and weirdest—high schools in America.

Where else is it cooler to be a nerd who aces a differential equations test than a jock who masters the touchdown jig? How many other high schools can boast that hundreds of seniors annually gain admission to Ivy League colleges? Or that their alumni include a handful of Nobel laureates, Oscar winners, and other luminaries of the arts, industry, and public service. In a glowing story about Stuyvesant, *Life* magazine once posed the question in its headline: "Is This the Best High School in America?"

And this is a *public* school.

Stuyvesant, on the eve of the hundredth anniversary of its first graduating class in 1908, remains a model of academic excellence—public or private—while educators and policy makers decry the state of education in America, including the nation's estimated 25 percent dropout rate, as U.S. students fall behind those of other nations in their mastery of such vital subjects as math and science. Which, by the way, happen to be Stuyvesant's great strengths.

Stuyvesant remains the alternate universe of high school, where students are proud to admit they pull caffeinated all-nighters to study, where they don't want to leave school at day's end. "We have to sweep them out of the building," says Assistant Principal Eric Grossman, the school's popular English department chairman. In a high school that feels more like a college, there are virtually no fistfights, mostly only tussles over grades, which students calculate to the second decimal place, and there are no official class rankings because, well, hundreds of students maintain a high grade-point average, so what's the point? While high school football is worshipped in places like Texas, the deities at this school near the southern tip of Manhattan are the science geeks and the math wonks, and if they don't win science and math championships, hell hath no fury like an overinvolved parent. To underscore the point: there is no football field, but the school has a dozen state-of-the-art science labs.

Thomas Jefferson might have called such a place an aristocracy of talent. Stuyvesant boosters call it a meritocracy. Any eighth- or ninth-grade student in New York City can take the test to gain entrance to Stuyvesant. Critics, however, say the test makes Stuyvesant nothing more than an exclusive club, where only about 3 percent of applicants gain admission, and they argue that acceptance is not a measure of academic skills but of financial resources for those parents who can afford to send their children to costly prep courses, tutors, and private academies, sometimes starting in elementary school, with the single aim of winning a seat at Stuyvesant.

Whichever is true, it's hard to argue against the powerful idea that Stuyvesant is a kind of educational lottery ticket—a free elite high school education for the brightest, or at least the best prepared.

Not that I appreciated the place. That is, until March of 2004, when the Stuyvesant High School Alumni Association invited me to speak on a panel about corporate scandals, the subject of my first book, *Stealing Time: Steve Case, Jerry Levin, and the Collapse of AOL Time Warner*. It was my first visit to the old stomping grounds since I escaped from adolescence relatively unscathed. Buried for years, that queasy feeling came back instantly: was I late to school again? That, and a sensation that what had seemed so grand as a teenager had been reduced in size now that I was an adult, even the romantic sweep of the staircase from the school lobby to the second floor, which no longer looked so grand or romantic. I couldn't remember a solitary thing I learned in high school classes, not even the Pythagorean theorem. But a dollop of reminiscence struck me: how, on the first day of freshman year, an upperclassman offered to sell me a pass for a pool that didn't exist. Of Ron Cancemi, a school counselor who believed in me when I didn't, rest his soul. Of the time I professed my love for a girl from a nearby high school by spray-painting in gigantic letters "I LOVE YOU" on the broken asphalt of her school courtyard. Her boyfriend wanted to kill me. Of Dr. Bindman, a Stuyvesant English teacher who handed back a creative writing assignment to me with high praise, including the subversive suggestion, "Why don't you become a writer!" (I recently found the paper on a sweltering summer day in a musty cardboard box deep in the bowels of my dusty garage.) It was just the tonic for a fifteen-year-old boy in need of an idea.

And then there was Frank McCourt, another of my high school English teachers before he became a literary phenomenon, who once burst out of the front doors of the school, his nose bloodied reputedly at the hands of a friend of a Stuyvesant math teacher. Mr. McCourt was tough on the reputed friends of math teachers, charitable with the students. He bestowed on me a grade of 98 on my report card (a faded copy of which I found in the same cardboard box).

Who knew at the time what a unique place this was? The Pulitzer Prize–winning McCourt wrote a brief but loving ode to his experience at the school in *Teacher Man*. The school has been stitched into the fabric of literature: "it was nerd, nerd, nerd," wrote Jonathan Lethem in his best-selling novel *The Fortress of Solitude*. But no one had ever taken an in-depth look at the school and what made it so different. And that visit to the old school got me thinking: what can be more important than our children and the future? Nearly nine out of ten students in the United States are educated in the public schools—more than 48 million students—and they affect everyone, whether you're a taxpayer, a student, a parent, a teacher, or an employer. Few things inspire more passion in people than the education of our children. Schools don't just determine what communities we live in. They tell us about ourselves, our values, whether in the strife of desegregation, one of my early subjects as an education reporter in the South, or in the debate over how to educate the gifted and talented, like the denizens at Stuyvesant. This bizarre high school, where the brainiacs prevail, nonetheless tells the universal story of high school. The question, though, was, how do I get to the heart of the matter? There seemed only one answer: return to high school.

It's a rare gift to go back without all the bad stuff that comes with high school: the unending battery of tests and homework, the looming Damocles sword of college applications, the confusion of peer pressure (do this) and parental pressure (don't do that), the pressure to succeed, to be all you can be, to fulfill your potential, yadayadaya. This time around, mercifully, I didn't have to take a drafting class to learn how to draw a straight line. But it wasn't until I returned to Stuyvesant as an adult that I saw with clarity how the school had given me the gift of opportunity. How, for one, I still write today because when I was fifteen, I was inspired by Shakespeare's *Othello* and wrote a school musical, a magical experience even though school administrators changed the title from *Dead in Bed* to the less risqué *Mystery Tonight*. It was only when I returned to Stuyvesant twenty-some years later that I saw clearly just how high school is a microcosm of our society, driven by our deeply held beliefs about competition and rugged individualism and the idea that the best will prevail, even if that notion is perhaps sometimes just an illusion. At Stuyvesant, I witnessed the drama of adolescence that I had forgotten about, that parents don't hear about: first loves, illicit drugs, sudden death. Broader questions about how we teach children played out below the surface: Is it better to separate gifted and talented students into their own school, like Stuyvesant? Or is this a debilitating case of elitism in public education? What makes Stuyvesant—the kids who pass the test, or the school that educates them? And how do students cope with academic integrity, sexual discovery, and the complex burdens of being smart?

This much is certain: Stuyvesant is to many the embodiment of the American Dream, a school founded more than a century ago as a manual training school for boys that has become a haven for immigrants and the children of immigrants who want a better life. Stuyvesant's roughly three thousand students—packed about thirty-four per class—represent a kaleidoscope of ethnicities. Today, with more than half the students of Asian background, the school represents virtually every nationality and socioeconomic level, offering a window into the ethnic politics that pervade not just schools but communities throughout the nation. The school also offers a window into the dark side of the American Dream—unyielding competition, massive pressure, chronic cheating, racial divisions—leaving no student untouched.

For this book, the challenge was focusing on a handful of people who represent the great breadth of talent inhabiting the school. They weren't hard to find, even if I stumbled into most of them: a ten-year-old prodigy who has the memory of a computer chip. A sixteen-year-old football captain who taught himself calculus. A seventeen-year-old heroin junkie whose gift is the beautiful poetry she scrawls on paper. A dedicated teacher who suffers from depression and isn't supposed to be teaching because he lacks a license. An assistant principal who regularly breaks the rules if it means helping the kids.

To his credit, the school principal, Stan Teitel, never told me whom to interview, nor did he ask for any control over the book; it was essential to have this freedom so that I could write a true and accurate account, however unflattering some of the passages might be. Throughout my time at the school, I was acutely aware that although I'm an alumnus, I was not there as an advocate. I was an outsider, a journalist, whose story would carry meaning only if it was fair and whole. Rarely do schools allow a writer such latitude over an extended period, if only because even in the best of places, things can and do go wrong. But I was given free rein to roam about the school, including an open letter tucked in my pocket from the principal asking his staff to extend to me "every courtesy" in case they were wondering what a thirty-nine-year-old man was doing wandering the hallways or attending class. I never needed to show that letter to the students. My real pass with them was simply that I had graduated from Stuyvesant. I *knew*.

Plus, I had gone to Brown University, a fact that I never thought carried much weight in my career as a writer but now finally paid off. It represented credibility in a school where many students and even more parents worship at the altar of the Ivy League.

There was little formality to the reporting process, although I did ask parents of students under the age of eighteen to sign a consent form allowing their children to be interviewed and photographed for this book. Other authors have employed fictional names in writing about teenagers and high school life, but despite the many delicacies involved, I never use pseudonyms in the book. The narrative is a faithful account of the time that I spent at the school, written in the present tense when the action occurred, with ages and other facts reflecting the time covered. Some parents asked for the right to review their children's quotes before the book's publication, fearing what their children might say; I refused in each case, explaining that such censorship would compromise the integrity of the journalism. One parent went so far as to ask me to sign a waiver before speaking to her. I didn't. What I did promise—to myself—was that I would practice compassionate journalism, which is to say that I would remember that I was in many cases interviewing children, not adults, and that as such, it was important to keep in mind the repercussions of what they said or did. When a student left what appeared to be a suicide note, my first duty was not to document it as a detached journalist but to rush to school to do something about it. Fortunately, the student was alive.

Little did I realize what I was getting myself into when the semester started. In the first week, I came to a swift conclusion: I had all the wrong accoutrements. I should have known as much from the undergraduate students to whom I teach journalism at Georgetown University. Out went the briefcase, in came the North Face backpack. When I began to renovate my wardrobe, my wife, Julie-Ann, became alarmed. "You're starting to morph into a teenager; suddenly you want new shoes. Before you never liked to shop. Now we go to J. Crew and you shop like a madman!" (She said this while lying in bed as I was at my nearby desk, firing e-mails back and forth with a high school freshman and a senior, just before midnight.) The next morning, when I showed her my new Stuyvesant photo ID, she worried that I was slipping into a midlife crisis and added, "No sports car!"

She needn't have worried. I wasn't entering midlife. I was reverting to teen life. I went back to New York City, living the life, experiencing that crazy high school ritual all over again, rushing to catch a crammed subway down to Chambers Street on a daily basis, along with the hordes of students. It didn't take me long to realize that students respond faster to e-mail than to phone calls, even though almost all of them have their own cell phones, that they respond even faster to IM (instant messaging, to those of you not in the know), and if you really want to know what's going on, check out their blogs. Within weeks, it became all too clear that high school has become decidedly tougher, more competitive, and increasingly professional, both the organization of the school and the students who learn to master it. A month and a half into the semester, I knew more kids than many of the kids, judging by the number of them I was high-fiving in the hallways on my way to my next class. Proof of my regression: more than twenty years after I left her precalculus class, my high school math teacher, Ms. Schimmel, who was still teaching math at Stuyvesant, mistook me for a student when I rushed past her on my way into school (late again).

Somewhere along the way, my point of view began to evolve, which is another way of saying I began to see things as a teenager, chief among them that everything is momentous—whether the question is where to go to lunch or where to go with the rest of your life; that even while everything is of great consequence, high school is made up of small moments, taken in incremental steps; that you're just trying to deal with loneliness and heartache and who you are; that some adults are inflexible; and that you have to endure the injustices of it all, though sometimes I wasn't quite sure what *it* was. Even peer pressure got to me. When an amiable freshman noted I had frequently worn a blue-checked button-down shirt, I proceeded to leave the shirt in the dresser for an extended vacation.

Never could I say I was immune from the harmless offhand comments of a fourteen-year-old. And never could I imagine what a chaotic and full-time job it was. I spent more than a year interviewing, researching, and writing this book, but I have focused the narrative on the spring semester—the most intense period for Stuyvesant students who were grappling with the school's great musical contest, not to mention college admissions, senioritis, prom, graduation, and all that other stuff that happens after the final bell rings. As Danny Jaye, Stuyvesant's beloved math chairman, likes to say, "The greatness of the school is what happens after three o'clock."

Every semester is packed with drama—it's the nature of high school—but I could never have anticipated that I was capturing a seminal moment in time, when great eras were coming to an end at Stuyvesant, when harrowing events would explode on the scene, and when new—and sometimes unwelcome—change was about to unfold. A semester that sped by so quickly at first descended into a grind by the latter stages. It's not easy being a kid today. Take it from an adult.

Near the end, I found myself asking students and teachers to sign my yearbook, even though it wasn't *my* yearbook (mine had become sealed shut by a suburban basement flood years ago).

"Enjoy being a kid again," scribbled senior Julie Gaynin in my yearbook before she headed off to Macalester College. "I hope you've had fun going back to high school. Don't feel embarrassed, lots of people need an extra year before graduating."

Wrote Harvard-bound Becky Cooper, "You've continuously asked me what it is exactly that drives me to work. Recently, I read a paper by

Faulkner that talked about why he writes. 'To appease the demons inside him' or something like that. Well, there aren't demons, but I would say I work for maybe the same reason you write. It's a long, sometimes painful process, but it's just something you have to do. (I think.) That's kind of what it's like for me. I work because I care and I care because I know nothing else."

Before moving on to Yale University, Stuyvesant Student Union President Kristen Ng wrote in my yearbook, "We're a diverse, and, dare I say, very odd bunch. Thanks for listening 2 us and deciding that diverse & odd is a good thing."

All along, I was aware of how foolish I probably looked, a veritable middle-aged man lugging around a yearbook meant for others. But I didn't care. That is the right of a veritable middle-aged man; I'm less afraid than teenagers to humiliate myself in public. I have had more practice in the art. Besides, the yearbook held a cherished place in my heart, for what it represented: the openness and innocence and the evanescence of youth. They tell the truth. They cry so easily. They thirst for knowledge, for connection, for beauty. They haven't become guarded, jaded adults yet. Thank goodness.

Alec Klein
February 2007,
Washington, D.C.

PART ONE: DELANEY CARDS

Early February–Early March

CHAPTER ONE

Romeo

IT'S 7:38 A.M., AND AN OLD MAN BOXES A PHANTOM
on Grand Street, jabbing and slicing the crisp air with his withered fists,
the first ambition of the day. The rest of the morning awakens in slow
motion on this unforgiving stretch of asphalt on the Lower East Side, a
hardscrabble neighborhood on the edge of Chinatown in Manhattan.
The Grand Spa down the block isn't open yet. Nor is the next-door
Liquor & Wines. Nor Chester Fried Chicken across the street. All that
can be traced on this gray February morning is the wisp of breath billowing like wordless cartoon bubbles from anonymous pedestrians as
they trudge to work, huddled against the coming snowstorm.

And then from out of a nondescript red brick high-rise, Romeo
emerges. Like the old man, he looks ready to wage combat against the
day. That's the message conveyed in his baggy black Sean John jacket
and baggy black Sean John jeans and black scarf and black skullcap and
black shoes. But it's just urban utilitarian fashion—black against the
muted gray hues of the rising day—which does little to disguise his
broad shoulders or his chiseled 195-pound frame or the ferocity that he
brings to the football field as a bruising tight end and defensive end who

also played running back last season because he's so good, the best on his team. Romeo can bench more than his own weight—225 pounds— no problem. Not that he needs to prove it. Jersey number ninety-eight commands respect, and the girls adore all six foot three inches of him— the swagger, the charm, the dreadlocks, the silver earring in the left ear, the dark brooding eyes, the ambiguous smile full of braces.

Romeo is an archetype of the high school idol, a popular, powerful captain of his football team, except for one thing—Romeo Alexander is also a sixteen-year-old math whiz.

He taught himself calculus by reading a tattered textbook. Then he got the top score on the advanced placement test and skipped a course in calculus to go straight into differential equations, the *really* hard kind of math. Girls flock to him for tutoring help, boys plead for help on homework.

Not your typical high school jock.

"I do a lot of math in my free time," he says without a hint of brag-gadocio. "After a while, it becomes a sport, fun."

If only the football team was as much fun. Last season, the team lost its first game sixty-four to zero, and it just got worse. The team stum-bled to a one-and-eight record, its sole victory earned by default: the other team couldn't field enough players. Romeo's team was lucky to eke out the one victory. The school doesn't have its own football field. The team has to take a yellow school bus from Manhattan to Brooklyn to reach its so-called home field at another public school. The practice field is about a mile away, and it's not even a football field; it's a *soccer* field. Players say a mutiny forced the head coach to resign. "Almost nobody on the team liked him," a teammate was quoted in the school newspaper, the *Spectator*, which cited accusations of the coach's "extreme emotional outbursts." And to top it off, on a good day, only about ten Stuyvesant parents show up for a game.

"Nobody really cares," Romeo says. "It has its down moments."

A defensive tackle adds that it gets so bad that teammates don't like to brag about being on the team: "We don't really go around advertising it."

Perhaps the worst indignity, at least to Romeo, is the team name: the Peglegs. The moniker comes from the school's namesake, Peter Stuyvesant, the crotchety Dutch colonial governor of New Amsterdam, a man who hobbled around on one good leg, the other having been blown off by a cannon shot and replaced by a wooden leg. Such associations don't seem to inspire athletic greatness on the gridiron. Romeo would've preferred "the Flying Dutchmen." That suggests a certain grace—nay, supernatural abilities—which are sorely needed on the field.

But then again, this is Stuyvesant High School. And here, football doesn't matter. The brainiacs rule.

Romeo understands that, embraces it. Football drills under a baking sun don't match the pain of the academic workouts under a small pool of lamplight, the relentless nights when Romeo sits hunched over his small wooden desk, cloistered in his room, studying until two, three, four o'clock in the morning—unless he dozes off while studying. His mother, Catherine Wideman, sleeps fitfully, knowing her son is up late studying, the only evidence a sliver of illumination emanating from the slit at the bottom of his shut door.

"Do you know it's two o'clock in the morning?" she will ask, knocking on his door.

"When the lights are off, I can relax," she says.

Not Romeo. Recently, he printed eight-and-a-half by eleven-inch signs from his computer and taped them up in his room, lashing Orwellian words to inspire, drive, compel.

Over his desk: "Discipline."

Over his bed: "Work is fun."

On his door: "The world is yours."

Conquering the world begins when he climbs aboard the overcrowded M22 public bus as it careens toward Stuyvesant on this chilly morning. "I was always the type of person who said I have to work harder, suffer," he says matter-of-factly.

For Romeo, an average of four hours of sleep has yielded a grade-point average on the high end of 96 out of a 100—near perfection. "Some people calculate it to the last decimal," he says. Romeo, however, doesn't debase himself with such picayune detail. "The way I see it, it's high."

Now all he has to do is maintain that near perfection during this, his junior year, the most critical period in his high school career, the sweet spot for colleges examining the almighty academic transcript of grades.

At least, that's his goal. That, and acing the dreaded SAT, required by most colleges, the single exam that can wipe out all his academic success in one fell swoop if he doesn't get a high score. It's not a question of bombing on the SAT: there's no chance of that, it doesn't compute. But even a slight misstep—a mathematical miscalculation, a reading comprehension snafu—could lower his score ever so slightly, which would ruin Romeo's goal, achieving a perfect 2400, a rarity not even reached by most supersavants.

"Above twenty-three hundred is reasonable," he concedes.

That still leaves precious little margin for error. Which is why, tomorrow, he begins his SAT prep course at school, a grueling process involving forsaken Saturdays leading up to the test in June. Romeo, the product of a modest upbringing—the son of a struggling musician and a struggling freelance writer—is keenly aware of the five-hundred-dollar cost of the class, even though it pales in comparison to the expense of other private tutoring courses, totaling in the thousands, if not the tens of thousands, the built-in advantage of the wealthy and privileged.

For Romeo, this is only the beginning of the price of admission to the college of his dreams: Harvard University.

But now, sitting in the back of the bus on his way to school, peering through the smudged window as City Hall scrolls by, Harvard is a mirage, and the only sound he's hearing is the remembered voice of his father. Romeo calls it "the famous speech," the time when Romeo was fourteen and his divorced father, a former funk singer still known as Prinz Charles, who lives in Harlem, lectured him on the realities of life, urging his son to grab the American Dream—to go to school, get a job, be comfortable for the rest of his life. Father told son, *You've got to rise up and take the reins.*

His mother, a French former journalist, offered a different vision of the future, one in which Romeo would become a great scholar-athlete, much like her second husband, John Edgar Wideman, a Brown University professor and venerated author who became Romeo's stepfather about four years ago. Mr. Wideman was himself a celebrated student in his youth. At the age of twenty-one, he was the subject of a *Look* magazine article entitled "The Astonishing John Wideman," which hailed his many accomplishments, including a Rhodes Scholarship following his

Ivy League education at the University of Pennsylvania, where he was captain of the basketball team and elected to the prestigious Phi Beta Kappa honors society. It was at Romeo's age that Mr. Wideman's son, Jacob, stabbed to death another boy of sixteen, for which Jacob was sentenced to life in prison. Romeo doesn't talk about the tragedy, or the shadow of expectations that comes with an accomplished stepfather. Mother told son, *I just want you to be happy.*

And what does Romeo want?

"I want to help save the world."

He makes such a startling declaration with the same equanimity as a boy simply saying he is going to school, and both statements are to be believed. He doesn't know it yet, but today at school he will meet a seventy-eight-year-old New York University professor dying of cancer for whom Romeo will volunteer his services in unraveling the secrets of fusion. To Romeo, it will be an experiment for a prestigious national science contest, but if it's successful—more of a wild dream than a remote possibility—the project could provide energy to light entire cities, which would certainly fulfill his mission to achieve greatness. As a career choice, Romeo didn't have any say in the matter, not when the decision was made for him before birth. Or so he will soon write in his autobiography, an assignment for an upcoming English class:

> My dad wanted me to become a star, in the most general sense. One way to make that happen was by giving me a name that would catch people's attention, that would constantly put me under the spotlight. My father was a star himself—a musician—that's how he seduced my mother in France. My mother, along the same lines, wanted me to become a great intellectual genius. That, I believe, comes from her father, who would be very pleased if all his grandchildren went to prestigious universities. Thus, Romeo was planned out and defined before I was even born.

His father, speaking to his wife's pregnant belly, recited simple math while Romeo rested in the womb: one plus one, two plus two, four plus four. "I did it, and we got some pretty good results," Charles Alexander says. He continued to challenge his son after his birth, speaking to

Romeo not as a child but almost like an adult. "I didn't baby-talk him," he says. And always, the mantra was the same: "You can get this," his father would say, urging on his son. If his parents had any concern about Romeo as a child, it was that he was not aggressive. "Very passive," his father says. "Gandhi," that's what his mother called him. She always had great expectations for her only child. "I was on his case," she says, laughing shyly about the days when he was in elementary school and she was sometimes "screaming" at him to do his work, threatening to throw his video game out the window. She still prods him when his drive begins to flag. "I'm very ambitious for him," she says.

Another secret of his success: she started Romeo in martial arts when he was seven, demanding he never miss a class.

Romeo: "It taught me to get used to pain."

She says it taught something else: "Discipline."

"There is a life of the mind in this house that we value," adds Romeo's stepfather, referring to the way that he challenges Romeo to think, asking questions the teenager can't answer and talking at the dinner table about intellectually enriching issues like politics and history.

For Romeo, though, all that doesn't exactly explain how he got to this point, riding on this bus, going to this school, on the cusp of this future.

"I think a lot about that," he says, giving credit in part to good luck and what he calls "social Darwinism." But he isn't sure how to explain his accomplishments, except to say, "I always like to see it as my own doing, that I did it myself."

Football wasn't part of the plan. Until he was twelve, he didn't even like football. He watched the Super Bowl only for the ostentatious television commercials. But then his father taught him how to play a football video game, and it meant something deeper. "It was the first time I started hanging out with my dad," he says. It helped too that his father came from Boston, and the New England Patriots won their first Super Bowl. Success bred interest, and now his father tapes every one of his son's football games.

Math, though, was the way for Romeo to pave his way to stardom. In the eighth grade he joined the school math team. Then the summer after his freshman year at Stuyvesant, he borrowed a friend's textbook to teach himself calculus, which he viewed as an exalted form of math because students often don't learn it until college, if at all.

"I always thought calculus was one of the secrets of the world," he says.

Romeo was also smitten with a girl a grade above him who already was taking calculus. If he could learn calculus on his own, he figured he could skip the first-year course and catch up with the girl, sitting in the same class with her for second-year calculus. His friends teased him about the bookish, bespectacled girl. More brains than beauty, they said. But no matter.

With trepidation, Romeo ventured online to sign up for the advanced placement test and pushed the button to pay the eighty-dollar fee. Like a football player drilling himself to perfection, Romeo practiced calculus over spring break. The result: "The test was so easy." He earned a five, the top score. He also zipped through the school's department final with a grade of 98, and the Stuyvesant math chairman saw no reason to waste Romeo's time with first-year calculus. Romeo was in love—with math.

"When I met math and logic, it was like, 'Wow, this is how I'm going to understand the world,'" he says. "Maybe that's why I like math. I was searching for something."

But he quickly made another discovery: "In higher math," he says, "there are uncertainties."

So too with girls.

A month ago, he met a sophomore at a party. She asked him to dance. And now he has the first girlfriend of his life. Last night, his father gave him the birds and bees speech—"the advanced course," Romeo quips.

The girl chose him; he didn't choose her. That's what he tells himself. Otherwise, it wouldn't have happened. He wouldn't have allowed it. Girls, he thought, would be a distraction, take him from work. His friends, on the same grueling academic mission, preach the same ascetic gospel.

"We talk about dominating the world and power and how women bring you down—adolescent stuff," he says, aware of his own foolishness.

Just in case he needs a reminder, there's always a girl, Xevion Baptiste, a fellow junior, frequent lunch companion, and self-appointed conscience, to put Romeo in his place—or at least try.

"I'm always telling him to put down his book, and he won't listen to me," she says. "I'll call him at midnight and say, 'Talk to me.' He says, 'All right, I have two seconds.' He's brilliant. He just needs to lighten up a little."

It's a struggle. Romeo has conditioned himself to suppress his emotions, to be strong, to be heroic, driven by a need to win, succeed, achieve. He's reminded of Raskolnikov, the tormented figure who neglects human emotion in Dostoyevsky's *Crime and Punishment*, which he's reading for fun. (He also subscribes to the *Economist* for fun.) The internal conflict even imbues Romeo's own fiction: "You know as well as anyone else that the only way for there to be any productive progression in the history of humanity, science, and technology, you must be willing to make a few sacrifices of the mind and body," the main character tells himself in a science-fiction story that garnered Romeo a national writing award.

Suddenly, though, Romeo's been thrown off kilter. Maybe, he thinks, it's chemical. He just read an article in *National Geographic* about the physiological reactions of people in love. Their brains look like "someone who has a disorder," he says.

The only symptom Romeo detects in himself is some kind of stomach pain. But maybe it's just because it's all beginning—the morning, the semester, his life. It's 8:23 a.m., and Romeo is about to disembark from the bus and enter Stuyvesant High School, ready to wage combat against the day.

CHAPTER TWO

The Gauntlet

AFTER ROMEO CLIMBS OFF THE RUMBLING BUS, HE shifts into automatic, taking morning steps choreographed by days of sheer repetition, from freshman to junior year, taking little notice of the immediate but unstated fact confronting him: that what he is fast approaching is an extraordinary place.

He begins by climbing a set of concrete stairs curving to the Tribeca Bridge. After he reaches the landing, for the next 250 feet, he is sealed in a 13-foot-wide passageway of glass above West Street, a hyperkinetic highway where drivers are hurtling in both directions. All the while, Romeo is oblivious to the enormity of the steel expanse he is crossing and the striving it implies—oblivious to the 5 tons of paint that it took to coat it, to the 250 tons suspended above Manhattan traffic, to its $10 million cost. What Romeo knows is, this pedestrian bridge is the only way students can enter and leave Stuyvesant High School—a span crossing an urban moat into a magical educational kingdom.

How else to explain the gleaming $150 million edifice that stands before him, one of the costliest high schools ever built?

At nearly twice its original price tag, the building replaced a dilapidated dwelling squatting unceremoniously across town on Fifteenth Street near First Avenue. The new building on the West Side opened to students on September 9, 1992, at 345 Chambers Street, where luxury housing was once intended, in the trendy milieu of Tribeca, haunt of well-appointed bistros, Robert De Niro, and New York hipsters with bank. Ensconced on the banks of the Hudson River, with spectacular views of the Statue of Liberty, the school sits near Wall Street on a land-fill packed with earth excavated when the World Trade Center was built. Now that site is Ground Zero, a crater four blocks away, an eerie, hollow reminder of the September 11, 2001, terrorist attacks that temporarily turned a traumatized Stuyvesant into an emergency shelter for rescue workers.

Bathed in early morning light, the school today sits majestically undisturbed, soaring from a base of limestone into a tan brick building ten stories high, twice the height of the usual New York City high school. Because it's wedged into a one-and-a-half-acre site, there was only one way to go: skyward.

The grandeur of the place is instantly conveyed from the first floor, a stately terrazzo entrance hall in black and gray accents, adorned with art deco lights and embellished with the following Latin phrase engraved in polished gray granite rising from a set of classic black columns:

PRO SCIENTIA ATQUE SAPIENTIA

For Knowledge and Wisdom. A pair of gray marble staircases climb to the second floor, a subtle nod to the sweeping beaux arts staircase at the old school building. On the second level, one-legged Peter Stuyvesant sternly gazes down from an oil portrait that once hung in the paint-chipped school building across town. But just beyond the school's namesake is one feature disconnected from the past: a series of escalators that rise through the building's core—rise, that is, when they're not malfunctioning or a student hasn't hijacked an escalator key (black-market price: $1) and derailed students from scampering to their next class within the appointed four-minute break.

The real action takes place throughout the building in a series of science labs, robotics workshops, drafting rooms, and shops for metalworking, woodworking, plastics, ceramics, and photography. Classrooms come equipped with television monitors. Walls are lined with fiber optics. More than 450 computers populate the school. Students almost take for granted the world-class facilities—the wood-paneled theater with orchestra pit, balcony, and movable partitions; the dining hall (so named because it's not merely a cafeteria) that commands panoramic views of the Hudson River; the library with the sun-filtered southern exposure and the columned loggia.

It's true there are no playing fields—no football stadium, no baseball diamond, no tennis courts. But, hey, this is Stuyvesant, and as Mr. Teitel, the principal, says, "The superintendent [of New York City schools] is not going to call me if we don't have a winning basketball team . . . no one's going to call me if the football team has a three-and-five record." On the other hand, if Stuyvesant fails to win a slew of national math and science awards, he says with a knowing, if beleaguered, smile, "my phone will ring."

Besides, it's not as if the school ignores athletics altogether. Stuyvesant does have two full-size gyms and a seventy-five-foot-long swimming pool, standard for Public School Athletic League competition. And by the standards of public education, where some schools look more like prisons under lockdown, there's little like it.

"It's like going to school at Club Med," writes recent Stuyvesant graduate Ned Vizzini in his published autobiography, *Teen Angst? Naaah . . .*

The school designers are more humble about their work. "Its architecture will never live up to the institution itself," says Karen Cooper, a principal at Cooper, Robertson & Partners, one of the building's architects, "because obviously it's a rather formidable institution."

Actually, the feel of the place is anything but formidable. The students have made it their own, reducing the towering citadel of learning into a veritable homespun bulletin board, covering the building on a daily basis with taped-up flyers announcing extracurricular activities, such as "Pie a Teacher!!!" (The raffle ticket proceeds will help "build schools in villages in 3rd world countries!") Flyers are also the province of abject public apologies by a boyfriend, identified only as "pathetic loser," to a girlfriend for a forgotten special occasion: "If you made your girl feel special, help a stranger in making my girl feel like the one in a million billion gajillion girls that she is. . . ." And on some occasions, the makeshift flyers attempt to inspire:

> *Life has a higher end,*
> *than to be amused.*
>
> —WILLIAM ELLERY CHANNING

In this free-flowing atmosphere, students sprawl out on hallway floors, camping out amid friends and the accoutrements of adolescence: iPods (playing the Beatles, cool again), North Face backpacks, cell phones with built-in cameras, and Sidekicks for instant messaging when spoken discourse just won't fly. And the language of the moment is a curious blend of slang where everything is "mad," if not "ill," or "sick," all of which are good things, while being "emo," or emotional, isn't cool, though "cool" isn't cool, but "hot" is, and the righteous "word" has made a strong comeback as a general affirmation and the perennial "whatever" suffices when nothing more need be said.

When language is too far removed from—or too close to—the idea being communicated, unspoken physicality still works, as in prevailing fashions, the gestalt of which seems to indicate that no effort was involved in the selection of clothes and accessories, that the ensemble was just thrown together, patterns butting heads with shapes, which, of course, is a complete lie, because it's all about coordination, cause and effect, especially among many of the girls. (The idea of fashion among the majority of boys is truly haphazard: a pair of jeans under an ill-fitting T-shirt.) Thick belts with massive buckles cinch around shirts so long that they serve as skirts. Frayed denim miniskirts cover a small amount of real estate over tights, thanks in part to teenage fashionista Lindsay Lohan, who helps give currency to the hip-hugging leggings and the dark nail polish painted on legions of like-minded girls. Owing to a teen icon of another generation, Jennifer Beals of *Flashdance* fame, sweatshirts torn at the neck and dripping off a shoulder are making a comeback. Of less determinate provenance, unless such purveyors as Urban Outfitters, Ecko, and Akademiks are to be blamed, are the frilly tops, the layer upon layer of cheap necklaces, the wisps of scarves, the cavalry of cowboy boots and those other throwbacks, Vans and Converse canvas white-tipped high-tops, particularly in shades of bright green.

But that could be any high school.

It could be argued that Stuyvesant is set apart from other schools by its more than two hundred clubs, ranging from the Bookworm to the N.A.R.F. (Neo-postmodern Artistic and Recreational Forum). Or by its thirty-some student publications, including *two* competing school newspapers and a third solely devoted to politics. Or by course offerings as diverse as the English department's existentialism and the biology department's vertebrate zoology.

But that's not it, not really.

"The *students* make Stuy what it is," says one who knows firsthand, Namita Biala, a senior off to Princeton University, echoing the sentiment of many students, teachers, and administrators.

Converging on the school from five boroughs, some traveling as long as two hours by subway, Stuyvesant students have compiled a stunning record of achievement. Laurels and trophies are regularly heaped on the math team—numbering about five hundred, or one in six students in the entire school—as well as the nationally recognized debate team and the official school newspaper, the *Spectator*, each claiming about two hundred members. Every year, Stuyvesant produces among the country's highest number of National Merit Scholars, whose distinction is based on students' performance on the Preliminary SAT/National Merit Scholarship Qualifying Test; in 2006, ninety-nine Stuyvesant students were finalists. By comparison, there is on average one finalist for about every two public high schools in America. Stuyvesant also consistently generates several semifinalists and finalists annually in the prestigious Intel Science Talent Search; the school has produced more than seven hundred semifinalists and over a hundred finalists since the contest's inception in the 1940s. And of the 2,800 advanced placement tests administered at the school yearly, usually more than 90 percent of the students earn at least a three out of five, school administrators say, a score that the College Board defines as meaning students are "qualified" to receive college credit or advanced placement. More than 70 percent achieve scores of four, considered "well qualified," or five, "extremely well qualified."

It's almost an afterthought that 97 percent of Stuyvesant students graduate within four years of the ninth grade, according to the New

York City Department of Education. But that's a notable achievement compared to only 75 percent nationally who graduate on time, U.S. Department of Education figures show.

Even more remarkable, Stuyvesant students' average SAT score is a 691 out of 800 in verbal and 725 in math, according to figures furnished by the school to the New York State Education Department. That places the average Stuyvesant student in about the 95th percentile nationally in both categories, according to statistics from the College Board, which administers the test. The average U.S. test scores are nowhere near—508 in verbal, 520 in math.

With such high SAT scores at Stuyvesant, it's not surprising that virtually all its graduates enroll in four-year colleges, school statistics show, compared to only 67 percent of high school graduates nationally who enroll in either two- or four-year colleges, according to the U.S. Department of Education. But what is stunning is that about one in four of Stuyvesant's graduating class of about eight hundred wins entrance to an Ivy League college, school administrators say. In some years, Harvard accepts more students from Stuyvesant—over twenty—than from any other public or private school. Many students view Ivies like Cornell University as a *safety* school. And Stuyvesant sends many students to several other popular destinations outside the Ivies, such as the Massachusetts Institute of Technology, Stanford University, and a number of other equally selective colleges.

Perhaps the truest measure of Stuyvesant's greatness is what its students do after they leave school. Four alumni have gone on to win the Nobel Prize: Joshua Lederberg, in 1958 for physiology or medicine, cited for "his discoveries concerning genetic recombination and the organization of the genetic material of bacteria"; Roald Hoffmann, in 1981 in chemistry, for theories "concerning the course of chemical reactions"; Robert W. Fogel, in 1993 in economics, for "having renewed research in economic history by applying economic theory and quantitative methods in order to explain economic and institutional change"; and Richard Axel, in 2004 in physiology or medicine, for "discoveries of odorant receptors and the organization of the olfactory system."

Few high schools can boast such an alumni lineup, which also includes Eric S. Lander, a leader of the Human Genome Project in the race to break the human genetic code, and Col. Ron Grabe, lead astronaut for the development of the International Space Station. He took a Stuyvesant pennant with him when the *Atlantis* space shuttle circled the globe in 1989. For a school traditionally strong in math and the sciences, Stuyvesant also has cultivated a wealth of artists and performers, such as Academy Award winners James Cagney and Tim Robbins, jazz musician Thelonious Monk, plus a number of Emmy and Grammy winners and even an international sex symbol, actress Lucy Liu.

Less heralded are the school's handful of Olympic medalists, members of Congress, federal judges, and industry titans, including Jeffrey Loria, owner of baseball's Florida Marlins, and Arthur Blank, cofounder of Home Depot, one of the largest retailers in the world. (See Appendix of Notable Alumni.)

Many who have gone on to achieve greatness share one trait: they first walked the halls of Stuyvesant as nerds.

The tradition continues today.

"I embrace being a dork," says Becky, a senior who scored a 790 in math, a perfect 800 in English, and a perfect 800 in the new writing category on the SAT, and carried a 97.79 average into this, the second semester of her last year.

As proof, Becky offers up the following joke: A neutron walks into a bar, and asks how much for beer.

The punch line: No charge.

Becky can get away with such a typical Stuyvesant joke because she's not only a nerd. She also happens to be a beautiful cheerleader whom many of the boys love. So she can be forgiven for going to Harvard.

Everybody's in on the joke, anyway, even late-night television comic Conan O'Brien, a high school dork in his day who also attended Harvard. As the commencement speaker at Stuyvesant's 2006 graduation, O'Brien paid tribute to the students by poking fun at them in the most appropriate way: "Today, Stuyvesant has a remarkably diverse and varied student body, ranging from math geeks to science nerds. Yes, you are a glorious, beautiful rainbow of brainiacs."

The laughter from the gallery was deafening—and knowing. The audience is all too aware that they derive from the same pool: a highly select group of students who passed the harrowing Specialized High Schools Admissions Test—otherwise known as the Stuy test. It's like the SAT, except that unlike the college admissions process, which also involves essays, teacher recommendations, and school transcripts, the Stuy test is basically an all-or-nothing affair. Make the test cutoff, and you're in Stuyvesant. If you come up short, no dice.

Stuyvesant is the most selective of the city's eight elite specialized public exam high schools. Of the estimated twenty-six thousand students who take the test annually, only those with the highest scores—about eight hundred students—gain entrance to Stuyvesant. (Students can be denied even if they reach the Stuyvesant cutoff, if they don't pick the school as their first choice.)

"It's harder to get into Stuy than to get into Harvard," says Wyndam Makowsky, the incoming editor in chief of the *Spectator*, the school newspaper. That's true at least on a statistical basis, since the high school accepts only about 3 percent of those who take the test, while Harvard admits about 9 percent of freshman applicants.

"You could theoretically buy your way into Harvard, but you can't buy your way into Stuyvesant," says Mr. Teitel, the principal.

The Stuy test is open to all New York City residents, although it's an open secret that some parents who live beyond the city limits will, to avoid expensive private schools or bad public ones, cheat on the residency requirement. For instance, they will have mail sent to a relative who lives in New York City to establish residency for the family and qualify their children for the test.

Such tactics hardly assure their children a seat at Stuyvesant.

The 150-minute multiple-choice test is divided into two grueling sections, verbal and math, each with its own twists and pitfalls.

The *Specialized High Schools Student Handbook* offers the following question as a verbal example of a logical reasoning question on the test:

There are five bookshelves on the wall. The bottom shelf is Shelf 1, the top shelf is Shelf 5. Each shelf is filled with books of one color.

1. The red books are above the green books.
2. The yellow books are below the blue books.

3. The orange books are between the red books and the yellow books.
4. The yellow books are on Shelf 2.

Which color books are on Shelf 1?

A. red
B. green
C. blue
D. orange
E. Cannot be determined from the information given.

(Answer: B)

The math questions are just as challenging. An example from the handbook:

What is the smallest positive odd integer that is not immediately adjacent to an integer power of 2?

A. 1
B. 3
C. 5
D. 11
E. There is no such number.

(Answer: D)

The competition for Stuyvesant's limited seats is so fierce that some students begin to prepare for the high school test several years in advance—when they are ten years old, or younger. Indeed, the demand to get into Stuyvesant is so great that a number of Asian academies designed to help students crack the test have sprung up throughout the borough of Queens, appealing to immigrants who see education—and Stuyvesant in particular—as the key to their families' future. Alexa Solimano, who is half Korean and half of mixed Irish and Italian descent, entered such an academy in the fifth grade, and she says, "I don't think I would've gotten into Stuyvesant without it."

Now a freshman, Alexa still attends the academy on Saturdays to get ahead, doing academy homework on top of her regular high school homework. While she is studying algebra and geometry at Stuyvesant this year, she's already digging into trigonometry and precalculus at the private academy to get a jump start on the next two years of math. She's also studying for the SAT, the first practice test for which she took in the sixth grade.

"College seems so far away," says the fourteen-year-old, "but I know it's not."

With such an attitude pervasive at Stuyvesant, what predominates are professional test-taking students who have accepted a culture of ambition, where pressure is a natural by-product. That pressure, though, is extreme and self-selective, like a rare strain of hyper-Darwinism, and it infects students in every grade.

Freshman Susan Levinson, at lunch, ponders, half kidding, the meaning of an algebra test she recently flubbed with a grade of 69, possibly the worst mark in her life: "I'm going to fail the class, which means I'm not going to get into college, which means I'm not going to get a job, then I'm going to live with my parents, then I'm not going to get a boyfriend, then I'm not going to have kids, I'll have nothing to live for, I'll do drugs and become a bum—because I failed a math test."

Sophomore Brittany DiSanto, at the school library, is pallid after her last class, in which she too thinks she just bombed her math test in algebra and trigonometry: "Everyone wants to have that good GPA." She says some students, though not she, smoke cigarettes "to relieve stress."

Junior Andrew Saviano, sitting in a third-floor hallway, shows no signs of fatigue even though he manages only about three to four hours of sleep a night. "I like to think of it as the mind doesn't get tired, the body does." Sometimes he works by the sole light of computer glare in the *Spectator* newspaper office so he won't get caught at school in the wee hours of the morning. He maintains a 97 average and nearly perfect SAT scores. He admits, however, "There's the stress, there's the not sleeping, there's the coffee and other stimulants," which, for him, means tea. He also admits there is a toll: "I do suffer from it. I don't grow." He has been five foot seven since the beginning of the school year. "I don't care about being tall," he says.

Senior Kristen Chambers, in a café outside school, ruminates about how she hates Stuyvesant. She tried to persuade her parents to let her transfer to a less stressful Catholic school in her Brooklyn neighborhood and can't wait to escape at graduation: "It's very competitive, it's not comforting to me, I'm always on edge."

Reminders of what's at stake are everywhere. An advertisement for the Kaplan test prep service in the school newspaper puts it in stark terms:

Higher score.
Brighter future.

Academic pressure is always in the air, a frequent topic of conversation in hallways, where the latest test is frequently followed by the refrain, "What'd you get? What'd you get?" Student publications bemoan students' obsession with tests, grades, and colleges. "In the midst of APs and college applications, many students have a hard time finding the meaning to it all," writes the opinions editor of the *Stuyvesant Standard* newspaper. "Classes are just taken for the grades, and those are only for the application to an Ivy League university." In another student publication, *Stuy Health*, a front-page article entitled "Stopping Stress at Stuyvesant" offers remedies that would be obvious to an otherwise normal student body, like having *friends*. The problem of pressure even comes up at a Parents' Association meeting, where students on a panel try to explain the Stuyvesant phenomenon. In a school of overachievers, "the pressure is crazy," one student says.

Teachers are acutely aware of the ponderous atmosphere weighing on students. Some are known to inflate students' grades, even unprompted. Others, like Michael Waxman, a popular social studies and foreign language teacher, can only wonder what the fuss is all about. He says that a student in his Hebrew class warned him at the beginning of the term that she "better get a ninety-six" in his class.

"Why?" he asked.

Apparently she was concerned about getting into college.

She was in the ninth grade.

As the semester wore on, she requested to see his grade book and demanded to know how he calculated her grade. During a Hebrew vocabulary test, she broke down crying, banged her desk, and rushed out of the room.

The problem? She couldn't remember a couple of answers.

Mr. Waxman gently tried to explain that it's okay not to be perfect, that she was allowed to get a couple of answers wrong. She wasn't convinced. Still upset, she proceeded to give him a negative rating on a popular Web site, www.ratemyteacher.com.

"The chutzpah," he says, resting his hand wearily against his forehead.

Chutzpah of another sort greeted Eleanor Archie, assistant principal for pupil services, from the moment she arrived at Stuyvesant in 1992 as a guidance counselor. Her first student barged into her office sobbing because of the grade she had just received in a math class: 97.

"I'm going, 'So where's the problem?'" Ms. Archie recalls.

The student had expected nothing less than perfection.

She too was a freshman.

"Then I realize, I'm in a population that's so stressful, everyone wants to get a hundred," Ms. Archie says.

"It is tempting, and easy, to become such a part of the system, to become so transformed by the work and the competition and the pressure that you lose yourself in them, so much so that, in the end, you yourself are responsible for sustaining them," Mr. Grossman, the English chairman, cautioned students in a graduation speech a couple of years ago. "It is dangerous too, because Stuyvesant's imperfections are the world's, it is a smaller city within a larger one."

But the pressure isn't coming only from students. "I have spoken to parents that will tell me, 'If my child doesn't get into an Ivy, I'm not paying for college,'" Ms. Archie says.

Irate, overbearing parents are a common phenomenon at Stuyvesant. One parent called Mr. Waxman, the Hebrew teacher, to ask, "Is there something wrong with my son?" There wasn't. The father then wanted an explanation for his son's grade. "Why did he only get a ninety-eight?" At the recent induction ceremony of the Stuyvesant National Hebrew Honor Society, one unscheduled feature was a parent who complained to Mr. Waxman that he moved too slowly in class for his daughter, after which the parent summarily left. And the mother of a student in his economics class wrote a note to Mr. Waxman, asking him to reschedule his upcoming test because her daughter had four other exams on the same day. As an incentive, the mother, who ran an Asian restaurant in Manhattan, offered to serve him sushi "free free free."

He declined.

"You can't make this stuff up," he marvels.

The school tries to counsel parents to ease up on their kids. At a School Tone Committee meeting, parents are given a handout entitled "Being a Stuyvesant Parent: What Your Kids Hope For."

Under the category "What You Shouldn't Be Doing," the flyer recommends against such common parental practices at Stuyvesant as

1. Demanding certain grades; instead ask that your child puts in his/her best effort;
2. Comparing your child's performance with other students or family members, or frequently asking how other students are doing;
3. Nagging underclassmen about college, portraying college as the be-all and end-all;
4. Deciding your goals for your child are synonymous with your child's goals for him/herself;
5. Pressuring kids to take more and harder classes. They should take classes in which they're interested, and should not take on too heavy a course load;
6. Worrying about college, numbers, rankings.

And under the heading "What Stuyvesant Students Consider the Greatest Sources of Stress," it ranks

1. Parents' expectations
2. College
3. Competition with other students
4. Workload

At times, the pressure gets so intense at Stuyvesant that Ms. Archie, the assistant principal, says some students "have a nervous breakdown" and are even "hospitalized, you know, because of the pressure."

Others resort to drugs, says Angel Colon, a school counselor. "Methamphetamine is becoming a big, big, big concern," he says. Some students are taking the illicit stimulant to help them stay awake to cram for tests, he says, but "eventually it really catches up with you." Some students say they have also resorted to using Adderall, a prescription drug intended to treat attention deficit disorder, to give them an academic edge.

It's hard to miss the bleary-eyed symptoms of students who've pulled all-nighters studying, if only fueled by Starbucks, conveniently located two blocks from school. The popular saying seems apropos: At Stuyvesant you can have only two of the following three—high grades, a social life, or sleep. Many forgo sleep. According to a recent survey by the *Spectator*, about 27 percent of Stuyvesant students say they use caffeine to stay awake during the day, while 60 percent say they get five to six hours of sleep a night, which is little more than half what is recommended for teenagers. And 75 percent say they sometimes or always sleep on a train, bus, or ferry, an indication that sleep-deprived students will doze whenever they can, even on the way to or from school.

Apparently, it's not nearly enough shut-eye.

Stuy Health reports that "students often complain about headaches, crankiness and feeling 'dead.'"

CHAPTER THREE

The Wizard of Oz

DEAD OF NIGHT CLOAKS A MODEST TWO-STORY BRICK town house in a quiet Brooklyn neighborhood, until 4:34 a.m., when out of the front door bursts a bolt of lightning, a whirling dervish, an anarchist, a rebel, a ringleader, and a gale force all wrapped in black spandex leggings, a blue fleece thermal jacket, a floral skullcap, rimless glasses, blue and gray sneakers, and a Yale baseball hat.

Otherwise known as Mr. Jaye.

He looks like he's ready to run a marathon this early February morning. And that's what he's about to do, in a manner of speaking, when he arrives at school, where he runs amok until late into the evening, gleefully creating havoc, breaking rules, and inventing new ones in the name of helping students as the assistant principal and powerful and adored chairman of Stuyvesant's vaunted math department, the school's heart.

"When you work with kids," he says, "you better stay young, or they get the jump on you."

Mr. Jaye—grinning like he can't wait to get started—looks about twenty-four years old. He's fifty-four.

But it's dark, and now he's pushing the pedal in a black Honda

Accord along a deserted stretch of asphalt where, at this predawn hour, he says, "Only the drunks and me are on the road." Though the avenues have changed over the years, he's been on the same journey since 1972, when he started as a student teacher at Stuyvesant. But all that may be coming to a screeching end in a matter of months. After thirty-four years at Stuyvesant, Mr. Jaye believes this may be his final semester.

"I'm really torn about leaving because I love this institution," he says. "If I leave here, there's a hole they'll never fill."

Mr. Jaye doesn't want to leave. But he feels he may have no choice. For the past few years, he's expected his friend and boss, Mr. Teitel, to retire as principal. Each year, it hasn't happened, and it doesn't look like it's going to happen anytime soon. Mr. Teitel, himself fifty-seven years old, just received a bonus that would have counted toward his retirement, if he took it, but he didn't, even though there's no guarantee he'll get the bonus next year. Mr. Teitel has made no noise about walking away from the "blue chair," his coveted seat as principal of the nationally recognized school. Mr. Teitel's news—or lack thereof—has sent Mr. Jaye into a tailspin this morning, at the beginning of the semester. He's tired of waiting to become principal, the job he aspires to, which students and teachers alike assume is his one day for the taking.

"I've been prepared to be principal for three, four years," he says. "My time is now."

It's 4:52 a.m., and Mr. Jaye rumbles off the Brooklyn Bridge, thinking about what looms ahead: the possibility of the principal's job at another prestigious public high school, Bergen County Academies in New Jersey. The wheels have already been set in motion. Bergen officials have been wooing him, he's visited the school five times, and he's awaiting the results of the New Jersey principal licensing exam he recently took. The numbers make sense too: if he retires from Stuyvesant, he reckons he'd collect about $80,000 a year in his pension and bring in another $130,000 as principal—almost double what's he's bringing in now.

What's not to like?

Still, the thought of leaving Stuyvesant tugs at an unseen emotion as Mr. Jaye turns onto a darkened Chambers Street, barreling across West Street and parking in front of the school, not a soul in sight. That unsettling thought will have to wait. Time to move on. It's 4:58 a.m., and there are things to do.

Tucked in a corner of the school overlooking the Tribeca Bridge, room 402—the cramped math department office—is much like the man who barges into it this morning, jam-packed. There is lots of stuff: six computers, two printers, five tape dispensers, three staplers, seven dollar bills, four pairs of scissors, an ivory bust of bearded philosopher-mathematician-hero Pythagoras. A red message light flashes unanswered on the phone. Mr. Jaye's desk is peppered with papers, files, and tons of yellow stickies, reminders of pressing to-dos. On a cabinet, a certificate is posted: "Jennifer Michelle Jaye has been awarded admission to Yale University Class of 2007." She is his oldest daughter, a prototypical Stuyvesant graduate for whom the Ivies were preordained. On the bookshelves are the usual props of a math man—*Elementary Algebra, Trigonometry, Precalculus, Calculus,* along with *Never Give In: The Best of Winston Churchill's Speeches.* Dozens of math trophies of various shapes and sizes collect dust and rust on top of a file cabinet, like forgotten toys for children who have too many, next to a clunky computer, circa late 1980s. More prominent is a photo of Mr. Jaye—same Cheshire grin but younger, with a thin, wide mustache long since gone—standing next to a grown-up Tim Robbins, the Oscar-winning actor, on a visit to his old math teacher.

This is the fiefdom where Mr. Jaye gets things done—things that other administrators won't dare, that teachers can't fathom, and for which students praise him. Which is why they call him the Wizard of Oz. He puts it more carefully: "When you help kids, you have to interpret rules favorably. Here's my motto: 'Make it happen.'"

Mr. Jaye has rarely seen an administrative roadblock he couldn't overcome, which is quite a feat in a complicated bureaucracy like the New York City schools, the largest public education system in the nation. If a student oversleeps and doesn't get to school on time for a math final, Mr. Jaye will arrange a makeup. He lets students—like Romeo—skip a math course to get into a higher level without any red tape. And when a student has surpassed high school math altogether, Mr. Jaye will find the course that the student needs, even if it's a PhD class at NYU. What's more, he will get that student high school credit for the college class, no matter how loudly the high school guidance counselors howl in protest. "In this department," he crows, "there's nothing we can't do."

That statement—a double negative—is just the kind of math equation expected of an unreformed troublemaker who failed algebra in the ninth grade.

Born in the shadow of Stuyvesant, Daniel Jaye lived and learned to be a wise guy just a couple of blocks from the vaunted public school when it was on East Fifteenth Street. The middle-class son of a commercial real estate broker, he passed Stuyvesant every day on his way to take the Avenue A bus to his regular public school, Seward Park High. But never once did he wish he attended Stuyvesant, a forbidding place to him because it was then an all-boys' school where the boys looked miserable from the heavy workload. Danny liked to have fun, and school got in the way of fun.

School was such a breeze that Danny skipped the eighth grade, but all the classes he cut in the ninth grade finally caught up with him. He failed algebra with an abysmal 55, a grade he matched in French class. In his junior year, he did it again, attending about a third of his classes and failing math while achieving the dubious distinction of a perfect score on the statewide algebra and trigonometry final. Details are sketchy, but somehow, Danny negotiated a retroactive passing grade in the course.

"I was not actively engaged in the institution" is the way he puts it.

The same could be said of his subsequent experience at the City College of New York, where as an undergraduate he had no idea what he wanted to do—other than to avoid the Vietnam War. Despite his high school run-ins, numbers came easy to him, and he decided to major in math. But he minored in education for more practical considerations. Teaching, he says, "was a draft deferment. That's what it was about."

Until his senior year of college. Then by accident—or fate—it became about something else.

As part of a math methods course, his professor took him and his fellow college students to observe a classmate practice the craft, teaching a fifteen-minute lesson at a Bronx high school, a rough place where it was an achievement if the students merely showed up. On this day, the surprise was that the student teacher didn't show up. So Danny, as reckless as ever, volunteered to teach the class. Of all things, it was ninth-grade algebra, the subject he had himself failed.

But not on this day. Instead, he quickly scanned the Delaney book, a time-honored New York public school seating chart named after Edward C. Delaney, a Harvard-educated public school teacher. The attendance and grade book was filled with Delaney cards, tabs about the size of a business card containing the names of the thirty-some hardened students blankly staring at him at the front of the room.

Looking back at them, Danny began by asking how many students were interested in baseball, a question intended to elicit a popular response since the school was a stone's throw from Yankee Stadium.

About a third of the class raised hands.

Not bad.

Then he called on a boy in the last row, in the last seat—by name: Alan. Danny had strategically memorized the names of four students, one in each corner of the Delaney book. The classroom buzz was palpable. A little boy in the front row said, in an aside to a buddy, "Oh shit, he knows our names."

And Danny thought, *I got 'em.*

He pushed forward, asking how many students had heard of Joe DiMaggio, the great Yankee slugger.

Again, more hands.

What was he famous for?

A boy volunteered: a hitting streak.

Right. A hitting streak of consecutive games. Like consecutive numbers, or integers, the subject of today's lesson. And Danny was on his way. "I was intoxicated with the fact that the kids liked me," he recalls. "I was really enthralled this came so easy to me." So was his professor, who approached Danny at the end of the lesson and predicted, "You will be a great teacher."

His professor was right, but he couldn't have predicted this: Danny would coauthor with that professor, Alfred S. Posamentier, a book called *What Successful Math Teachers Do, Grades 6–12.*

The book now sits on a shelf, a relic of the past lost in the din of teenage voices streaming into and out of Mr. Jaye's office at 8:35 a.m. Already, he's accomplished a lot, including taking his first morning bike jaunt of the semester on a path along the West Side Highway, from Stuyvesant to Harlem, with a colleague, Mike Zamansky, a Stuyvesant graduate who loved the school so much he's now its computer science coordinator. Mr. Jaye rode a Trek 6000 mountain bike spangled with two high beams and a flashing light on the front end, two flashing lights on the back side, and lights powering out of each end of the handlebar, a dazzling array of portable illumination that prompted his bike partner to say, "Danny's like a Christmas tree."

Now, though, Mr. Jaye is showered and garbed more appropriately for a math department chairman: black wing tips, black slacks, a massive ring of keys on his right hip, a blue collared shirt with "DJ" embroidered in white initials on the breast pocket, and a blue tie. In his pocket: five hundred dollars, just-in-case cash. And he's in the thick of it: he peeks from his doors at the line of students snaking out of the math department and yells to no one in particular, "Why does my line get bigger? I'm not giving anything away."

Well, he is.

Students know Mr. Jaye isn't just the math chairman. He's the fixer, the man you go to at the beginning of the semester to get your class schedule changed when you don't have the course you need or want, or when you have a class (or teacher) you want to get rid of. Word gets around.

"I hope I don't get in trouble for this," says a senior for whom Mr. Jaye just switched schedules with the stroke of a computer key.

He laughs it off with a math joke to distract her: "If your sister loves you and you love me, by the transitive property, she loves me."

The senior, still worrying about the schedule tinkering, isn't laughing. "It's, like, all done? It's perfect?"

"It's perfect," he assures her.

They high-five.

His next customer, a worried boy, asks, "Did my mom call?"

"No," he deadpans, "we don't talk to parents."

A teacher pokes her head in his office, looking for aspirin. His wife calls on his cell phone. He steps out into the hallway to rally the troops, "to spread my cheer throughout the building." He ducks into a secret elevator beyond an aqua green door marked, "Notice—Keep This Door Closed." He's corralled in the hallway by a student who wants to drop statistics, a killer course. He writes a note on the back of scrap paper and tells her to stop by his office.

"I love these kids," he says.

Adults are another matter.

At 11:45 a.m., Mr. Jaye is sitting at a long wooden table in a conference room adjoining the principal's office, and he's not happy. Nobody is. Sitting with him are the principal and the assistant principals of English and social studies, advisory members in a private gathering of the principal's inner circle—the "kitchen cabinet."

Today's burning issue: faculty uproar over a new school rule requiring them to flip over time cards to indicate their presence at school. Teachers don't want to do it. At Stuyvesant, where students are treated like adults, the adults complain that they feel as though they're being treated like children.

Mr. Jaye, sitting at the head of the table, as if he's already principal, takes charge, suggesting a compromise, that they require teachers to flip over time cards once, when they arrive, but not when they leave.

The idea seems to garner support.

Mr. Teitel, the principal, sitting to Mr. Jaye's side, suggests that they write a letter to the faculty, dictating out loud what he imagines to be the opening: "This has been a very upsetting week—"

At which, Mr. Grossman, the English chairman, interrupts, "Start with something positive."

Mr. Jaye adds, "Reflect on our successes."

Mr. Teitel piggybacks on the positives, deciding not to use the term "time cards." Sounds too . . . officious.

"Time check-in?" Mr. Grossman suggests.

"The truth is, I'm under direct order from the superintendent," Mr. Teitel says.

"Do this in the least intrusive way," Mr. Grossman offers.

Mr. Jaye's idea wins the day: one flip a day, whatever the time card is called.

"I can only lose my job once," muses Mr. Teitel, who, in his seventh year as principal and his twenty-third at Stuyvesant, looks like Abraham Lincoln after the Civil War—shaggy-bearded, emaciated, and incredibly tired.

The conversation devolves into group commiseration about new rules in the teachers' contract requiring them to do what many consider menial jobs, like monitoring the library. Mr. Teitel mentions that someone recommended that he bring in a conflict mediator to deal with a faction of angry English teachers. Someone received a dreaded "U"— "unsatisfactory"—teacher performance rating, which has roiled some on staff. Mr. Teitel says he couldn't eat after the last contentious faculty meeting.

On a wall across the room, a bank of head shots of the previous dozen principals of Stuyvesant—a select club of eleven men and one woman—gaze down on Mr. Teitel, as if sympathizing with his plight.

Then Mr. Jaye finally shows his cards, revealing what he really came here for, saying he wasn't consulted when one of his best teachers was assigned to patrol—*babysit*—the library during seventh and eighth periods instead of using those free periods to meet with students in math research, room 401.

Mr. Teitel knows better than to duke this out in front of everyone. At 12:28 p.m., he dismisses the cabinet, save Mr. Jaye, leaving the two of them like brothers ready to roll up their sleeves and kick dirt in each other's face, such is their mutual admiration. Mr. Teitel begins with the obvious salvo, explaining why he assigned the teacher in question to library duty: "He's a school aide."

The argument has the benefit of being true. The teacher is *not* a teacher, at least not officially. He's a school aide—not much higher in the school hierarchy than a custodial worker. Not that such labels stopped Mr. Jaye from assigning the school aide to teach a math research class to Stuyvesant freshmen and sophomores. Mr. Jaye hired the aide for his mathematical genius, ignoring minor details, such as his lack of a teacher's license because he hasn't been certified, which he can't be because he hasn't graduated from college, which he has flunked out of.

Mr. Jaye appealed to the college dean yesterday to get the aide reinstated, but so far, the college is unmoved, even though the teacher's aide recently won a Putnam Fellowship, making him one of the top five undergraduate mathematicians in North America.

"He's the smartest person in the building!" Mr. Jaye screams at the principal.

"Someone has to do it," Mr. Teitel says of the library duty.

"But the person who answers the phone can't do what [he] can do!"

"Stop," says Mr. Teitel, burying his head in his hands.

Mr. Jaye suggests installing security cameras in the library to catch vandals.

But Mr. Teitel moans, "We spent a fortune on the library. What do you want me to do? I need to supervise [students] in some way."

Now Mr. Jaye's worked himself into a lather. "We're not employing a genius and having him do security!" Then his anger dissolves into a well of tears in a set of deep brown eyes. "I'm not going to make him flip fucking burgers."

Mr. Teitel downshifts into a softer, conciliatory tone, saying how he respects Mr. Jaye more than anyone else, how they go back a long way. But he says, "The reality is, I've got to run a school." And here, emboldened, Mr. Teitel begins to build an argument about how he gets a set school budget from the city every year and how he can't foresee every eventuality, but then he falters, at first imperceptibly, and now he's agreeing what a terrible waste of talent it is to have a math genius police the library, and in the end, he says he'll try to get him out of there.

Mr. Teitel smiles wanly. "Okay," he says, "we'll find somebody."

It's all over. Mr. Teitel nods his head ruefully, sighs. Mr. Jaye rises to leave, renewed. Crisis averted. On his way out of the principal's office, practically skipping, he turns back and, with a lascivious grin, calls out to the secretaries, asking whether they want to join him in a "cuddle puddle."

Cuddle puddle?

> *Duck and COVER!*
>
> —desktop graffiti, Stuyvesant High School

CHAPTER FOUR

Cuddle Puddle Muddle

BEHIND CLOSED DOORS FIVE DAYS LATER, MR. TEITEL is hunched uneasily, marooned in a maroon armchair in his office, speaking in urgent tones to a small gathering of lieutenants, as if hashing out military strategy in a hastily convened war council. And in a sense—just a week into the semester—he's already in a pitched battle.

Some teachers are still refusing to flip over their time cards. What's more, some are resisting the menial tasks of patrolling the various byways of the school, prompting an assistant principal to suggest a dire prospect: that the school may be forced to fire some teachers so it can free up money to hire aides who will perform the odious monitoring duties. But that's the least of Mr. Teitel's worries on this February day.

The bigger problem: parents are up in arms, deluging him with e-mails complaining about a just-released *New York* magazine cover story on Stuyvesant that dropped like an unexpected public relations bomb on his coffee table. The title: "Love and the Ambisexual, Heteroflexible Teen."

The cover photo features a high school principal's nightmare: a recumbent, bare-chested boy, à la Calvin Klein advertisements, right

45

arm bent at the elbow, his other embracing an impish girl with golden locks and a Mona Lisa expression of mischievous ennui.

The story delves into a Stuyvesant subculture involving a handful of students who heap themselves and their backpacks in a "cuddle puddle" on a second-floor hallway where "[t]here are girls petting girls and girls petting guys and guys petting guys." The author writes that it is "just one clique at Stuyvesant" but says the "cuddle puddle is emblematic of the changing landscape of high-school sexuality across the country," citing a recent survey showing that 11 percent of U.S. girls from fifteen to nine-teen years old have had "same-sex encounters." Then the writer goes on to discuss the vague sexual boundaries of teenagers who call themselves "polysexual, ambisexual, pansexual, pansensual, polyfide, bi-curious, bi-queer, fluid, metroflexible, heteroflexible, heterosexual with lesbian tendencies . . ." Details ensue, such as an ice cube dropped down various pants.

How does Mr. Teitel, the principal, explain this away on a legal pad?

He reads aloud his scribbled attempt, a draft of a letter to one per-turbed parent, acknowledging that sex, drugs, and alcohol do exist even at an august institution like Stuyvesant. But he adds that one of the great traditions of the school "is the almost college-like environment" of freedom. And he notes that "Stuyvesant has always been and will always continue to be a magnet for this kind of thing because of its 'elite' status."

But here, Mr. Teitel can't resist an aside to Mr. Grossman, the English chairman, who is sitting with him in commiseration. "They're teen-agers!" Mr. Teitel says. "This is what happens!"

Mr. Grossman agrees and gives Mr. Teitel a good grade on his letter composition: "It's perfect."

Mr. Teitel isn't soothed. He buries his head in his hands, uttering, "God, I'm not going to get through these weeks."

It's remarkable that he's made it this far. If not for his weight, Mr. Teitel might be a retired cop today.

A Brooklyn boy, Stanley Teitel was the son of a New York police officer who grew up poor, selling apples on the streets, a searing memory that prompted the father to encourage the son to join the men in blue, stressing the steady paycheck and the early retirement, which he could take at age thirty-eight if he started at eighteen. Stan was willing. But there was one major sticking point: the teenager weighed 129 pounds—reed thin on a six foot one inch frame.

"I was tall enough," he says, "I just didn't weigh enough."

Stan was so underweight that he was pronounced 4-F—unfit for military service—which thrilled his mother because it kept him out of Vietnam. But that left Stan in a quandary about his future, the unfolding of which put a new wrinkle in the adage that those who can't, teach, or in his case, become the principal of one of the best high schools in America. He applied to dental school but didn't get in because of his mediocre college grades. He tried his hand briefly as a private investigator, but that didn't take either. He sold men's clothing. Then he took a flier on teaching. It was supposed to be a temporary gig. His high school alma mater needed a biology teacher to fill a vacancy until the end of a term, and young Stan had a knack for science going back to his childhood, when he idolized Albert Einstein and helped his dad fix carburetors for extra money. So he took the teaching job, which came as something of a surprise to the principal, who remembered young Stan as the former student whom he had suspended for five days. The former troublemaker won't say for what, for fear of encouraging naughtiness in his own students today. He says only, "I did something bad."

It wasn't bad enough to get him kicked out again. Teaching, he soon learned, shared some of the stability that his father had admired in the police force. And then there was this bonus about teaching: "I like summers off," Mr. Teitel says.

Today, though, is no vacation. The controversial cuddle puddle story spreads like a virus throughout the building, from the first-floor principal's office to the second-floor senior "bar," a lozenge-size block behind which a gaggle of girls is sitting cross-legged on the floor, gawking at the candid photos from the torn-out article as if they were contraband.

"That is so unnecessary," says Becky, the brainy cheerleader, glued to the page.

Fellow senior Nikki Bogopolskaya worries that she'll be mistaken for a sexually free girl named Nikki in the cuddle puddle. And the article mysteriously reminds another onlooker, senior Molly Ruben-Long, "I've come to the realization that I'm going to prom by myself." Though no one disputes the assertion, she quickly adds, "No, it's okay."

The angst levitates like a magic trick to room 640, where students in a journalism class debate the article's merits. Few are found.

"The journalism didn't seem morally correct, or ethically correct," says one editor of the *Spectator* school newspaper, criticizing how the *New York* magazine writer entered the school without the principal's authorization and used pseudonyms in the article. The author, Alex Morris, says later in an interview that she didn't realize she needed to obtain permission to enter the school. "I just walked in," says the twenty-seven-year-old author, noting that this was her first article as a freelance writer. She says she used pseudonyms to protect the students, especially those who had not told their parents about their sexuality. "One of our concerns was not 'outing' kids." She says she did not seek parental consent before interviewing the students, a general practice when writing about minors, but says the magazine did obtain parents' permission before publishing photographs of the students.

In class, the journalism students seem even more bothered by their perception that the story casts Stuyvesant as a sex-crazed school whose students struggle with ambiguous gender tendencies.

"We're not all like that," one girl says.

Another calls it cheap "entertainment."

A third says that her concerned mother asked whether she was a lesbian, eliciting nervous tittering in the classroom.

Alair, the sixteen-year-old *New York* cover girl, isn't here to air her own grievances about the article, but she has many. She says the story contains a good message about tolerance, but "it used sensationalism to cater to people's eyes." What's more, she says that she and her friends asked the *New York* magazine author not to use the term "cuddle puddle." Ms. Morris disputes that, saying, "They never asked me not to." Alair also takes exception to the way the students were characterized, saying, "It's not soft porn. We're just hanging out in the hallway."

Ms. Morris says, "I know some of them were upset," but she stresses, "That was never my intention." She acknowledges, though, that the article "is about teenagers and sex, you're not going to have a perfectly

Junior League article" and that the story lost "some of the more tender moments" during the editing process. "It's always a hard thing, being written about," she says.

Lately, Alair, the menthol chain-smoking junior, has taken to wearing sunglasses at school. Celebrity is not everything it's cracked up to be.

But the story has legs. The term "cuddle puddle" instantly enters the Stuyvesant lexicon, both student and teacher versions, becoming a derisive term of endearment. Overnight, the magazine cover shot becomes iconic, like a bad reproduction of Michelangelo's *Creation of Adam* in the Sistine Chapel. In a parody of the magazine photo of the two teenagers clutching each other, the Republican Club of Stuy tapes up flyers throughout the building, showing a shirtless boy draped in the American flag, a girl resting on top of him, grasping a doll of former President Ronald Reagan. Promoting its next meeting, the flyer touts "News and the Ambipolitical, Conservative Teen."

The *Spectator* takes a more serious tack, dissecting the *New York* article under the headline "Cuddle Puddle Muddle." A survey of students finds that most believe the school was misrepresented. Rounding out the general disapprobation, the *Spectator* also runs a student opinion piece, "Sex and Sensationalism at Stuy." None of which stops *New York* magazine from following up later with another salacious item about Stuyvesant. But then, perhaps this piece falls under the category of don't-shoot-the-messenger, as the article merely reports on a just-published book, *The Notebook Girls*, written by four girls during their recent years at Stuyvesant. It just happens to be chock-full of teenage talk about oral sex and lesbian lusts.

Fact is, talk of sex—or the engagement in it—isn't hard to find at Stuyvesant, or any other high school, for that matter. The topic, for instance, comes up casually during a meeting of the advisory School Tone Committee of parents, faculty, and students, one of whom talks about the distribution of condoms in school as if she were talking about handing out an item as ordinary as a lollipop. The topic of sex is just as breezy in the school library, where a sixteen-year-old honors student says that on an upcoming date, he plans to take his girlfriend to a shop that sells condoms to "check that out, then go out to eat." The junior also mentions that he recently ripped a condom while in use, and his parents simply told him to get his girlfriend a morning-after pill as an emergency contraceptive. His attitude: no big deal. "My dad knows," he says, "it's a natural thing when you're sixteen, you have a lot of sex."

Backing up that assertion is an article in the *Spectator* at the beginning of the semester. Ostensibly, the story is about the little-used Hudson staircase at the back of the school. But it's really about not how *little* it's used but *how* it's used. "The Hudson staircase is synonymous with sexual activity in the eyes of many students," the student reporter writes. School administrators acknowledge as much, saying in the *Spectator* that security guards patrol the stairwells to prevent unacceptable behavior. Nonetheless, a sophomore is quoted as saying the Hudson staircase is where students "go to have sex in," the details of which are left to the reader's imagination. Someone edited out of the story a graphic term for oral sex, according to a faculty member.

Someone else, meanwhile, manages to keep the cuddle puddle off the agenda at an after-school meeting of the School Leadership Team—known as the SLT—an advisory committee of students, teachers, and parents. But on this day in early February, when the *New York* magazine article reverberates throughout the school, Mr. Teitel, the principal, knows other trouble awaits at the SLT meeting. The first giveaway: as he enters room 615, it's claustrophobically hot from overactive radiators. "I can see the heat's up," he remarks, opening a window, which does nothing to cool off about twenty-five simmering parents and students—his "constituents," as he calls them.

The first order of business is another brewing controversy—the introduction of "kiosks," a euphemism to many frowning members of the committee for "lockdown." Stuyvesant, joining many other schools, is preparing to install computerized identification scanners, which would require students to use cards to swipe into and out of the building. No longer would teachers be required to keep a paper record of attendance; no longer would students simply flash a photo ID at a somnolent guard standing by the school entrance. Proponents, who seem to consist of school administrators and few others in the room, say the kiosks will automatically record students' attendance and enhance security by keeping track of exactly who is in the school at any given time—and who shouldn't be.

"It only takes one person to mess up a school," says an official of the kiosk manufacturer, a featured speaker at the committee meeting.

Left unsaid are new facts of school life: the threat of terrorism, the menace of a Columbine High School–type carnage.

Opponents, who seem to include almost everyone else in the room, say that the scanners will only send a message of mistrust from the very moment students enter the school. The devices, they fear, will also invade students' privacy, collecting personal data that could be abused. And at a cost of about sixty thousand dollars for the scanners, the opponents want to know, aren't there higher-priority expenses for a high school like Stuyvesant, which boasts nearly no student violence and a 97 percent attendance rate?

"We don't need this," says impassioned committee member Marty Davis, an involved parent of a senior. "We need more money for teachers. We need more money for space." The scanners, he says, will make the school look less like an academic setting than "the subway system."

Nothing is resolved. The agenda item is tabled until the next meeting. But rumblings are already sounding elsewhere. The Student Union government is planning to fight the installation of the scanners. Protest marches—effective in past student clashes with the administration—could erupt. The *Spectator* has weighed in as well, criticizing the school administration in a student editorial that begins, "You may have heard that Stuy is being put under lockdown." Andrew, the newspaper's managing editor, says the scanners threaten to extinguish the school's freedoms.

"It's kind of like prison," he says.

Despite the principal's attempt to maintain a collegial atmosphere of student empowerment, many students and teachers believe a strict law-and-order force is gaining momentum under the direction of Randi Damesek, the effective assistant principal of organization.

There's a leaden mood about her that is more than the sum of her parts, something about the way she prowls the halls cloaked in a dark sweater over her shoulders. Believed to be forty-one years old, she would be pretty if she didn't look so owlish—pale-faced, her raven hair pulled back severely. Last semester, Ms. Damesek fired off a Grinch-like faculty memo, effectively banning food from class parties around Christmas, that became front-page fodder for the *Spectator*. Mr. Jaye, her equal as an assistant principal and her opposite in spirit, put the kibosh on her measure, as he likes to do, saying he intended to party it up with his students. Ms. Damesek promptly followed up at the beginning of this semester by ripping down a star-studded student banner on a second-floor wall. The infraction was unclear; the poster merely welcomed back seniors. With that swipe, Ms. Damesek again made the front page, which she trumped with a cameo appearance in a subsequent student editorial under the headline "Ms. Damesek, Talk to Us." For several years, she has refused to comment to the school newspaper, which complains that she is leaving students in the dark about such important issues as the pending installation of scanners. "We ask Damesek to consider talking to the *Spectator* in the interest of the Stuy community," the editorial implores, "for we are the body that serves to inform it."

Ms. Damesek's reply: deafening silence. (She also declined repeated requests to be interviewed for this book—the only teacher or administrator to do so. She later threatened, among other things, to sue this author and have the principal fired if she were cast in a bad light.)

It hasn't been an easy transition for Ms. Damesek since she arrived at Stuyvesant as an administrative intern about four years ago. Little could prepare her for the oddity that is Stuyvesant, not even her eleven years as a math teacher at Fiorello H. LaGuardia High School of Music & Art and Performing Arts, an acclaimed New York public school and the subject of the movie *Fame*. (LaGuardia has its own selective admissions based on auditions.) From the beginning, Stuyvesant students bristled at Ms. Damesek's restrictions on bake sales and hallway traffic even when such rules are the norm at other public schools.

Things have been particularly difficult for Ms. Damesek lately, according to school colleagues. Her father, a principal in the New York school system, passed away not long ago. By all accounts, clashes with Mr. Jaye only add to her tension. And even Mr. Teitel admits that Ms. Damesek holds the unenviable position as the school's strict disciplinarian by default—because no one else, not even he, fills that role. "In every organization, someone has to be the heavy," he says. "In this one, she's it."

Mr. Grossman, the English chairman, says that Ms. Damesek has the best intentions even if students and teachers sometimes question them. For instance, he says, she will repeatedly remind students of a deadline, such as their payment for the advanced placement exams, but if they fail to hand in their checks on time, she won't budge. Ms. Damesek guards her privacy so well that few know that she will give students a few dollars when they need it or call students to get them out of bed in the morning, according to Mr. Grossman. "In her own way, she really loves the kids," he says. Mr. Teitel adds that she stretches the school budget as far as it will go, finding ways to save money. When students owed about seven thousand overdue school books, he says she came up with the idea to give them a couple of days of amnesty, but then take away their out-to-lunch privileges if they didn't return their textbooks. Within short order, students returned most of them. "This is a girl who works tirelessly for these kids," Mr. Teitel says. Arms akimbo, Ms. Damesek often stands outside her second-floor office, intently watching in silence over students, though they sometimes take the stance to mean something less than charitable.

If Ms. Damesek isn't forthcoming, one of the best chances for students to find out what the adults are up to is to attend a meeting of the School Leadership Team, which has moved on from the controversial scanners to a discussion of another perennial problem at Stuyvesant and other high schools: cheating.

Call it the ugly stepchild of excruciating competition in an excruciatingly competitive school. Some students will tap their desk, in a sort of Morse code, to transmit answers to nearby friends. Others will use M&M candies, each color representing letters A through D on multiple-choice tests, to convey to other students the right answer. Then there are the more primitive techniques, such as writing test answers on a leg or an arm or the brim of a hat, or on the back of a label of a bottle of water, one of the few objects allowed on students' desks during exams.

The problem is so institutionalized at Stuyvesant that it's parodied. A front-page article of *The Broken Escalator*, an underground student publication, once blared, "Students Cheat on Math Final, Sun Continues to Rise and Set." The story went on to say, "Much of the student body has responded with shock. 'I simply can't believe that at such a prestigious school, cheating goes on,' said a deaf, blind baby in an incubator."

Cheating makes it into more mainstream reading, including the School Leadership Team's handout, under the rubric "School Goal 6": "To improve ethical practices among the students, and the school tone, at Stuyvesant High School." The Academic Honesty Committee, which was "working to devise a policy on plagiarism and other forms of academic malfeasance," has been folded into another school-related organ, but the issue remains as intractable as ever. "I was told by students this was not a subject that could even be fixed," says a concerned mother at the meeting. "The problem is so big."

A school official agrees, blaming cheating on Stuyvesant's stressful environment. "It's more acute in a school that has higher academic standards," she says. A parent blames it on the awesome quantity of tests foisted on overwhelmed students. Another says it's the media's fault for glamorizing the rich and famous, some of whom got that way by compromising their integrity.

Students on a panel discussing "Life at Stuy" at a subsequent Parents' Association meeting explain that some of their peers justify cheating by saying there's too much pressure to achieve, too much emphasis on grades, and that the system is unfair to begin with: bad teachers give bad tests; tough teachers grade too toughly. Students also say they take many advanced placement classes because it looks good to prospective colleges, but the workload can be too much, prompting some to cheat.

"There's so much stress and so much work," says one student on the panel.

"Everyone wants to get the highest grade," says another.

The school culture fosters the idea of achieving "by any means necessary," says a third.

Whatever the cause, cheating is as difficult to stop as teen acne. It can be abated, but it will rear its ugly head again, even if students are threatened by the daunting prospect of having the incident placed in their permanent record. Usually, teachers handle the situation on their own. One says she designs a different test for each class so that students can't pass answers on to their friends who take the exam later in the day. Another teacher says he requires students to sign a document assuring their academic integrity. Matt Polazzo, a popular teacher of comparative government and the coordinator of student affairs, makes cheaters sign a contract vowing never to cheat again, then requires them to sing the contract aloud. None, he reports, has been caught cheating a second time. Other teachers have turned high-tech to ferret out classroom culprits. A service that's gaining traction at Stuyvesant and other public schools is www.turnitin.com, a Web site that detects plagiarism in student papers by comparing them against countless works found on the Internet and other databases.

But for every high-tech tool to prevent cheating, students find a way to foil it. One such method lies just a block from Stuyvesant, where hawkers pass out business cards offering to write students' research papers for sixteen dollars a page. Another advertises:

NO JOB IS TOO BIG; NO JOB IS TOO SMALL!
SAME DAY & NEXT DAY SERVICE IS AVAILABLE

Standardized tests can be gamed just as easily. A recent Stuyvesant graduate became the subject of a *New York Post* article entitled "Confessions of SAT Test Faker," in which he boasted how he became a test-taking gun for hire, armed with a fake ID and a student's social security number, helping high school students obtain the high scores they want on college entrance tests and other exams.

"The only complaint I've ever gotten was that I scored too high," he told the *Post*.

The intricacies of cheating are the subject of a class project documentary by junior Ada Ng, who wanders Stuyvesant's hallways interviewing students, using a Sony video camera resting on a tripod.

"Have you ever cheated before?" she asks a nervous girl on camera.

"Yes," the girl says, then quickly adds, "I don't recommend to do it all the time."

How do you cheat?

Glancing at another student's test from "the corner of my eye," the girl says.

Have you ever been caught?

No.

Have you helped others cheat?

Yes. Sometimes, the girl says, she will memorize the answers to questions on a test, then give those answers to friends who have the same class later in the day.

How do you feel about cheating as a way of getting by?

"It's not," says the girl, "the best method to use."

> *This isn't kosher*
>
> —desktop graffiti, Stuyvesant High School

CHAPTER FIVE

Jane's Addiction

THERE'S NO METHOD TO JANE'S MADNESS. IT'S ALL rage, and pain, and poetry, and love, and hate, and a childhood lost, and a father gone, and a search for something, a yearning for anything, or a hope for nothing, to simplify, to reduce, to forget everything in the unyielding vortex of a hit of heroin.

"My hobby is self-destruction," she says impassively.

A fight breaks out—something about how her mother is going to lock her in forever—before Jane takes off, instantaneously proving the point that forever doesn't even last a day, the day, incidentally, that she is supposed to take an advanced placement calculus test. For five days, seventeen-year-old Jane stays with a friend before returning home. By then, she has some explaining to do, not just to her mother, but to Stuyvesant, for her unexcused absences. So mother and daughter head down to the school in early February, first thing in the morning, first period. While her mother waits in the first-floor lobby by the school security guard, Jane marches into a nearby bathroom, brazenly leaves it unlocked, and injects herself with a shot of heroin.

The next day, Jane takes the makeup math test—and passes.

That day near the beginning of the new semester, Jane also decides to stop using heroin. For one, she says, "I ran out, I didn't have any money, I just got sick and tired." It helps too that waiting for her at the end of the day is a homemade detoxification concoction: the prescription painkiller OxyContin and a sleeping pill.

It doesn't take. The following day, Jane can't get out of bed, doesn't go to school, couldn't care less. It's noon. She's unconscious. Then suddenly, she's screaming and kicking and crying, and she's being rushed into an emergency room, fighting against the flow of methadone.

"I don't remember anything else," she says.

What follows is a blur, too—detox at the hospital, then home, then back in detox. And now here she is, back at school, barely hanging on to her senior year, oblivious to the scanner controversy, mildly amused by the cuddle puddle brouhaha. What sustains her is not the antidepressants, which she periodically pops, or the outpatient group therapy—rehab—which she considers a joke, but her will.

"Right now," she says, "I'm just trying to put back the pieces."

The pieces of Jane are so delicate and small—all five foot two inches and ninety pounds of her—she almost looks like fragile porcelain, too beautiful to break. And yet the feline ferocity in her eyes conveys the sense that the waiflike girl could tear you to shreds for looking at her the wrong way: with sympathy.

Such a ferocious effect could be owing to Jane's various contact lenses—purple, blue, green, hazel, gold, moonlight, or the gray of today. Or maybe it's the net effect of the incongruous purple baby's pacifier dangling below her form-fitting T-shirt, the long, golden-dyed talons of her dark hair, and her bare midriff. It could also be her earrings, which label her a "Rebel." Or her two arrests for carrying stilettos, which she calls "a nice accessory." Or her cell phone voice mail announcement, which tells you to "leave your message or fuck off."

The truth is, Jane isn't even sure how she came to this point. "I never saw it coming," she says.

Problems began just beyond Beijing, where Jane was born and raised in large part by her mother's grandparents. "I had a messed up childhood," she begins in Dickensian fashion. Her earliest memory, she says, is "pushing open a door, wondering why after you wake up, you're weak." Her father left Jane, an only child, in China when she was two so he could pursue a career in Europe as a painter. Her mother left a year later to join Jane's father. Over the next several years, Jane shuttled back and forth between China and Europe, living with a confusion of relatives, until her parents brought her to the United States in the sixth grade. Her father stayed for a couple of months, then left. Jane, meanwhile, barely spoke English, not even small conversation; she was limited to clipped, stultified sentences, as awkward as Eliza Doolittle uttering "How do you do?"

But Jane was gifted. Attending a Chinese academy in Queens to learn English, in just two years she achieved the highest score in her middle school on the Stuyvesant exam, gaining entrance to the elite school.

That, however, was all prologue to the pain of high school, where vicious rumors about her and a football player quickly made her an outcast, only motivating her to become even more of a pariah.

"I never even tried to fit in," she says, even though her mother always reminded her that the bird that stands out the most likely gets shot down first.

By her sophomore year, Jane stopped praying, became an atheist, and dated an Asian ghetto gangsta who dealt knives. The relationship did little to free her from an abiding sense of despair, the origins of which she could never locate. "It's like fighting an invisible enemy," she says, "but the enemy is yourself." The more that others at Stuyvesant pushed themselves academically, the less she tried. If they cared about grades, she wouldn't. The more the academic pressure mounted, the less she gave in to it. Rage consumed her, unspecified, unearthed. She hated her father in his absence. She screamed at her mother in her presence. She didn't learn of her parents' divorce, a secret for several years, until she was about thirteen. It was a lie—her parents' marriage, her place in it, role models, all of it. At the age of sixteen, Jane decided that it would be better to end it all. To be dead. Looking for ways to kill herself, she searched online, where she struck on the idea to overdose on heroin. Someone gave her a stash of the illicit drug, which she viewed as "sort of like your last meal before the prison execution." But it didn't work out that way. Instead, she says, "That's when I learned self-destruction is really fun."

Others at Stuyvesant have come to the same conclusion. While drugs plague high schools everywhere, the problem becomes especially striking when smart, successful students are caught in the act: Jane's classmates are generally otherwise well behaved. Violence of any kind is almost nonexistent at Stuyvesant, with zero "crimes against persons" reported in 2005. Suspensions are negligible as well, with fourteen reported in 2005, less than 10 percent of the average for a school its size. What few suspensions are doled out are usually for what Ms. Archie, the assistant principal, calls "silly things." Sometimes students will buy an escalator key on the black market and activate an escalator when it's supposed to be at a standstill.

"They think it's cool to turn it on," she says.

Some students also think it's cool to trade in illicit substances. Blared a *New York Post* headline a couple of years ago,

EASY BUY AT STUY 'HIGH'

TOP KIDS RUNNING AN OPEN DRUG MART

"The school, considered one of the best in the city and which has produced four Nobel laureates, has an outdoor black market where students brazenly exchange drugs, get high and sell illicit cigarettes in broad daylight," the article said. The *Post* writer went on to describe students exchanging what appeared to be LSD and marijuana and inhaling nitrous oxide a block from school on a long, mural-covered wall known simply as the Wall.

It's still called the Wall, or more specifically, the Stoner Wall. And Johnathan Khusid, incoming president of Arista, the Stuyvesant chapter of the National Honor Society, believes that the majority of students have tried pot. But he adds that academics temper drug use.

"If you have a calc test," he says, "you're not going to light a jay."

Many students view cigarettes as more evil than marijuana because tobacco "can give you cancer," he says, while the popular perception is that marijuana isn't a threat "aside from [causing] memory loss."

Demonstrating pot's popularity, one self-professed stoner says he arrived at Stuyvesant on a Monday with about twenty-seven dime bags of marijuana and by Wednesday, after brisk sales, he had one left. Business is expanding. "Acid, hallucinogens are big in this school," the sixteen-year-old says. One day, he says, he came to school with $6 and left with $231 after selling hits of acid at about seven bucks a pop.

Jane, for her part, is trying to abstain from drugs. Already, she says, "the amount of heroin I've done would kill a normal person," and the withdrawal is painful in a way she can't describe. Clarity, though, is beginning to pierce her general fog. "In a strange way," she says, "I've become the kid I always wanted to be. I always wanted to become the coolest kid, the rebel." But she blames no one but herself: "I chose my own path, I just didn't realize the repercussions."

What buoys her now is what's clutched in her pale, thin hand—a dog-eared copy of James Joyce's *A Portrait of the Artist as a Young Man*, a life raft of sorts and required reading in her "Great Books" class, which is taught by the one person in the building she respects, Mr. Grossman, the English chairman. Hers is a curious selection. Where Jane is all fire and fury, her English teacher is soft-spoken and understated. But she is not alone in her high opinion of Mr. Grossman. Many a schoolgirl finds him dreamy, his big blue eyes, his gravelly baritone voice, his gold earring in the left ear. At thirty-nine, he retains a youthfulness with which students can identify. They sense that he understands. That he's been there. That once he himself was a smart kid, a classic underachiever who was adrift in school and in love with music, despite an awful singing voice.

"I didn't want to be a teacher—it wasn't that I didn't want to be a teacher—I wanted to be a rock star," he says.

Teaching, strangely enough, grants him many of the same rewards that being a rock star would have: a stage on which he performs great acts before an adoring audience, an arena where creativity is rewarded, where ideas and art are exchanged, where he can feel his influence on others, like Jane.

They met in her freshman year, Jane and Mr. Grossman, before everything went haywire, when he was observing her class's discussion

on Shakespeare's *Much Ado about Nothing*. Jane's hand shot up to volunteer a comment about how such comedies resolve in people pairing
off romantically and how one of the characters was like a puppet master. Impressed, Mr. Grossman jotted a note, which he passed to her, saying that maybe Shakespeare was doing the same thing, pulling the play's
strings. Mr. Grossman is pulling the strings now, allowing Jane to take his
course even though it's supposed to be open only to upperclassmen
with at least a 94 average in English, which she doesn't have, not nearly.
But he still believes—wants to believe—in Jane. Rarely does he come
across a student like Jane, who has what he calls that elusive "spark," a
special intangible quality, a gift. So he is giving her one more chance.
"I've got my fingers crossed," Mr. Grossman says.

Jane's gift is evident in her poetry:

> *I wish to bestow upon you God's most gracious gifts to me.*
> *no faith*
> *no comfort*
> *no response*
> *no escape*
> *no rescuer*
> *no hope*
> *no happiness*
> *no freedom*
> *no relief*
> *no air to breathe*
> *no will to live*
> *no means to die*
> *every intention of suicide*
> *no one who understands*
> *no conscience*
> *painful pleasure*
> *guilty secrets*
> *shameful truths*
> *disgusting habits*
> *grotesque interior*
> *decaying soul*

banished father
dark thoughts penetrating every cell
poisoned blood screaming for
more poison
hungry veins
unsatiable appetite
disappointed disapproving dishonest
mother
and of course no one
but voyeurs
and most worst intentions
my loving curse
my cursed love
no peace
no rest
no sleep
eternal stupor
no way back
no lighted path
lost best friends
fake best friends
wasted affections
waking in waste
basking in hate
waiting for revenge
on God
whom I
don't believe
no real words to express
anguished pain.

The rage in her poetry isn't far from the surface, never is. Fuming, Jane can't wait for the day she turns eighteen—just a few months from now—because then she can escape from her mother's supervision.

"The only thing she has over me, except love and shit like that, is that I'm underage," she says.

Jane can't wait to leave high school either. "I'm not sure Stuyvesant was a good thing or not," she says, thinking back on how her depression sank its teeth into her in freshman year and never let go.

"I represent the best and worst about Stuy," she says.

Jane doesn't have to say why. She's smart—fantastically smart—but the question is, will she graduate? She thinks she will, thanks to a surprisingly respectable 86 average, due largely to strong grades she earned before diving into drugs. Some of her teachers are less certain. College seems even more of a question mark. Jane, naturally, did well on the math and verbal sections of the SAT, with a combined score of 1470 out of 1600, but she has no extracurricular activities to speak of and even less of a will to go to college. A photographer recently approached her on the street. He took pictures of her. And now she's thinking of taking off a year before college to become a model.

"He said I was totally gifted," she says of the photographer.

Maybe Jane needs to hear that now, at the beginning of the semester, a time to begin again, when everything is new and possible. Yet she is less certain of herself, especially when it comes to her drug recovery.

"I don't think it's very sustainable," she says, and you can almost hear the echo of a clinician.

"I've gone through this before," she says, then parrots words thrown at her, how one day she will be "liberated from this addiction, blah, blah, blah." But Jane has a different take on her problems.

"I know me," she says. "I'm not optimistic."

> *The Who*
>
> —desktop graffiti, Stuyvesant High School

CHAPTER SIX

Open House

ROMEO, THE FOOTBALL CAPTAIN, EXUDES NOTHING BUT optimism as he stalks the escalators and hallways of Stuyvesant on the afternoon of February 16, week three of the semester. And why not? He practically owns the joint like an action hero in his own domain. Last Saturday, he took his first practice SAT, scoring in the 98th percentile. *Pow!* He just received his report card from last semester: a 97 average. *Bam!* This week—and it's not over yet—he's aced tests in biology, French, and math. *Whap!* He still had time to stay up late one night talking with his dad about "stuff," which translates into "girls." He's even allowed himself to hang out with friends after school—a novelty for him—chowing cheap Mexican food and making one-dollar bets on who will get the higher test scores in class.

He's already owed a buck.

And then there's next week. The pilgrimage to Harvard. He'll take the bus to Cambridge, Massachusetts, sit in on classes as a prospective student, and imagine himself there as a college freshman, his hope, his future.

But the present beckons. It's just an hour until Stuyvesant's "Open House," an orchestrated event for next year's incoming students and their parents, a chance for eighth and ninth graders to find out what's in store for them at the legendary pressure cooker of a high school. It's also an opportunity for Romeo to recruit football prospects, which is why he's patrolling the hallways after school, decked out in his royal blue and crimson football jersey—number ninety-eight—searching for the early arrivals.

"We need to get the younger guys," he says, always thinking of the future.

It wasn't so long ago that Romeo himself was recruited. Not for football, though. Stuyvesant was searching for something more important to it than athletes: diversity. Romeo was an ideal candidate. He is half black, half white. That makes him a rare commodity. Nearly thirty years ago, in 1979, 12.9 percent of Stuyvesant's students were black. By 1995, the numbers had dwindled: blacks made up only 4.8 percent of the school—even though nearly 40 percent of the city's public school students were then black.

"The racial demographics of the school have been a source of great embarrassment to educators in New York," says author Jonathan Kozol in *The Shame of the Nation*. Those educators included Ramon C. Cortines, New York City's schools chancellor at the time, who tried to address the troubling trend by launching a little-known program in 1995 called the Math and Science Institute. "As educators, we have a responsibility to ensure that every child has an opportunity to excel," Mr. Cortines said.

School administrators handpicked minority students with potential, like Romeo, for rigorous studies beginning in the summer after their sixth grade and continuing through the seventh and into the eighth grades. They were exposed to everything from algebra to great literature to chess until it came time for them to take the elite public high schools exam, the Stuy test. The idea was to avoid controversial quotas but to level the playing field for students who might not have the resources to hire tutors, attend private academies, or take special test prep courses. The rest was up to them.

"I see that as the beginning of my career," Romeo says.

Little compares to the constant pressure of a program of about sixteen months leading up to a high-stakes test for a boy of thirteen, which is why the pressure of getting into Harvard doesn't compare for a young man of sixteen today.

"I've been through worse," he says.

Romeo is reminded daily of those trials, especially when he eats breakfast, shoveling a tray of scrambled eggs and orange juice while sitting in Stuyvesant's dining hall, overlooking the glistening Hudson River beyond. This is where it happened. He studied for the Stuy test right here at Stuyvesant, a wondrous haven of panoramic views and shining escalators and sparkling students, all of which fueled the ambitions of a prepubescent boy.

"I loved this building," he says. "I knew this is where I wanted to be." So did his mom.

She still smarts over the indignity of Romeo's rejection from UNIS, the private United Nations International School, when he was about five years old. He had lived with his grandparents in France from the ages of two to four, and when he returned to the United States, he spoke a mix of English and French that school officials took to mean that his verbal skills were not sufficiently developed.

"I wanted to prove them wrong," she says.

What's more, she wanted to prove that her multicultural, biracial child could succeed. "I wanted Romeo to be proof to the world that it can be achieved," she says.

It can and he was. But while he has succeeded, the program that helped prepare him for Stuyvesant hasn't. Black enrollment did inch up almost a percentage point to 5.5 percent by 1997, but it's been in decline since then.

Today, in a school system where more than 70 percent of the students are black or Hispanic, only 2.2 percent of Stuyvesant's students are black, a precipitous drop from 4.8 percent little more than a decade ago, while the number of Hispanics is down from 4.3 percent to 3 percent. White enrollment has dipped from 40 percent to about 39 percent of the school. Asians remain the majority-minority, growing from half of Stuyvesant to about 55 percent of the student body today.

All of which adds up to this: the Math and Science Institute didn't fulfill its mission. Instead the school system changed its name to the Specialized High Schools Institute and expanded its goal beyond preparing only black and Hispanic children for the test, as parents of white and Asian children clamored to gain the same advantage. The unintended result, though, was a decline in blacks and Hispanics at Stuyvesant.

"If you look at the program now, you see very few kids of color," says Ms. Archie, Stuyvesant's assistant principal of pupil services.

Other attempts to balance Stuyvesant's minority enrollment have fallen by the wayside, if not because of ineffectiveness then as a result of changing political winds. For several years, the Discovery program—as unheralded as the Math and Science Institute—allowed students who barely missed the Stuyvesant exam cutoff to get into the school if they took special summer classes and performed well. While the program didn't specifically target minorities, it had the same effect by qualifying what it termed "disadvantaged" students, whose families, among other things, relied on public assistance or were recent immigrants speaking a primary language other than English.

As many as twenty students a year gained admission to Stuyvesant even though they scored sometimes as much as fourteen points below the cutoff, school officials say. But as academic quotas have come under fire in recent years, the Discovery program has quietly taken a hiatus at Stuyvesant. Over the last two years, school officials say they have not accepted any students who failed to reach the exam cutoff. They say, however, they have not abolished the Discovery program.

The issue of diversity still percolates in full view at Stuyvesant. In a meeting of the advisory School Leadership Team at the beginning of the semester, students, teachers, and parents are given a handout that includes the explicit goal of a "more proactive outreach to minority student candidates, and new organizational resources necessary to increase enrollment of African American and Hispanic students." And in a subsequent page-one story, the *New York Times* reminds readers of the intractable problem at Stuyvesant and two other public exam high schools. Under the headline "In Elite Schools, a Dip in Blacks and Hispanics," the author writes, "City education officials said they were at a loss to explain the changes at the three high schools despite years of efforts to broaden the applicant pools."

Policy makers and others strain to identify the cause as well. Some say that private schools more aggressively recruit promising minority students, siphoning prospects from high schools like Stuyvesant. Others say schools and teachers in predominantly black and Hispanic neighborhoods sometimes fail to adequately prepare their students for the kind of math needed to pass the Stuy entrance test. And then there is the perennial problem of resources: white and Asian families have in many cases the financial wherewithal that others don't to pay for the costly tutoring needed to help their children win a seat. Ms. Archie, also the assistant principal in charge of admissions programs, remains perplexed by the problem.

"There's so much more that has to be done," she says.

The problem is not only that there are few blacks and Hispanics at Stuyvesant: that fact is also glaringly obvious. Students of different races and ethnicities segregate themselves in the school.

"Race is part of Stuy, no question, everyone has a label," says Mr. Polazzo, the coordinator of student affairs.

Predominantly white seniors stake out territory by the second-floor "senior bar," prime real estate near the school's bridge entrance, and underclassmen don't dare tread there unless invited. "We were told not to sit there because we'd be likely to get beaten up," writes a freshman in an opinion piece in the *Stuyvesant Standard* newspaper.

About ten feet away, Asian seniors have a lock on space along a wide hallway, and nary a non-Asian walks through. From there, status works in inverse relation to floor number: the higher the floor, the lower the caste. Asian juniors have territory by the gym on the third floor that is dubbed the "Asian atrium." Indians and Middle Eastern students—known here as "brown people"—occupy parts of the fourth floor. Blacks and Hispanics have a slice of land on the fifth floor by the dining hall—an area known as the "ghetto." Asian sophomores own the sixth-floor "Asian bar."

As for freshmen, they have such low status, regardless of race or ethnicity, they have to climb up to floors seven, eight, and nine for refuge. Apparently the highest floor, ten, is too toxic for anything but actual classes. White freshmen have lately carved out a niche near the second-floor staircase landing that looks more like a romper room where small bodies collide with high frequency.

The city's boroughs demarcate several other Stuyvesant cliques: Jews from Manhattan's Upper West Side, Russian immigrants from Brooklyn, and gangsta Asians from Queens. But there are no designations for the typical high school divisions—nerds or their opposites, the beautiful people—and that's hardly a saving grace. Virtually everyone's a nerd at Stuyvesant, even the beautiful people.

"At Stuyvesant, it's cool to have a higher average; at other schools it's nerdy," says freshman Samantha Whitmore, who is a nerd and a member of the beautiful people. "You can raise your hand a lot [in class], and people are not going to say you're a nerd." Even more, she says, "people disdain you if you have a low average."

The others who make up the rest of Stuyvesant's diaspora include people who go directly home from school, people who do drugs, people who do drugs but do well in school, people who play the fantasy Magic card game, the theater crowd, and now the recently anointed cuddle puddle, who are squeezed on the second floor between the white and Asian senior factions.

"The school is completely segregated," says junior Kieren James-Lubin, who is half black and half white like his friend Romeo. Then he quickly amends his statement, so stark are its implications. "Not completely, but mostly."

When an Eastern European girl tried to sit on the sixth-floor Asian bar, she says, she was summarily told to leave. A Korean girl who made friends with white students says she drew dirty looks from Asian friends, who called her a "twinkie"—yellow on the outside, white on the inside. An Indian freshman called an Asian boy a "chink"; the Asian boy responded by punching him in the eye, Ms. Archie says.

Students blame the problem on themselves.

"I think we self-segregate ourselves," says senior Liana-Marie Lien, the daughter of Vietnamese and Chinese immigrants, who settles in the second-floor Asian sector.

"At Stuy, it seems like more often than not, we stick to our own segregated cliques without a second thought," says an opinion piece in the *Spectator* newspaper. "We must strive to eliminate the sense of division."

Students do try. A talent show that celebrates the school's ethnic and racial melting pot invokes students to "Get your diversity on." A junior of Indian descent says she attempts to be color-blind: "I try not to define myself" through ethnicity. Her friends, however, do it for her, defining her as "the brown girl who hangs out with the Asians." And she says, "That's what I don't like about Stuyvesant. There are a lot of cliques." It's hard to avoid reminders. A flyer for an upcoming Black Students League meeting asks, "Have you ever been discriminated against b/c of your race?" Someone felt inspired to scrawl on it an emphatic answer: "Yeah!"

And yet, in a reflection of the contradictions and complexities of Stuyvesant, a tradition of tolerance persists. Being different is the norm. One out of five students is a first-generation American, and about a third are themselves immigrants, most commonly from distant points of the globe, including China, Russia, and Bangladesh. That explains why there is a Bengali Culture Club, not to mention the Chinese Students Association, the German Club, the Guyanese Culture Club, the Indian Culture Club, the Japanese Honor Society, the Romanian Club, the Filipino Club, the Greek Club, and the Korean Club.

The immigrant experience, where education is king, is infused in the Stuyvesant culture. So is the American Dream, which junior Katherine Kim can attest to. Her parents journeyed from Korea to the United States in the hopes of giving their children a better opportunity. "They came here for me," she says.

Her parents toil seven days a week running a Broadway deli, hoping for nothing less than Ivy League colleges for their two children. Her father, Katherine says, "wanted us to study; he didn't want us to taste the reality he was going through, the harsh reality." Katherine's brother made it, garnering a perfect SAT score and a scholarship to Columbia University. Now it's Katherine's turn.

"It's junior year—do or die," she says.

Six days a week, she attends a private Korean academy to get a leg up on the competition, taking classes in physics and precalculus. But it's not simply the coursework that sets the place apart. When Katherine enters the Kappa Community Center, a tidy little building hidden away from a main thoroughfare in Queens, it's as if she's been instantly transported back to an Asian sanctuary, led by tradition, respect, and a strict adherence to the rules.

At the threshold, Katherine removes her shoes and bows respectfully to the academy's revered principal. Inside, it is as quiet as a temple. Students shut doors with a light touch so as not to disturb others in deep academic contemplation. There is not an iota of desktop graffiti. Students clean up after themselves. A sheet of paper taped to a wall informs, "Excuses must be legitimate and true or consequences will follow." Outside the principal's office, a bank of thirty-two television monitors keeps track of every classroom, every student, every study hall. Classroom doors are adorned with gold labels of the names of famous American colleges to remind students of their goal: MIT. YALE. HARVARD. BROWN. UPENN. CORNELL. JOHNS HOPKINS. UC BERKELEY.

There should be another door: STUYVESANT. For many immigrant parents, that's why they first bring their children here. It's a collective mind-set, to get into the great American high school, the key to the great American college, which leads to the great American Dream, which is becoming a doctor or a lawyer or a professional of another ilk and taking care of the rest of the family. But first, parents clamor to get their children into this Asian academy, the demand for which is so great that despite its $300 to $400 monthly cost, it doesn't advertise. It doesn't need to. It is forced to turn away droves of applicants because it doesn't have enough space for them.

"They're all crazy about sending their kids to Stuyvesant," says the academy's principal, Michael Son, who is himself one of those parents. His oldest child is entering Stuyvesant next year.

If you get into that school, he says, the thinking goes, "You're on your way."

For other immigrants, like fifteen-year-old Daniel Alzugaray, the way to Stuyvesant is a solitary path. He started studying for the Stuy test a year before he even arrived on these shores.

Born in Cuba, the son of a Russian man and a Cuban woman, Daniel was living in Portugal with his mother and his American stepfather when they told him about Stuyvesant, the famous American school. So he went out and bought a study guide to prepare for the entrance exam. Just months after settling in the United States, he took the test and passed. But it still feels like a dream to Daniel, as it did when he first caught sight of the Hudson River from the windows of Stuyvesant.

"When I saw the view from the lunchroom, I said, 'How can it be?' It's surreal," Daniel says.

He still finds himself marveling at the sights. "I see the Empire State Building and say, 'Wow.'" Sometimes the freshman daydreams about the Internet service Google Earth and imagines how it shows the globe from the great distance of a satellite, then zooms in to Stuyvesant to where he sits, daydreaming in art class.

It might be a marvel that Daniel made the cutoff for Stuyvesant, given that he didn't even start speaking English until he was about ten, except that such circumstances are common at the school, where students are fluent in more than fifty-nine languages. The staccato of foreign speech that echoes through the hallways is part of the messy, discordant life of Stuyvesant, where students are anything but homogeneous. Different religions coexist, whether represented by the Seekers Christian Fellowship or a "Grand Shavuot Ice Cream Party" for the school's considerable Jewish population. Meanwhile, middle-class and upper-middle-class students regularly interact with poor kids, who make up nearly 17 percent of the student body, a figure based on the number eligible for free lunch.

And in one of the most visible signs of Stuyvesant's diversity, students openly express their sexual orientation. That includes members of the Gay Lesbian and Straight Spectrum. Once a year, droves of students commit to a "Day of Silence" to express their support for gender diversity. If you ask, they will hand you a slip of paper:

Please understand my reasons for not speaking today. I support lesbian, gay, bisexual, and transgender rights. People who are silent today believe that laws and attitudes should be inclusive of people of all sexual orientations and gender identities. The day of silence is to draw attention to those who have been silenced by hatred, oppression, and prejudice. Think about the voices you are not hearing. What can you do to end the silence?

Faculty don't interfere. Sometimes, actually, faculty get in the act. Such is the case with "Gay Day," an event in the first-floor lobby, where a teacher strums a guitar in solidarity with students. The affair has the staid feel of an ordinary PTA meeting, where chocolate-chip cookies are sold, except for a few telling details. A girl in a white satin robe presides over a twenty-five-cent marriage booth where same-sex kids kiss. For sale are T-shirts that read "Captain Fabulous!" and "LESBIONIC WOMAN." And a gaggle of cross-dressers enter in full regalia: high heels, purple spandex, gold chains. A teacher passing by mutters that such a spectacle would never fly in a more conservative place like Kansas: "Only in New York," she says.

Such an event wouldn't always play well at Stuyvesant, which may be why it occurs in June, near the end of the school year, not on this afternoon in mid February when hundreds of parents and incoming students are packing the auditorium for the school's Open House. Mr. Teitel, the principal, is standing at the podium in a conservative black suit, saying, "I've never seen any other school like it." He's talking about Stuyvesant's wealth of course offerings in math, science, and the humanities. But he could just as easily be talking about the school's wealth of diversity.

CHAPTER SEVEN

Like a Polaroid

FOURTH PERIOD, ROOM 401. MATH RESEARCH CLASS. The room contains all the telltale signs of a typical high school class: boys in peach fuzz, straining to reach adulthood. Girls scribbling notes not having anything to do with classwork. A poster of wild-haired Einstein, who's quoted saying, "The truth of a theory is in your mind, not in your eyes." But off to the side, by the front of the class, listening intently to the teacher discuss arcane math, is an anomaly that betrays the eyes: a little boy topped off by bed-head vectors of blond fluff, not unlike the messy mop Einstein reflects back. At four feet five inches and fifty-five pounds, the little boy is dwarfed by many of his classmates. His feet barely touch the floor from the perch of his swivel chair. Buried inside a big blue parka to ward off the mid-February chill, he doesn't look anything like a surly teenager, and he's not. He's not even old enough to be a member of next year's incoming freshman class. He's ten years old. And if the principal is right that there's nothing like Stuyvesant, there's certainly no one like Milo Beckman.

Named after a family friend's cat, Milo was born with a compulsion to learn, process information, master knowledge. At the age of two, while staying at a Florida hotel with his family, he would run from door to door, reciting four-digit room numbers. By two and a half, he was reading. When he was three, he would wind down at night in bed by reciting numbers in sequence: four, eight, twelve, sixteen . . . Or if that didn't work, then one plus one equals two, two plus two equals four . . . until he reached into the thousands, or into the ether of his dreams.

In preschool, Milo couldn't fathom why other children couldn't read and write as he did: "I remember feeling, 'Why aren't these kids writing normally? Why aren't they reading?'" All the other children would gather around Milo, like their teacher, as he read a story to them. By four, he wrote a novel, science fiction about an evil babysitter. Around then, friends encouraged his parents, struggling entrepreneurs who run the New York International Children's Film Festival, to test his intelligence. But the test failed: he hit the ceiling in every category. So he took another test designed for gifted children. The result: Milo was off the charts, somewhere between one in ten thousand and one in a million.

"It's not like there's something you can do to make it happen," says his mother, Emily Shapiro, who teaches a birthing class. "His memory is unlike anything I've witnessed before."

Adds Milo, "Dad said I have a memory like a Polaroid camera."

On his fourth birthday, Milo stared at a subway map and, from his mind's eye, wrote seventy pages about all the possible permutations of getting from Coney Island in the far reaches of Brooklyn to their home, then on Fulton Street in Lower Manhattan. "I couldn't get him to open any of his presents," his father says. His mother would take Milo on some of his elaborate subway routes, and the longer the trip, the better. Sometimes, when they reached their stop, they didn't even bother stepping off the platform; they'd just turn around, hop on another subway, and head home. It was about the journey, not the final destination.

Around that time, his parents were surprised to discover that Milo had created a spreadsheet of the solar system and written several chapters of a book he had never mentioned. So his parents decided it was time to hire a tutor. Neighbor Tim Novikoff, then an undergraduate student at NYU majoring in math, would come over, sit on the floor with Milo, and the two would talk math, practicing arithmetic without the aid of pen or paper, reciting such exercises as two times two equals four, two times four equals eight, two times eight equals sixteen.

"A four-year-old doing arithmetic in his head, that's nuts, that's crazy," Mr. Novikoff says. "He was born that way."

Milo would grasp concepts immediately and run with them. He knew how to compute area. He quickly learned prime factorization—that, for instance, twenty-four equals two times two times two times three, leaving Mr. Novikoff in awe.

"I'm thinking, on a selfish level, I can't believe I'm getting a chance to have this opportunity," he says. "It almost felt like an honor."

Sometimes it felt like a struggle. Milo's mind was so supple that he was easily distracted, his hyperactive brain wandering to random objects in his room while the tutor tried to lasso his charge's attention back to math. Eventually, Mr. Novikoff told Milo's parents that the little boy wasn't ready for a math tutor. A few years later, when Mr. Novikoff was in his first year teaching at Stuyvesant, he agreed to tutor Milo again. It was a matter of mercy. Then seven, Milo was distraught in his elementary school math class. It was too easy. He was bored. He broke down in fits.

"I used to drag him, crying, to school . . . literally yanking his arm," his mother says.

Milo had already taught himself elementary school math, using a computer program to plow through multiplication, long division, fractions. Mr. Novikoff took him to the next level, teaching Milo high school math, including algebra, geometry, number theory. Finally, Mr. Novikoff felt that Milo was ready to take a math class at Stuyvesant. Maybe it was genius meeting good fortune. A neighbor becomes a math teacher, recommends Milo to Mr. Jaye, a math chairman who has a congenital disregard for school rules and regulations and, thus, has no compunctions about allowing a ten-year-old prodigy to take classes at Stuyvesant without passing the entrance exam or being officially enrolled.

Milo started taking classes at Stuyvesant when he was eight. This year, his parents officially pulled him out of his fifth-grade class at P.S. 234 a couple of blocks from Stuyvesant. He was getting little out of it. Now he's homeschooled in English, history, and science, while he attends four classes at Stuyvesant, making him, in effect, a freshman without official

portfolio. In addition to his math research class, Milo's taking a
Stuyvesant course called math team and another in trigonometry. He's
also in a class where students learn to build stereo speakers because Mr.
Jaye simply thought it would be fun. But Milo can't get enough math. At
home, Milo helps his older sister, Willa, with her seventh-grade math
homework. "Only when she asks," he notes. She asks for help on problems like, if you know the radius of a bicycle wheel, what is its circum-
ference? Milo practically frowns at the simplicity of the answer: multiply
the radius by two, then multiply it by pi, which he recites to the twenty-
fifth decimal place:

$$3.1415926535897932384626433$$

"It's a mixed blessing, and I think Milo knows that," his mother says
of his gift. "It comes with pressure. It comes with feeling odd. It's not
been easy and glamorous. . . . There was a period he hated when people
called him a genius."

Milo adds, "It's sort of like name-calling." It's odd to see him nodding
in agreement with his mother. He looks too young to comprehend the
complexity of his situation. He looks like a fifth grader, small and cub-
like and unformed, or not fully formed, not even close, and he sounds
like a fifth grader, complete with the squeaky voice of a little boy, and
yet what comes out are the elaborate words of an adult, the end product
of a thought process too advanced for someone housed inside a ten-
year-old's body.

"He didn't ask to be born with this brain, and he didn't necessarily
want it," his mother says.

When she thought about asking a psychologist to evaluate Milo in
the third grade, he responded in horror: "But, Mom, everyone will *know*."

"It was like a deep, dark secret," she says.

Only rarely does Milo betray his age. It reveals itself at the most
unexpected of moments, when he pauses from, say, proving the
Pythagorean theorem and chirps that if he does well in school, his father
will reward him with a pizza party. Even when you are a child prodigy,
prizes like that still matter.

They also almost reaffirm that Milo is just a regular fifth grader, except that he is all too aware that he's not. Mr. Novikoff, his former math tutor, was heartbroken when Milo once confided, *I wish I was normal*. Milo still wrestles with the separation from his fifth-grade friends. "It's sort of, I mean, I'd like to be with kids my age," he says. " . . . It's kind of weird because I'm not with them anymore." What's also strange, he says, is that he's attending a high school where students are nearly twice his age—and twice his size. "I'm kind of used to doing this when I'm talking to people," he says, demonstrating how he has to crane his neck, his big brown saucer eyes staring up at the fictional teenager standing before him, an imposing giant.

High school is tough enough for teenagers; for a ten-year-old, it's exponentially harder. Not that Milo grapples with the subject matter. Math is still a piece of cake. It's just that he's not used to getting an hour of math homework a night. His fifth-grade pals get about twenty minutes of homework altogether.

"It's intense, you could say."

Though he doesn't say it, high school is also lonely. It's not easy to find a teenager who wants to hang out with a ten-year-old. There is one, though—Daniel, the fifteen-year-old Cuban immigrant, who takes math research class with Milo. One day they went to get ice cream. Milo ordered chocolate-chip cookie dough, his favorite. At the counter, Daniel asked Milo how to spell the word for ten to the hundredth power, or the number one followed by a hundred zeros. Milo coolly replied, "*G-o-o-g-o-l*," not "*G-o-o-g-l-e*," the famous Internet search engine. Daniel was impressed. It was a trick question. "No one ever gets that," Daniel said. Milo brushed it off, saying, "That's my typical quiz question." Daniel upped the ante. What, he asked, is 36 times 36? The ten-year-old thought for a split second, then blurted it out: 1,296. How did he compute it so quickly in his head? Simple. His formula: $(30 + 6) \times (30 + 6)$, or $(30 + 6)^2$.

A friendship was born.

Milo has made another friend, his math research teacher, Jan Siwanow-icz. They make an unlikely pair. At six foot three, Mr. Siwanowicz towers over Milo. A bedraggled, hulking figure with long, stringy blond locks and clunky tortoiseshell glasses hiding eyes red from sleepless nights, Mr. Siwanowicz has trouble remembering how old he is until he's reminded what year it is. He computes the math, then emits an output: he's twenty-nine years old.

But Mr. Siwanowicz used to be Milo.

Mr. Siwanowicz too was a math whiz. The son of an engineer and a statistician, he was born and raised in Warsaw, Poland, where as a child he read math books for amusement. In preschool, he counted not the traditional way—one, two, three—but in binary, using zeros and ones, like a computer program. After his family moved to the United States, he made it through several qualifying rounds in high school to represent Poland in the international mathematics Olympiads, winning bronze. Later he confirmed his extraordinary talent, becoming a winner in the prestigious William Lowell Putnam Mathematical Competition, effectively making him one of the top undergraduate mathematicians in North America. There was only one hiccup: he had already flunked out of one college and was well on his way to failing out of another.

"I stopped caring," he says.

While attending college in Poland, he stopped showing up to class. He stopped studying. He stopped eating. He doesn't know why. Alarmed, his parents brought him back to New York to convalesce and enrolled him at City College, where he proceeded to fail out again. In one course, he didn't attend any of the classes but aced the final, and still failed. In another, he was so incensed by the contents of a final exam, which he felt didn't reflect the coursework, that he handed it in blank. Just shy of gaining his undergraduate degree, his grade point average stands at a paltry 1.6.

Mr. Siwanowicz isn't supposed to be teaching. He doesn't have a license, which requires a college degree. He only has a high school diploma. He lives in a dusty room in his parents' apartment in Queens. He barely gets by on about $1,300 a month after taxes as a school aide at Stuyvesant, which is why he has to patrol the library, despite the efforts of Mr. Jaye, the math chairman, to release Mr. Siwanowicz from the lowly monitoring task. Mr. Jaye, ever the troublemaker, hired Mr. Siwanowicz to unofficially teach math research to freshmen and sophomores for one compelling reason: Mr. Jaye recognized Mr. Siwanowicz's math gifts in the same way he understands that ten-year-old Milo needs a place like Stuyvesant if he is to reach his potential. So a student who doesn't belong is being taught by a teacher who's not supposed to teach, and yet the two of them may be the most innately gifted people in the school.

Mr. Siwanowicz still struggles with bouts of depression. The episodes last about a week, then release him for a few weeks before ineluctably returning. He tries to cope by isolating himself in his cluttered room at his parents' home, listening to a relentless, orderly techno beat from Internet radio, which sounds to him like the reassuring rhythm of a march. The hard part comes after night falls, when he ponders the morning and the bright light of the day again.

"I know I'll wake up tomorrow and forget everything," he says, expressionless, a single tear streaking down his cheek.

Mr. Siwanowicz doesn't know if he'll finish college. He doesn't seem to care. He glazes at the mind-numbing thought of all the paperwork involved in being reinstated as an undergraduate student at City College. "I just don't have the mind to comprehend the bureaucracy," he says. And yet he wonders how he'll become a licensed math teacher, which is all that he wants, a calling he discovered when he was a high school senior and volunteered to teach a class. That moment, however, seems far away. He barely remembers the details of his own past. He seems almost embarrassed by the present.

"I'm not a role model," he says. "The last thing I want is the kids to grow up like me." But it's the kids who sustain him, "saving his life, giving him purpose," Mr. Jaye says. It gets Mr. Siwanowicz up in the morning, the urgency of getting to "the kiddies," as he affectionately calls them. In return, he imparts his sophisticated knowledge of math in gentle doses.

Mr. Novikoff, Milo's former tutor, once remarked how lucky Mr. Siwanowicz was for being so good at math, a strange compliment coming from someone who as a math teacher is skilled in the subject himself. Mr. Novikoff will never forget how his colleague responded. *Yes, I am lucky, but everything has its price*, Mr. Siwanowicz said. Mr. Novikoff just hopes Milo turns out well. He has every confidence that the little boy will find his way. Milo is motivated, he's well-adjusted, he's resilient. But like Mr. Siwanowicz, Milo suffers from bouts of insomnia, and if his teacher's experience is any guide, genius alone isn't enough to overcome life's intractable problems.

CHAPTER EIGHT

Sing!

PROBLEMS ARE ESCALATING IN ROOM 339 AT 5 P.M. ON Friday, February 17, where a defiant girl is surrounded by a group of frustrated students. The girl, sitting cross-legged in a black swivel chair, won't budge. Neither will those circling her. The shades are nearly drawn, leaving a stark fluorescent sheen on the gathering. A window is cracked open, though it does little to let the tension escape.

"I would love to do something I'm proud of," says the girl, Xevion.

A boy shoots back that this isn't about doing earth-shattering work. Xevion frowns. That's not what she wanted to hear.

Then it comes out: Xevion, the best singer in the junior class, doesn't want to sing Aretha Franklin's classic, "Respect." It's about her own self-respect. Xevion doesn't only like to challenge her friend Romeo at lunch. She wants to challenge herself, and she thinks the famous R&B vocal is just too "cheesy." She'd rather perform something less obvious from the more contemporary R&B pop singer Deborah Cox. Xevion is thinking that the idea is to move people, and if you don't, what's the point? She isn't about to be intimidated by this group.

"When you're dealing with my mother," she says, "a room full of teenagers won't scare you." Her mother, a Jamaican immigrant, always told her daughter to look people in the eye and speak her mind. Which she's doing now, assuring the juniors surrounding her that she will find the right song: "Give me until tonight."

Such is the plight of an idealistic diva and a school play in progress, which is what they are rehearsing after school on this icy February day. The stakes of putting on a play are high at Stuyvesant because this isn't an ordinary high school production. This is one of the biggest events of the year. Seniors, juniors, and a combined sophomore and freshman class engage in fierce competition against one another to stage the best musical. Several hundred students from every grade mobilize in a rare show of class unity to create virtually every aspect of each production, from intricate costumes to ornate sets to original scripts to a dizzying array of dance numbers ranging from hip-hop to Irish jigs. The only things the students don't create are the melodies, which are borrowed from famous songs, but even then, they invent new lyrics to fit their story line. The competition—three plays a night repeated over three days—is such a big deal that an exclamation point is a permanent appendage of its name: Sing! Every performance sells out—filling more than eight hundred seats a night—generating a whopping school profit of about $30,000. But for the students, the prize is something vastly more precious to them: class bragging rights.

For the adults, Sing! is little more than a distraction, especially on this Friday when Mr. Jaye has his own problems. For one, Mr. Siwanow-icz is still patrolling the library, despite Mr. Jaye's impassioned plea to the principal. For another, Mr. Jaye just emerged from a kitchen cabinet meeting, where he's still fuming about butting heads again with his nemesis, Ms. Damesek, the assistant principal of organization. She wants more faculty to patrol the hallways. He doesn't. "The perfect school for her would have no students," he says. Ms. Damesek's stance on school security especially galls Mr. Jaye because he recommended her for the job at Stuyvesant, and now all they do is argue. He's called her unmentionable names; she doesn't take the criticism lightly. So it goes.

Meanwhile, Mr. Jaye recently received word that he passed the principal's licensing exam, bringing him one step closer to taking the top job at the New Jersey high school—unless Mr. Teitel, Stuyvesant's principal, retires, a prospect with no hope, even though Mr. Jaye continues to harbor some.

"It's frustrating knowing you're ready to be the starting pitcher but you have to watch the World Series," he says.

Mr. Teitel has no intention of retiring, despite this Friday. As principal, he sees himself as the equivalent of a chief executive of a corporation with a budget of about $14 million, and right now, that budget is looking tight. He's preparing to hire counselors for the short-staffed guidance office, but that means he may have to let go of as many as a half-dozen teachers. It's the immutable law of any school budget: what it giveth in one area, it taketh away in another.

On top of that, Mr. Teitel is just beginning to realize that he underestimated student vitriol over the looming installation of scanners to record attendance. What's more, he's still grappling with the fallout from the cuddle puddle controversy, which seems to have the half-life of a nuclear meltdown, and it's gone all the way to the top of the food chain. He's already had a personal sit-down with New York City Schools Chancellor Joel I. Klein to discuss the controversial article. And before February's done, he'll find himself trying to placate worried parents on the School Tone Committee and at a Parents' Association meeting who want to know what in the cuddle puddle world is happening to their children.

At least, though, Mr. Teitel has resolved a couple of other controversies. Teachers have reluctantly agreed to take on the various monitoring duties stipulated in their new contract. Even better, they have agreed to flip over their time cards once a day, which leaves only the question of who will flip them back at the end of the day. Mr. Teitel has found an ideal candidate: himself. He is not above a little flipping. That, he can live with. But his job as principal is another matter. "It's hard," he says. "It'll be the nights that will force me to retire."

Mr. Grossman, the English chairman who helped the principal defuse the time card imbroglio, is preoccupied with a grave matter of his own: Jane. Until the senior recently returned to school, Mr. Grossman worried she would turn up dead. When she did turn up, after a stint in drug rehab, he was shocked by how "scary skinny" she was. On her first day back in his English class, she raised her hand but didn't get called on. It wasn't his fault. The students are so advanced that he lets them call on one another. Her turn never came up. She felt slighted, as if her fellow students weren't willing to take her back. She cried a little. "It was just heartbreaking to me," he says. Mr. Grossman can't help but think that she's smart, that she's a great kid. He just doesn't know if she's going to make it in this class, let alone in life. For now, though, he is thankful for the little things. Jane is coming to class.

"I can feel the tension in my chest," he says.

Such concerns make Sing! seem almost trivial. And yet, the outcome of the musical competition weighs heavily on scores of students, especially seniors, because the way they see it, what hangs in the balance is history, or an attempt to avoid making it. The seniors never lose—well, almost never.

"If the seniors don't win," says Liz London, executive producer of their musical, "that would be horrifying."

According to school lore, when Sing! first replaced a popular student-faculty talent show in 1973, the seniors revolted by stumbling onstage drunk—or at least appearing so—as part of an over-the-top parody that offended the judges' sensibilities. Even with Paul Reiser, the future television star, as band director, the seniors couldn't avoid a last-place finish. The combined freshman and sophomore classes put on a good show, featuring a young Tim Robbins in the lead role, but he hadn't won an Oscar yet, and his thespian talents couldn't overcome a production that ran way too long. The contest came down to this: the juniors "sang well, their story was peppy, and so they won by a landslide," according to *Stuyvesant High School: The First 100 Years*, a project of faculty and alumni.

Seniors have never taken the competition lightly again. Since their debut debacle, they have dominated Sing!, except when struck by a peculiar affliction that they refer to in hushed tones: the six-year curse. About every six years, so goes the curse, the stars are misaligned, up is down, and the seniors lose in an ignominious Stuyvesant upset worse than ending up at their safety college. It's been seven years since they lost.

They're overdue.

Making matters more precarious, the performances have been moved up to late March from early April, bowing to Ms. Damesek, the assistant principal of organization, who makes the unpopular but wise decision to give students more time to focus on studying for the AP exams in May. The Student Union throws its own monkey wrench into Sing! by changing the scoring system this year. Each play will be rated on a scale from one to ten instead of one to three to give judges more latitude to express subtleties in their scoring. But the scoring changes could inject an element of uncertainty as well, foiling the predictability of the seniors' triumphant finish, which is just the way the upstart juniors want it.

"We're definitely going to win," crows eleventh grader Liam Ahern, who looks the part of confident codirector, which he is, ready-made in a red turtleneck, silver necklace, and dark-rimmed rectangular glasses.

Liam has reason to be confident. A few days have passed, and Xevion, the great junior vocalist, has relented and agreed to sing "Respect."

"I caved," she says, but then considers the upside. "It's a challenging song, and they promised if I did this song, we could do a different type of Sing!, more meaningful" next year when they're seniors. The prospect seems to buoy Xevion. She's given up her dream of becoming president of the United States. "He doesn't make enough money, and he's always under fire," she says. But perhaps hashing out vocal choices is good practice in the art of negotiation for a girl who now aspires to be a diplomat.

Confidence is at a lower ebb a couple of days later in the auditorium, where scant freshmen and sophomores are huddled in darkened front seats, trying to make sense of a script in which the main character, Pandora, gets fed up; organ transplants are plentiful; people live too long; Michael Jackson, John Lennon, and Napoleon intermingle in the underworld; and it's up to Hades, ruler of the netherworld by way of Greek mythology, another esoteric Stuyvesant specialty, to save the day.

Codirector Taylor Shung is wondering where everyone is. "We have some people absent, and it's frustrating," she says.

It doesn't help matters that a glass display in the nearby first-floor lobby lists the previous winners of Sing!, reminding her that soph/frosh, as they are known, has never come out on top. She isn't optimistic about their chances this year. But then again, she and her cadre of underclassmen have trafficked a secret copy of the juniors' script, which they think is weak. And in this topsy-turvy year, with all the rule changes, she believes that just about anything is possible.

> *IN HONOR OF ALL WHO DIED*
> *WAITING FOR THE BELL TO RING*
> —desktop graffiti, Stuyvesant High School

CHAPTER NINE

The Natural

OUTSIDE, IT'S SNOWING. INSIDE ROOM 231, DURING fifth period, it's the late nineteenth century, a topsy-turvy period in history when an acquisitive United States, ordained by "manifest destiny" and the "white man's burden" to bring civilization to the rest of world, is looking overseas to conquer new lands.

"Who wants to be Santa Claus?" the teacher asks.

A hand volunteers in the back. Who wants to play the part of the Cuban boy? Who wants to be the Filipino girl? Others pitch in. But a student interjects, saying he sees stereotypes in the class handout, a cartoon of children representing nations that are the objects of America's desire. In the drawing, the Cuban boy is depicted with Jheri curls. The Filipino girl is in tattered clothing. Santa Claus, a stand-in for the United States, is condescending, asking, "Have you children been good and behaving yourselves?"

"Do you see a modicum of racism?" the teacher asks.

Suddenly, even though dancing snowflakes beckon beyond the windowsill, she has riveted their attention. No longer are they talking about stultifying, antediluvian history that has no bearing on their teenage lives. Now the conversation is about racism and stereotypes, pertinent issues in a class of thirty-two students, twenty-one of whom are Asian, many immigrants or first-generation Americans.

It's about here, now, Thursday, March 2, just over a month into the semester.

"What if God is black, or Asian?" wonders an Asian boy in the back.

It's not quite on point, but it doesn't matter; the teacher has them thinking, and she goes with it, grabbing the momentum, punctuating the air with small, chalk-smudged hands, exhorting her students to speak, as if she were a conductor, eliciting the right combination of notes from an orchestra.

"My, my, my, I couldn't have done that any better!" she enthuses at one student.

"The man, Chris!" she emotes at another.

"Give it to you, excellent!" she showers praise on a third.

Jennifer Lee is in her element, a diminutive teacher in perpetual motion who commands complete authority in this U.S. history class—except for one thing: she isn't their teacher. She isn't even being paid to stand before them. At twenty-six, she barely looks older than the students: a beautiful young woman with long, silky black hair framing a delicate, open face. Ms. Lee is herself a student, earning her master's degree at Teachers College, the vaunted program at Columbia University uptown. As part of her graduation requirements, she has to instruct a class as a student teacher, which is why she's here at Stuyvesant. She isn't just teaching. She's gaining classroom experience. But already, she's a natural. The strange thing is, she didn't intend any of this.

"I never saw myself as a future teacher," she says.

Nor did others, like attorney Jim Cocoros. But then, "You come to a point in life when you're completely miserable," he says. About seven years ago, he asked himself what he liked to do and the answer wasn't the law. It was math. Now thirty-three, he teaches precalculus at Stuyvesant, and notwithstanding his student loans from law school, this is where he's meant to be.

The same, however, cannot be said for all his colleagues.

While the students have to take a test to gain entrance to the school, the teachers don't. In fact, Stuyvesant draws from the same pool of teachers as any other school in the public school system. Some parents and teachers themselves say Stuyvesant has drawn a handful of weak teachers, blaming the teachers' contract, which for many years set aside vacancies for teachers with the most seniority. Teachers looking to transfer from one school to another could also bump a teacher with less seniority out of a position. The result, in some cases, was that older teachers who were looking to coast in their final years before retirement would transfer to Stuyvesant as a kind of final resting place—a vacation of sorts—where the common wisdom was that students would learn no matter what, in spite of bad teaching or even no teaching, say many parents, teachers, and school administrators.

"I'll be honest and tell you, the transfer system was a mixed bag," Mr. Teitel says. "Some people came and they were terrific and others came thinking this was going to be a three-year retirement before 'I decided it's time to retire.'"

When Mr. Polazzo, the government teacher and coordinator of student affairs, arrived at Stuyvesant six years ago, "teachers told me, a hundred percent of the students are smarter than seventy percent of the teachers." He adds, "Stuy can hide the flaws of some teachers."

Author Sol Stern, who graduated from Stuyvesant, as did his two sons, calls it "the school's dirty little secret" in his book *Breaking Free: Public School Lessons and the Imperative of School Choice.* "Incompetence was randomly distributed at the school," he writes.

The complaint is echoed nationally. "With a few notable exceptions, teaching is attracting fewer top college graduates than it once did," says the spring 2006 report of the Teaching Commission, a group that comprises leaders in government, business, and education, citing problems with inadequate teacher compensation and training programs.

In the mid-1990s, then Stuyvesant principal Jinx Cozzi Perullo complained that she had no say in filling as many as half the school's teacher vacancies in a given year because of the rules of so-called "seniority transfers." School administrators also complained about "integration transfers," another provision of the teachers' contract that gave black and Hispanic teachers preference in switching into schools, like Stuyvesant, lacking diversity. Their complaint wasn't about diversity but about the unintended consequences of the policy, that less qualified minority teachers would supplant more qualified minority teachers. "Integration transfers frequently displaced younger, dedicated minority teachers at Stuyvesant who had been groomed by the principal but had no seniority rights," Stern says.

Recent changes in the contract now empower the principal and department heads to hire those they consider the most qualified. But Mr. Jaye says, "We're still dealing with" vestiges of the old system. He cites the example of a teacher who used the seniority transfer to obtain his job at Stuyvesant and continues to be a problem this semester, giving students tests that are too long and unfair. Mr. Jaye tries to work with him, even though he knows there's little chance of improvement, because the alternative—firing the teacher—is "a huge headache," he says. It would require compiling massive documentation for the principal, fighting the teachers' union, and in the end, he says, he would end up feeling that it was his own job on the line.

"It's like you're on trial," Mr. Jaye says.

Mr. Grossman, the English chairman, knows the feeling. Last year, when he took the rare step of firing a teacher whom he determined to be incompetent, a small faction of angry teachers took up the cause, fighting to reverse the decision. The skirmishing has turned so nasty behind the scenes this semester that a teacher who supports him received an anonymous note smeared with what looked like feces.

"The most difficult part of my job is ensuring the quality of instruction," says Mr. Grossman, who was himself temporarily bumped out of a teaching job early in his career at Stuyvesant by a teacher with more seniority.

With a faculty of nearly two hundred, Stuyvesant boasts a battalion of dedicated teachers who make an average salary of about $72,000, and the best include the likes of rookie math teacher Oana Pascu, rising English teacher Jonathan Weil, and Robert Sandler, a tough but popular social studies teacher. Many of the best found the profession by accident, like Mr. Grossman and Mr. Jaye. Their meandering path stands in stark contrast to the beveled ambition of students whose compass was set toward Stuyvesant from an early age. But maybe that's what makes them such good teachers. The profession found them. So have the students, who know where to find the good teachers, as do their parents, who frequently jockey behind the scenes to get their children into classes with the best teachers. They also know who the bad ones are, including one teacher who is known less for instruction than for surfing the Web for dates.

And then there is French teacher Marie Lorenzo, the longest-tenured instructor at Stuyvesant. Such was her beauty that students and teachers nicknamed her "Legs Lorenzo." Today, decades after she started teaching here, Ms. Lorenzo is a stooped, bespectacled, gray-haired veteran who still teaches French. Though the right intentions are still there, to be sure, it is difficult to see any teaching happening on a recent day in her eighth-period class in room 505, where a volley of student voices drown each other out.

"Why are we talking all at once?" Ms. Lorenzo screams, to no avail.

She shuffles directly in front of a chattering girl in the front row and folds her arms, giving the student her best severe look. "One more word out of you, and you'll be failing this class," she seethes.

That takes care of that. But chattering continues to emanate from the back of the room, where freshman Sammy Sussman is boasting about how he received a 96 in Latin last year in middle school. His grade—or chatter—sends Ms. Lorenzo into a frenzy, which only worsens when another boy dispatches a paper airplane across the room, mysteriously prompting Ms. Lorenzo to send Sammy, not the airplane thrower, to the dean's office and order him to report to her after school.

"What did I do?" he asks.

No answer is forthcoming. Sammy mopes out of the class. Another paper airplane whizzes over Ms. Lorenzo's head. She is oblivious. A boy asks her about homework, which prompts her to yell at him, then she orders him to sit further back in class for no apparent reason. Outside the classroom moments later, Sammy is sitting on a bench, left hand on chin, rust bangs hanging low over moody blue eyes, in *The Thinker*'s position. He's come to the conclusion all on his own that his actions don't warrant a visit to the dean's office. He doesn't plan to meet Ms. Lorenzo at 3 p.m. either.

"She'll probably forget," he says, then adds, "This is my weirdest class."

But as soon as he hands down that verdict, Sammy seems to feel almost bad about it, as if it's his fault, all this weirdness. So he says he's learned some French already, like the word for "leave."

How do you say it in French?

Suddenly, he can't remember.

Sometimes it's hard for Ms. Lee, the student teacher, to remember things too. For her family, the past is marked by pain and disappointment, beginning when her father left Korea to find a better life in the United States.

"He was lured into this American Dream," she says.

But it didn't materialize. Barely able to speak English, he first worked in a deli, then as a stock clerk in a drugstore. When he made his big move, launching a Korean golf magazine, it failed. A second venture, making blouses, went down the tubes. Now he drives a yellow taxi in New York City.

The dream didn't die, though. It just took a different form, in his daughter. Ms. Lee would achieve academically. A poor grade would be met with the parental silent treatment until Ms. Lee internalized the ambition, making it her own. In the summer after sixth grade, she attended a private Korean academy, drilling in math and English for more than a year with the single aim of winning entrance to Stuyvesant. But a day before the test, her cherished aunt died of breast cancer, and Ms. Lee fell just short of making the cutoff for Stuyvesant. She did qualify for the Bronx High School of Science, a great school in its own right but considered a runner-up in the exam derby. It was a family disaster.

"We cried that day," she says.

In high school, Ms. Lee disappointed her parents again, achieving a respectable 89 grade point average, which wasn't high enough to win her acceptance into the college of her family's choice, Columbia. Her father's pronouncement still rings in memory. Father told daughter, "You failed one part of your life."

At Stony Brook University, Ms. Lee pushed herself to pass the next phase, gaining acceptance to the prestigious Phi Beta Kappa academic honors society. But when she applied to Columbia again, this time for a master's degree in political science, she fell short again. She wasn't dissuaded. Instead, she bided her time, living at home and tutoring Korean high school students, before applying to Columbia again. And again she was rejected. Still she remained unbowed. When she heard that she might have a better chance of getting into Columbia's Teachers College, she applied to that master's program, even though she had no intention of becoming a teacher. She simply thought it might be a springboard to a higher degree in political science. Finally, Columbia accepted her.

The day she found out, she stayed up until about two o'clock in the morning to greet her father returning from the taxi night shift. After she told him she had gained admission to Columbia, he gave her a high five. He had never done that before.

"I found an oasis," she says, on "a journey through the desert."

If Columbia's Teachers College wasn't part of the plan, neither was Stuyvesant. As a high school student, she had fallen short of its cutoff; as a student teacher, Stuyvesant just happened to be a practical place for Ms. Lee because of its relatively easy commute from Columbia. But once she arrived at the high school, she discovered an odd thing: joy. She loves teaching, and she loves Stuyvesant.

"I'm just having so much fun with this," she says. "Now that I'm here, I know why I'm here. Two years ago, I never would have imagined I'd be here." For the devoutly religious Ms. Lee, it was fate: "Was this an accident? I don't think so."

She doesn't know, however, whether she will remain at Stuyvesant. As a student teacher, she is, by definition, temporary. With graduation from Columbia looming just months away, Ms. Lee needs to find a permanent job, and she can picture herself teaching at only one place, Stuyvesant. But there are no openings. She is lost. That is, unless Mr. Jaye, the Wizard of Oz, can work his magic.

PART TWO: DETENTION

Early March–Mid April

CHAPTER TEN

Lost in *Gatsby*

"ALL THESE PEOPLE SEEM LOST," ROMEO MUSES.

The football captain is talking about the damaged characters in *The Great Gatsby*, required reading in English class, but his thoughts drift to a moment in time that has fossilized into a postcard of the mind. An indigo ocean. An idyllic seaside town in France. Arradon. Summertime. And centered within the frame is an eight-year-old boy named Romeo, who scampers down to a beach, where one of his teenage cousins is laughing with Romeo's mother about frivolous things like shoes. On his arrival, the two women rise to leave, as if not wanting to be bothered by his presence, which wounds the little boy, and a resolution instantly forms. "I promised myself I would never be a teenager like her," he says of his cousin. Instead, Romeo finds a role model in another cousin, an earnest teenager who harbors great academic ambitions. That summer in France, the two boys find a treasure map hidden inside the broken handle of a racquetball racquet. His cousin forgot that he had stowed the map there five years earlier. Curious, the two boys trace the clues to a tree under which they find the treasure—a smooth, round rock worth absolutely nothing but priceless to Romeo, who is transfixed by the idea that a place in time had been recaptured.

"My destiny started a long time ago," he says.

That destiny brings him to this day, eight years later, in early March, to this place: Stuyvesant, where teenagers like him are apt to be discussing the literary virtues of *The Great Gatsby* not only in class but in the dining hall over a slab of chicken, Spanish rice, and a helping of angst.

"I've been in a spell all week," Romeo is saying. "People say it's a history piece, but it relates to me." He sees Nick, the central character in Fitzgerald's classic novel, as a man tired of the artificiality of life until he meets Gatsby, a man of passion.

"Gatsby is incredibly idealistic," adds Romeo's lunchmate, Xevion, the great junior singer, putting aside her chicken lunch, what she refers to as her "mystery meat." Then Xevion, fresh from making a stand to sing a meaningful ballad in the school musical, finds a connection between Gatsby and herself. "I tend to be idealistic," she says.

Lately, Romeo has come to see himself as a "stoic romantic." It has something to do with an experience that he shares with another high school friend, Kieren, who also is half black, half white.

"We feel alienated from the world," Romeo says, his voice tinged with a vague sense of unease. "We claim we hate all of our peers."

Xevion, who is also black, pipes up, "Present company excepted, I hope."

Romeo lets the implied question linger unanswered as he finishes a thought. "At the same time, there's a yearning for passion, for love, but a reluctance to admit it," he says. Then he releases Xevion from suspense: "You're good."

She exhales audibly. "I feel better," she says.

Gatsby has Romeo thinking about his future too. So inspired is he by the novel that he's wondering if he should incorporate more literature in his college curriculum at Harvard. That he will be attending the famous American college in two years is accepted as fact, although he hasn't applied yet. Even Xevion, who'd be the first to downsize Romeo's ego as his self-appointed conscience, doesn't bother to dispute the notion because it seems so inevitable.

"I have my first year planned out, all the classes I want to take," he says of Harvard.

Romeo ticks off a course load of economics, advanced calculus, physics, and expository writing. Ivy League imaginings are hard to resist because he just returned from a tour of the Harvard campus, where he bumped into four other Stuyvesant students, who, like him, were casing out the university.

Romeo likes the fit. His SAT prep class is humming along. So is his nascent project for the Intel science contest. Romeo was immediately taken with an NYU professor who gave a recent lecture in his Stuyvesant math research class, and now the two of them are about to start working together on Saturday mornings in an attempt to unravel the mysteries of magnetic fusion. Romeo shows off his new NYU photo ID, which identifies him as a "Visiting Scholar." He seems to like where he's heading with that moniker.

Romeo seems to like where the Peglegs are heading too. The football team starts lifting weights next week. Several players from last year's junior varsity team have moved up to varsity, and camaraderie is high. Romeo is feeling daring enough to allow himself to think of a football season with a winning record. "I'm excited," he says. "I'm surprised."

Xevion is less sure of herself. Later, during tenth period, she wanders into room 133, looking for an empty space to practice before her rehearsal for Sing! For Xevion, it wouldn't do to show up for rehearsal without being properly prepared. There are appearances to keep up, especially for one who has already sung at the hallowed Apollo Theater in Harlem. So she navigates around three seated students who are gossiping among themselves, apologizing for the intrusion, calling them "honey," even though they are contemporaries who don't comprehend such a term of endearment unless it comes from a parental figure. They pay her no mind until she abruptly breaks through the low drone of their conversation by belting out the first stanza of Shania Twain's "From This Moment On." They stop speaking. It can't be helped. It's the soprano voice. Piercing and perfect. They look up. Xevion is strutting before the blackboard, as if this classroom were the Apollo and these were her fans, and in a way, it is and they are.

A music teacher barges in to pick up a Delaney book and just as quickly halts, listens, and dissolves into a beatific smile. Xevion's eyes are shut, her right hand modulating to the mellifluous sound of her voice, the ethereal feel of the music. When it ends, the students and teacher applaud.

"You're not in choir," says the teacher. "Why not?"

"That's a long story," Xevion says.

"It was an attitude problem, wasn't it?" says a student in the audience, one of her new fans.

"I don't have an *attitude*," she says with an attitude.

Xevion wouldn't be at Stuyvesant if she didn't have an attitude. When her middle school principal told her it was unlikely that she'd get in because she had only a few weeks to prepare for the entrance exam, Xevion took it as a challenge, studying from a textbook every night. "I just wanted to prove to her I could," she says. "I want to thank her. She did me a huge favor."

Her attitude, though, didn't do her any favors a year ago when she had a run-in with a choir teacher at Stuyvesant. Xevion had waited until the last minute to sign up for chorus class, which was not a good idea because the teacher was just heading out of the room and didn't have time to speak to her. When Xevion returned, the by-the-book teacher, known as something of a diva herself, wouldn't permit her to join the choir: it was too late. Xevion persisted. The teacher took doggedness as recalcitrance. Positions hardened. Xevion came back a third time, an assistant principal in tow, but it did no good. The teacher adamantly refused to let the best singer in her grade join the choir. Xevion shrugs it off now. She's singing, chorus class or not. "I feel sorry for her," she says of the teacher. And off to Sing! rehearsal Xevion goes.

If there's anyone who should be feeling sorry for himself, it's Mr. Siwanowicz, the brilliant school aide, who is on his hands and knees a day later, Friday, March 3, in room 406, the math storage room, pulling inky pages from the bowels of a Risograph CR1610 high-speed copier.

"What were they thinking?" he wonders aloud, and he could be talking about the offenders at school who broke the copy machine—or the dullards who gave him the task of fixing it.

Either way, Mr. Siwanowicz is agitated. The look is written in his pallid expression, in his eyes, which are fissured red under drooping lids. But it could be that he's simply fatigued. He's been playing online board games. He helped his parents repaint the living room. But he can't sleep, still. It's the depression and the debilitating inertia that grip him, at least when he contemplates resuming college so he can earn a degree so he can obtain a license to teach so he doesn't have to fix copiers anymore. He dismisses the thought with reverse logic. "College generally gets in the way of people's education," he grumbles. "College is not that necessary."

Mr. Siwanowicz fixates on the present, the math research class he unofficially teaches. He's encouraged by Daniel, the Cuban immigrant, who asks great questions. And Milo, the prodigy, who reminds Mr. Siwanowicz of himself when he was the same age, except that "Milo is a lot more social," he says. "I was more creepy." Mr. Siwanowicz is troubled by another student who is cutting his class, but he says, "There's nothing I can do." He fails to see the parallel to his own experience as a student who didn't show up to class. And he fails to see the perversity of being a brilliant mathematician, a Putnam fellow, who failed out of college.

"I don't see an irony," he says flatly, moments after fixing the copier.

Mr. Siwanowicz also can't fathom what he needs to do to get reinstated at City College. "I have absolutely no idea," he says. He blames it on his preoccupation with Stuyvesant. "I have way too much work," he says. Doing what? "I have copiers to fix, lightbulbs to replace," he says, deadpan.

He overlooks one other task: monitoring the library during two of his free periods. He's still doing that too.

Mr. Jaye hasn't given up on the fight to dislodge Mr. Siwanowicz from library duty so that the teacher's aide can do something more productive, like talk to kids about math. But at the moment—a period later—Mr. Jaye is sitting in his office, fuming about his other perennial problem: Ms. Damesek.

They've been at it again. In a meeting yesterday with the principal, Mr. Jaye had explained that he wanted to enlist parents as volunteers to proctor a prestigious international math contest, involving more than three hundred Stuyvesant students who had qualified for it. But Ms. Damesek, who is responsible for such matters, had refused, saying she didn't want to leave students in a room alone with a parent who could be a problem. At which point Mr. Jaye said, "I'm not asking for your *permission*, I'm *telling* you." Not backing down, Ms. Damesek said she didn't like the idea of kids hanging around after school unsupervised. To which Mr. Jaye retorted, "You don't like kids *in* school." Mr. Teitel, the principal, who had remained on the sidelines during the skirmish, couldn't help but laugh. Ms. Damesek didn't think it was funny. Nor was she amused this morning when she bumped into Mr. Jaye, who resumed the offensive when he suggested that she had been usurping Mr. Teitel in their last meeting. "I thought Stan was the principal," he said. "Was there something that happened I'm not aware of?"

That time, they refrained from exchanging further indelicacies.

Jane, the senior struggling with a drug addiction, has no such compunctions. By ninth period, she's in full battle mode, wearing a blue hooded jacket, blue jeans, and black sneakers, while her dark mane has been pulled back in a severe ponytail and her jewelry removed, the better to attack when the time comes. She's sitting in the sixth-floor library, waiting to finish a fistfight with a boy in the second-floor senior Asian territory.

They used to be friends. But after her latest bout with drugs, when she returned from detox, he told her he wouldn't put up with her anymore. "You pushed us away," he told her. "You chose drugs over us." Jane responded the only way she knew how: defiantly. "You owe me ten dollars," she told him. He looked back at her sadly. They moved into different groups, settling a safe distance apart on the floor until Jane couldn't help herself, started talking trash, marched up to him, and demanded, "Stand up and fight me." The large boy looked at the little girl and wouldn't move. She kicked him. She punched him. Finally, he said, "You pushed me away."

"Don't blame it on me!" she screamed at him. "Do you know what it means to be addicted?"

Jane lunged at him again, but another student held her at bay. The boy walked away.

Now, sitting in the library, Jane thinks of others who've abandoned her, fed up with her drug addiction—a best friend who ditched her, another good friend who wrote her off. "None of my friends had the capability of being there for me," she says, thinking of last semester when she was bedridden at home and no one called. A sense of discomfort casts a dark shadow over her thin, pale face. "When I say I don't have a conscience, maybe it's true," Jane says. "I'm a bad person."

The bell rings for tenth period. She has no intention of going to her next class, history; dismissing a lesson on the past, she instead grimly heads to the future, down the echoing stairwell to the second floor in the hopes of finding the boy.

"I'm not," she says, "afraid to die."

A day later, a bitterly cold Saturday, March 4, tension of another sort pervades the school, except now it emanates from room 735, where a group of students is wondering if they measure up. Dressed in ill-fitting grownup clothing—jackets and ties for boys, skirts and blouses for girls—students from various schools are participating in Model UN, a simulation of the United Nations where they play the role of ambassadors in the world of diplomacy. Ostensibly, they are discussing "Land Tenure Reform in Southern African Countries" and "Debt Reduction and Assessment Strategies." But the real discussion is occurring during the break in the hallway, where students visiting from other public schools are gawking at the magnificence of Stuyvesant's soaring structure.

"This is huge," says the Djibouti delegate, a sophomore at the David A. Stein Riverdale/Kingsbridge Academy, a neighborhood public school in the Bronx. He had studied a year for the entrance test, hoping to attend Stuyvesant. When he didn't get in, he was crushed. But now he's not so sure, given what he's hearing about the school's intensity. "The work at Stuyvesant is much harder, it's more competitive," he says. His classmate, a senior representing Malawi, is glad he didn't end up here. "Stuyvesant kids are pushed to do work," he says. "We have to take our education in our own hands."

School pride, of course, is in evidence among students at high schools across the nation—and for good reason. Many other schools, public and private, have established a national reputation, rivaling Stuyvesant in academic laurels and honors, such as Boston Latin School, a public school in Boston; Hunter College High School, a public school in New York City; the North Carolina School of Science and Mathematics, a public school in Durham; Phillips Academy, a private boarding school in Andover, Massachusetts; Phillips Exeter Academy, a private boarding school in Exeter, New Hampshire; Walnut Hills High School, a public school in Cincinnati; and Walt Whitman High School, a public school in Bethesda, Maryland.

There are many other great high schools, including those cited on *Newsweek*'s annual list, which is based on the number of advanced placement or international baccalaureate tests taken by all students in a school divided by the number of graduating seniors, a formula devised by education authority Jay Mathews, a *Washington Post* writer. While educators don't agree on how to accurately measure high school greatness, not surprisingly, many of the schools with the highest academic achievers share several traits with Stuyvesant. Many, for instance, are public schools that admit students based exclusively or in part on competitive exams, including Gretchen Whitney High School in Cerritos, California, where the stated mission is to get its students into the colleges that best suit them. Students there averaged an impressive 1344 on the old SAT, and the school is on a first-name basis with university admissions officers, while panels of school counselors and administrators interview every senior to find out where each wants to go to college. "We make no apologies about that," Whitney principal Patricia Hager says of the school mission. "There's no argument about whether you're going to go to college."

As at Stuyvesant, athletics remain on the sidelines at Whitney. Where there is no football field at Stuyvesant, there is no football *team* at Whitney. "We like to say we're undefeated," the principal quips. And in an atmosphere of freedom where academic achievement is expected, students feel good about themselves, a result that creates its own momentum, echoing another Stuyvesant strength. "You can't get them to go home," Ms. Hager says. "Our custodians leave at eleven [p.m.], and we still have kids floating around. This is their home."

The same can be said about students at New Trier High School, a top public school outside Chicago, where students averaged 1270 on the old

SAT. Long after the last bell, they can be found in the well-buffed hall-ways, pursuing their passion, whether it's working on displays for an AIDS awareness initiative or just hanging out with friends. Though the school doesn't impose an admissions test, it benefits from a different kind of selective process: you have to live in the neighborhood to attend the school, which sits on two campuses, and if you live in the neighbor-hood, there's a good chance you're well-off, a familiar phenomenon in other affluent suburbs across the nation.

With a strong local tax base, New Trier has the luxury of reducing teachers' workload so that more than 40 percent of them can serve part-time as "faculty advisers" to its more than four thousand students. Every morning, for twenty-five minutes, advisers meet with students in groups of about twenty-five, talking with them about their hopes, dreams, and fears. "We do an excellent job in the social and emotional connection of our kids," says Debra L. Stacey, principal of the main campus in Win-netka, Illinois. Advisers even make a "home visit" to talk to the students' parents during their sophomore year. "This is New Trier's attempt to make it a small school," says Jan Borja, principal of the freshman campus in Northfield, Illinois. School administrators acknowledge that the adviser system is expensive, but it's a tradition that dates back to 1928, and students love it. "It's so smart," says eighteen-year-old Cara Harsh-man, a senior off to the University of Wisconsin–Madison next year. "It's a support system. You all look out for each other."

At San Francisco's Lowell High School, a public school where admission is based in part on exams, students posted a solid 1236 aver-age SAT, benefiting from another support system: a cadre of parents intensely active in their children's education, much as Stuyvesant's par-ents are. In the wake of California's budget cuts, for instance, Lowell parents stepped in, raising funds to hire about a dozen teachers in such areas as the arts and counseling—a financial achievement in a school where about a third of the students are eligible for reduced-price lunch.

Parents are "critical not only to their kids' success but to the institu-tion," says Paul Cheng, the Lowell principal for sixteen years, until 2006.

Another top public school, Thomas Jefferson High School for Sci-ence and Technology in Fairfax County, Virginia, where admission is partly test-based, boasts a wealth of extracurricular activities much as Stuyvesant does. At T.J., as it's known, extracurricular activities are even built into the curriculum as part of an extended school day so that students can explore their interests, whether it's swing dance or math team. Students, whose average score well exceeded 1400 on the old SAT, can create their own extracurricular activities if they obtain administrators' approval. The result is that "the kids are there because they love to be there," says Principal Evan M. Glazer.

School pride is especially pronounced at Bronx Science, Stuyvesant's main competitor. The rivalry is a function of New York City's specialized high schools exam. After Stuyvesant, the toughest public high school to gain entrance to is Bronx Science. Students who barely miss the cutoff for Stuyvesant often end up at Bronx Science as their second choice. Lisa Ha knows this well. She attended a private Chinese academy, preparing a year for the test, goaded by her mother, a Chinese immigrant, whose goal was for her daughter to win a seat at Stuyvesant. "You have to be the best," she told her daughter. "You have to go to the best school." As an eighth grader, Lisa didn't care whether she made it into Stuyvesant as long as she earned a spot at one of the specialized schools. And she did, ending up at Bronx Science. Now a sophomore, Lisa is a top member of the school debate team, and whenever she beats Stuyvesant, which is often, she is sure to let her mother know.

"It's always good to point out, 'Oh, I beat Stuy.'"

The two schools compete in just about everything, not just debate, but also in the Intel science contest, admissions to the Ivy League, and even sports, like swimming, gymnastics, and soccer. The only thing that Lisa will concede is that Stuyvesant has a better-looking building than Bronx Science, an old, musty school. But she's quick to note that Bronx Science, whose students averaged a strong 1290 on the old SAT, has generated seven Nobel Prize winners, three more than Stuyvesant.

"We make do with what we have," Lisa says. "Imagine what we'd do if we had spent [$150 million] on our building. We might find the cure for cancer."

One of Lisa's debate teammates isn't convinced of Bronx Science's superiority. So Jerry Wang is transferring to Stuyvesant next year as a sophomore after reaching the cutoff on her second try on the entrance exam. But now that she's achieved her goal, Stuyvesant doesn't look so appealing.

For one, the freshman is filled with anxiety as she thinks of Stuyvesant's maze of ten floors and pictures herself getting lost, arriving late to math class. Friends whom she'll miss at Bronx Science have left graffiti on her locker, calling her a traitor for leaving their school for Stuyvesant. "Both of the high schools are, like, nerdy, but Stuy is, like, the nerdy-nerdy," she says. "We're, like, the nerdy-cool."

And then, there's the dreaded pool.

Jerry hasn't gone swimming since the fourth grade, which could present problems when she takes Stuyvesant's swim test. The prospect of failing gym weighs on her. So does the burden of work about to befall her. Stuyvesant recently notified her parents that it may behoove them to buy various math tomes so that Jerry can prepare for the placement test. The freshman couldn't believe it. As it is at Bronx Science, she had three tests last week, four this week, and she wakes up at 5 a.m. every morning just to keep up. "When do I have the time?" she appealed to her mother. Suddenly, the reality of Stuyvesant dawns on her. "The competition," she says, "is going to be so hard."

The reality of competition is just beginning to dawn on Stuyvesant freshmen and sophomores who are downstairs in the auditorium rehearsing for Sing! on this Saturday. The rehearsal is distinguished by one overriding feature: there is no rehearsing going on. Students are late, sick, out of town, or doing homework that will be eaten by the dog—anywhere but where they are supposed to be, which is here, less than three weeks before the curtain rises. Codirector Gui Bessa isn't getting much sleep. "It's so stressful," the sophomore says despondently. "We have to turn it on."

Boys trickle on stage to practice a hip-hop dance routine. It has nothing to do with the script's story line. But there is a rationale. "You put it in the plot because it looks awesome," says Alexa, the freshman coproducer.

At the time being, it looks less than awesome. Sammy, the freshman who drew his French teacher's ire for doing nothing, shows up late for the hip-hop routine. As a way of explaining, he wordlessly shrugs in his huge black parka, and it practically swallows him up. Hardly anyone notices. There are bigger issues with which to contend. The audio is so bad that singers can't be heard. Dialogue is indistinguishable. People are running on and off stage, out of sync, too early, or too late. Shell-shocked, Gui has wandered to a first-floor bench outside the auditorium, a quiet perch where he can slump in perfect misery. The codirector can't comprehend how they could be so bad. He doesn't know if there's enough time to turn the play around. He isn't convinced they will measure up to the juniors and seniors. "Terrible" is all he can say. "Nothing went right."

CHAPTER ELEVEN

Great Expectations

NOTHING HAS GONE RIGHT LATELY FOR SOPHOMORE Mariya Goldman, who broods during fifth period on a thawing Monday, March 6, as she sits Indian-style on the second-floor landing, munching on a small bag of baked Lay's potato chips and digesting her failure to instigate a schoolwide rebellion. What had started as a promising petition drive to end homework during vacations has fizzled out quietly. In the span of a week, Mariya collected 117 signatures, which wasn't bad. But her coconspirator, another disgruntled student, gathered all of 5 names. Few cared. Worse, few thought the petition would work. Worst of all, some students welcome homework, even during vacations, because, after all, this is Stuyvesant. "It's sort of dead now," she says morosely, wearing gothic black, as if dressed to mourn the petition's passing.

Mariya looks drained. At fifteen years old, it's easy to fall into a tailspin for any number of reasons, including her dislike of being five foot eleven; she seems unaware that being a statuesque beauty will be an asset one day. She doesn't like boys staring at her—at her big brown eyes, her network of freckles—oblivious to the admiration that it implies. Not even the prospect of her upcoming two-month anniver-

sary—an eternity in high school—with her first love, a boy named Tom,
can lift her spirits. "He's still my boyfriend," she says, as if the clock is
about to run out.

Mariya refuses to emerge from her funk, struggling to let go of the
homework ban, the inspiration for which was an English teacher who
had the nerve to assign her humanities class what she calls a "really crazy
project" over the recently ended midwinter recess. The homework: evaluate two translations of *Antigone*, the ancient Greek tragedy, and a poem
based on it, in three essays.

"I hate Greek plays and stuff," Mariya says, grimacing at the recollec-
tion. "I really didn't want to do it. I wanted to come up with an excuse
not to do it."

In the original version of the petition, she referred to teachers as "stupid" and "not understanding" and "evil monsters." Once she exorcized
that from her system, she handed out a politer version, addressed to the
principal and faculty:

> It has come to our attention that most teachers confuse the meaning
> of the term "vacation," or "time off," with "time off to do work." We
> would like to point out that a more accurate definition would be
> "time off to rest," and therefore insist that the multitude of projects,
> essays, and papers inevitably assigned during any such vacation are
> actually counterproductive to the purpose of such a period of time
> existing in the first place. Thus, in order for students to return to
> school rested and prepared to learn, as opposed to, say, on two and a
> half hours of sleep, we recommend that the following rules be put in
> effect immediately.

The proposed rules boiled down to this: no homework during vacation. Ending with a dour warning, the petition stated, "This rule should
actually be followed all of the time, as opposed to certain other
rules . . . that are sometimes followed."

Mariya, the undersigned, could have been addressing the petition to
other taskmasters: her parents.

When Mariya recently came home with her report card, they were
not pleased. For the last semester, she earned a grade point average of

94.86—practically straight As. That, however, was down from 95.29, a drop of less than half a percentage point—.43—from the previous marking period. Mariya could have made the argument that the difference was statistically insignificant, that a couple of mistakes on a single test could have ever so slightly skewed the report card results—a blip caused by poor sleep, a bad hair day, anything. More to the point, she could have argued that the marking period just ended doesn't count *because it doesn't.* Those grades are not factored into a student's overall grade point average; they're simply an indicator of how a student is performing during the course of the semester before receiving final grades at the end of the term. But such arguments, no matter how reasonable, wouldn't have made any difference. The way that Mariya's parents viewed it, their daughter's grades slipped, which warranted a punishment right where it hurts: they took away her cell phone.

"It's sort of ridiculous that it'd be a big deal," Mariya says, grousing about how her parents "expect me to get a full scholarship to a fancy Ivy League thing," which will lead to a fancy job so one day she can buy a fancy house. But Mariya is just venting. When she really thinks about it, she doesn't blame her parents for creating such great expectations for her. The family had less than a hundred dollars to their name when they left their home in Ukraine, arriving at Kennedy Airport little more than a decade ago in the aftermath of the collapse of the Soviet Union.

In Ukraine, her parents had sold leather necklaces, lacquer boxes, and other knickknacks at a street stand; in America, they thought life would be easier. It wasn't. Her mother became a maid, her father delivered pizzas. Now her father is an electrician while her mother is a clerical worker, and money is still tight. They sleep in the living room of their small Brooklyn apartment so that Mariya and her nine-year-old brother, Mark, can have their own bedrooms.

"I dream about *three* bedrooms," says her mother, Yelena Goldman, in clipped English.

In the dream, Mariya attends Columbia and grows up to work for a big company, with customers aplenty. Mariya would also have a daughter, whom Mrs. Goldman would secretly teach to speak Russian. And together, the family would move to a glorious house in Manhattan in a calm, quiet area, where Mariya's parents would live in the . . . basement.

The *basement*? Mariya is appalled. Her mother isn't. "The basement is good enough," she says resolutely.

The basement of the future will have to wait. Mariya doesn't even know how she'll pay for college. She thinks she may have to join the military reserve to help defray the cost, but she worries about the possible price—being compelled to go to war. At the moment, though, there are more immediate concerns. The school bell is ringing, and Mariya has a chemistry test in two periods for which she has yet to study. She doesn't have to answer only to her parents. She faces the expectations of the parents of a classmate, another immigrant from the former Soviet Union, part of a growing demographic at Stuyvesant. Mariya is supposed to help fifteen-year-old Mariana Muravitsky, who is camped out on the second-floor landing with her, prepare for the same class. "If you don't help me study for the chemistry test," Mariana warns, "my mom is going to kill you."

As they rise to leave, Mariya mutters hopelessly, "It's a death threat."

Down the hall and around the corner, Milo, the ten-year-old prodigy, is leaving his speaker-building class in a decidedly better mood. There is something different about him this morning, though it is difficult to detect at first. He is still buried deep inside his big blue parka. His tuft of blond hair still diverges in Einstein-like fashion. But then there it is: the backpack. Red and blue and strapped to both narrow shoulders. Milo has ditched his old backpack, which he used to wheel around school by a handle, like a piece of carry-on luggage, such was the burden of his academic paraphernalia.

Milo says he threw out the old backpack because it had a hole in it. "It was kind of a drag to be dragging it," he says. Therein, he proves two things with one backpack: Milo is beginning to fit in at high school not just in his choice of luggage but also in his lingo.

But that's not all that accounts for the newfound levity in his step this morning. Milo has just made it to the semifinal round of a citywide high school math fair. Only a small number of Stuyvesant students who submitted papers gained entry to the contest, and only a handful of those who participated in the first round made it to the second, including Milo. In his paper, he invented a thesis on what he calls the "fair distribution of things," using seven different kinds of chocolates—Reese's, Hershey's, Butterfinger, and Baby Ruth among them—as examples.

"The judges are suckers for candy," he says.

What he created, he points out, is "not your normal math." Milo devised two formulas to determine what is fair in a scenario involving a number of "players." One formula he called "happiness":

Happiness = True, if the player's final portion is greater than, or equal to, 100 minus S over N, with N = to the number of players and S = to sympathy [a term "which I made up," Milo says].

The upshot is, "A lot of people have negative sympathies," he notes, apparently drawing from personal experience. That could include high school students who have no idea what it's like to be a little boy in their midst.

It's an overlooked luxury that at a school like Stuyvesant, administrators can find a place for a ten-year-old genius who isn't officially enrolled, while other public schools are not even sure whether they can find their students at all. It's a concern based on recent—and troubling—trends in education in America today.

Almost all Stuyvesant students graduate, compared to only about 70 percent of high school students across the nation, and that number has remained virtually unchanged since the 1970s, according to the Manhattan Institute for Policy Research.

In an April 2006 *Time* magazine cover story with the blunt headline, "Dropout Nation," the author writes, "the most astonishing statistic in the whole field of education" is that nearly one out of three public high school students will fail to graduate, and that the number is close to 50 percent for Latinos and blacks. "Virtually no community, small or large, rural or urban, has escaped the problem," the author says.

At about the same time, a 2006 study on behalf of the Bill & Melinda Gates Foundation calls the problem *The Silent Epidemic*. While the causes are endlessly debated, the researchers of this study isolated some of the problems, surveying nearly five hundred high school dropouts.

Most said they had passing grades and could have graduated, but 69 percent said they were "not motivated to work hard" and 66 percent said they would have "worked harder if more had been demanded of them." In addition, 71 percent of high school dropouts said they favored "better communication between parents and schools and more involvement from parents," which is exactly what Stuyvesant already experiences in spades.

The ramifications of dropping out of school are all too well known: students without a high school diploma risk falling into low-wage jobs or unemployment lines—unsavory prospects compounded by rising competition in a global marketplace where even cheap jobs are being exported. But if there's a crisis of competence in American education, it doesn't apply only to dropouts. Students are slipping in some of the most basic—and important—academic subjects in an increasingly complex, technological society, where many jobs over the next decade are expected to require more science, engineering, or technical training. For instance, in science, one of Stuyvesant's traditional strengths, 54 percent of twelfth graders nationally scored at or above the basic level in 2005, down 3 percentage points from a decade earlier, according to the U.S. Department of Education, which administered the test. Meanwhile, U.S. eighth graders score lower in science than those of seven other nations, four from Asia (including Hong Kong) and three from Europe, according to the closely followed Trends in International Mathematics and Science Study, an international education project.

"Our superiority was once the envy of the world," says *Time* on its February 2006 cover about America's decline in science achievement. "But we are slacking off just as other countries are getting stronger."

American students are faring little better in math, another key subject—and another Stuyvesant strong suit. U.S. eighth graders showed "no measurable change" in their math performance in recent years, according to the same international education project. Running in place, these American students have fallen behind their advancing counterparts in math in nine other countries, five from Asia (including Hong Kong) and four from Europe, including the tiny nation of Estonia.

Things don't improve when U.S. high school students reach the age of fifteen. Even then, they continue to post lower scores in math and science literacy than most of their peers from the Organisation for Economic Co-operation and Development member nations. That means America is lagging behind the bulk of the industrialized world. No longer does it seem that there are great expectations for today's U.S. high school student.

What's happened to American education?

"No one really knows the answer," says Tom Loveless, director of the Brown Center on Education Policy and a senior fellow in governance studies at the Brookings Institution, a think tank in Washington, D.C. "I mean, I can speculate, but the serious, true answer is, people don't know."

Dr. Loveless reckons it's a "cultural thing," meaning that in the United States, many students—and parents—don't take academic achievement seriously while "in other countries, teenagers have a job, and that's going to school."

Other experts attribute the decline in American education to a variety of causes, including schools that are too big, teachers who don't have enough training, or parents who don't expect enough from their children. Mr. Teitel, Stuyvesant's principal, largely blames the decline in math and science achievement on the students themselves. "The problem we face now is that, you know, a lot of kids really don't want to go to the math and science field because it is, to some extent, more difficult than some of the other subject areas," he says. ". . . Kids don't want to take the tough subjects and struggle through them and parents don't want to see the kids struggle that hard." Which is why he won't diminish Stuyvesant's traditional emphasis on math, science, and technology, or MST, as he calls it. "I will not pull any punches to tell you that I am sure that many of my parents would not have any qualms about me just turning this into a school for gifted and talented, 'forget the MST part, pal. Just a school for gifted, pal, we could be very happy.' The reality is, I won't allow it." That's because he firmly believes such difficult subjects are needed.

Whatever the causes of the decline in American education, many policy makers and education leaders believe the long-term consequences may be great. "Unless we start figuring out far more effective ways to teach basic and high-level skills in our public schools, we will pay a serious price in economic competitiveness and social and political upheaval," says former chairman and chief executive of IBM Louis V. Gerstner Jr., chairman of the Teaching Commission, a group of leaders in government, business, and education, in its spring 2006 report. ". . . If we do not go far further, far faster, we will all soon be talking in the past tense about America's greatness."

The consequences of falling behind preoccupy a battalion of seniors after school on March 7 on the third floor, where they are rehearsing for Sing! with the grim determination of former juniors who nearly upset the seniors last year and aim to avoid such a dishonor now.

"Ready, from the top!" screams a stern choreographer leading a group of spandex-covered girls who are intently practicing a hip-hop dance step to Michael Jackson's "Smooth Criminal."

"I want to see energy and I want to see it good!" berates another fearsome senior, leading a group of grave girls nearby who are waving multicolored scarves in an intricate Indian dance step.

Observing off to the side is Liz Livingstone, the lighting director, marveling with a suggestion of trepidation at how quickly opening night is approaching. "Sing! is in two weeks, which is crazy," she says.

Upstairs in the fifth-floor dining hall, freshmen and sophomores are playing a Jackson 5 song, "ABC," though Alexa, the coproducer, doesn't like what she's hearing. The chorus needs to be louder, the band needs more practice. "It's not good," she says with a frown.

Hope, however, isn't lost. Based on the latest intelligence, word is that while the seniors are hungry after losing as juniors last year, this year's juniors are cocky and lazy, a notion reinforced today when the eleventh graders ended their rehearsal early. Some underclassmen sense a slight opening. "We might have a chance at beating the juniors because we're working hard," says freshman Erica Sands, a chorus member.

It's part of the life of Stuyvesant that after school on this day, as on almost every other, students are working hard throughout the building in a beehive of extracurricular activities. That includes the second floor, where a group of student boosters called Building Stuy Community is sitting in a semicircle discussing how to improve school life. The topic today: how to make the Stuyvesant Web site, www.stuy.edu, better.

Spurring them on is a comparison to rival Bronx Science, which possesses a more robust Web site, including a student resource section. What Bronx Science has, Stuyvesant students believe it is their right to have, in this instance a Web site that offers useful information about, say, the guidance office. Can it be done?

The question puts the students' featured guest on the spot. Eddie Wong, assistant principal of technology services, squirms in his student desk-chair before he says, without making any promises, that he will see what he can do. "This is high school," he kids. "I'm not sure you want to make it, like, interesting."

It's no accident that at the same time students are working to improve the school community, some of those students' parents, deeply enmeshed in Stuyvesant life, are doing the identical thing four floors above at a meeting of the advisory School Leadership Team. As at last month's meeting, it's stifling hot in room 615, and a small rotating fan does little to move the stilled air or stir the parents, who remain calcified in their positions. Mr. Teitel is backed in a corner—this time literally sitting in a back corner chair—still trying to explain the imminent introduction of the controversial computerized identification scanners to mark students' attendance.

"I don't know how long it will take to work the bugs out," Mr. Teitel is saying.

"Will they magically appear?" questions Kristen, the Student Union president, one of the principal's favorite students despite her frequent—and open—challenges to his authority.

Mr. Teitel explains that the hardware is already here and just needs to be tested, which prompts a parent, concerned about privacy issues, to ask, "Have you decided what information you will collect?"

The principal assures him that the school will only track students' comings and goings, but that prompts another parent to note Stuyvesant's nearly perfect attendance record and question "why this is a priority."

The question goes unanswered.

> *5 minutes till bell*
> *4 minutes till bell*
> *3 minutes till bell*
> *2 minutes till bell*
> *1 minute till bell*
> *where is the bell?*
>
> —desktop graffiti, Stuyvesant High School

CHAPTER TWELVE

The Real World

ON WEDNESDAY, MARCH 8, STUDENTS ARE DISCUSSING greatness in literature in the same room, 615, where last night parents grilled the principal on the merits of attendance scanners. While topics have changed overnight, the room retains its basic character—the institutional white walls, the functional wooden chairs, the glaring fluorescent lighting, the dirty white tiles. A poster on the wall commands, BE PART OF THE EXPERIENCE. That seems to speak to the one incongruent element in this English class: Jane. She practically begs to be seen—witnessed—in her tight baby blue T-shirt, in her pink cotton-ball-like rolls on either side of her head, broadcasting like airplane warning lights, and the dozens of plastic multicolored bracelets—pinkyellowgreen—stacked along her left wrist, all the way up to her elbow, hiding the soft crease.

Jane's present. That's the amazing thing. She isn't punching anyone. She isn't screaming at someone. She's not shooting herself up. She's holding on to her book, Joyce's *A Portrait of the Artist as a Young Man*—her life raft. "Page fifty-six," calls out Mr. Grossman, the teacher, her father figure. "Stop there," he says. "Jot down what you notice." Students start calling on each other. Jane raises her pale, slender right fist, clutching a pen. Finally, a fellow student calls on her, and she says, "A person is defined by what he does." She is talking about Stephen, the novel's main character, not herself, and no one in the classroom says otherwise as Jane, fully reabsorbed in the culture of this classroom after her bout in detox, calls on another student, who passes the proverbial baton to another, and all is good. Words fly across the room as if this were a college seminar, substantial terms like "antipathy" and "intrinsic" and "crisis of conscience" and "ingrained" and "constrained." Mr. Grossman barely can get in a word—which makes it easier for him to resist the temptation to "chew the scenery," as he dubs it. When the bell rings at seven past eleven, not a single student rises to leave for the next class. It's a strange phenomenon: no one leaves—no one *wants* to leave—until Mr. Grossman dismisses them, hastening them out with the admonishment, "For tomorrow, up to [page] ninety-one."

He's all business, but within him is a profound sense of happiness at the depth of his students' insights when things in class go so incredibly right. But the joys of teaching are tempered by the immediate realities of his other duties as English chairman. A student comes to him to complain about a teacher in a different department who made inappropriate comments about religion, and when that student spoke up, the teacher made life difficult for her, which is not Mr. Grossman's problem, except that students know him to be fair, so they trust him. What they don't know is that this problematic instructor is aligned with other faculty members who are allied against Mr. Grossman for firing another teacher, which created a controversy that has just begun to die down.

With the school preparing to hire about six guidance counselors, Mr. Grossman is facing another controversy: some English teachers—he doesn't know how many yet—may lose their jobs in the cold calculation of public school personnel decisions. That number includes possibly some of his best, those he has spent the most time training and cultivating. It's an unintended consequence of a school system that eliminated seniority transfers but preserved a provision in which the last-hired teacher is the first fired. Such layoffs are based on length of service. "Fair?" He lets the word linger. "'Fair' is such a hard word," he says. There is no easy answer, not when the countervailing argument against keeping a qualified young teacher is the retention of a qualified veteran teacher. There is little consolation for Mr. Grossman in losing either kind.

"It's just a train barreling down," he says.

Barreling down too is the thought of what will happen to Jane. Even though she's showing up to class again, Mr. Grossman cringes at the possibility that she may succumb again to the nihilism of heroin. And yet lately she seems more coherent, not quite as frenzied. In a quiet moment of reflection, she says, "I get a sense we're not in the real world yet." She's aware that for all the strife of high school, it's make-believe in the sense that it doesn't quite count the way adulthood does, that mistakes are forgiven, expected, and that do-overs are permitted even if, in her case, she already has lived a life all too real. Her incipient clarity is helped, perhaps, by the Subutex tablets she pops to deal with the heroin withdrawal. Already, she can feel a difference. She can climb a set of stairs without asthmatic laboring. The grayness of her skin is dissipating. She's even being friendly with classmates. Jane's newfound felicity is amplified by the prospect of graduating in three months, which she believes will happen if she passes all her courses this term, and so far, she's doing fine, a few class cuts notwithstanding. Things have settled at home too, where she's stopped fighting with her mother. So she makes an allowance for herself, tempting the devil, occasionally smoking marijuana, convincing herself that it's not that bad, that it's just a taste, that it's harmless. Anyway, she's still writing, she still has her poetry:

> *aromatic amnesia is incessant*
> *oso redundant oso redundant*
> *one is too many and never enough always*
> *more*
> *constricted pupils—the instantaneous closed door,*
> *complete voluntary constricted movements*
> *of the heart*
> *sealed off heart secretes*
> *no tears to eyes,*
> *no need for blurred disguise*
> *the crossed broken line*
> *acuteness of a knife*

charismatic adept lies
comes always
so easy
goes always
so hard
constricted
vision for reality
where the next line
breaks and what's the last word said
where the next step can only be intended and not
located
the uncertainty and inevitability
and this dichotomy persists

Hiding the truth, Jane tells Mr. Grossman that she's keeping sober. He wants to believe her, but he knows. "I've seen this pattern before," he says. For the moment, though, he must attend to his duties as English chairman, withdrawing into his office in room 601. Waiting to speak to him is a senior who has a beef with the school administration. Its relationship with students is "horrendous," she says, citing the unwelcome arrival of the attendance scanners—due any day—which she believes is threatening the school's greatness.

"It's going to be more than monitoring attendance," she says, fearing a Big Brother scenario, where students' privacy is invaded. "If we were having attendance problems, that would be one thing," she says, "but it's unnecessary. It doesn't make sense."

That's why she and other student leaders are putting up a fight. As heads of Stuyvesant's Big Sibling program, an influential group in which upperclassmen counsel younger students, they are using their clout in writing a letter of protest to the New York City Department of Education. "Instead of being rewarded for our excellent performance and highly regarded reputation, our student rights are being infringed upon," they write. "We see the new ID Scanning System that Mr. Teitel plans to install as an unfair way for the administration to discipline the students." They go on to say that the principal didn't consult student leaders and others before presenting the scanners as a fait accompli and add, "This money would be much better spent on new textbooks, extracurricular activities, electives, additional college advisors, guidance counselors, etc."

The object of the students' scorn, Mr. Teitel, finds refuge in room 829, where he removes his principal's hat, forgetting for the moment the uncomfortable exigencies of attendance scanners and the rising tide of student ire to teach physics to a freshman class, a job that isn't required of a principal but one that he wants, needs. It gives him credibility among his faculty; it means he's still one of them. Then there's this unstated factor: Mr. Teitel is still in love with teaching.

Gone is his principal's mask of weariness; in its place is a broad smile from which booms a scratchy voice discussing the mysteries of current electricity, electron flow, and the way electrical energy is expended.

"What's that last word?" a student asks.

"*E-x-p-e-n-d-e-d*," Mr. Teitel says.

Grasping a piece of chalk with a clear plastic glove, like that of a surgeon, he inscribes a long, arcane equation on the blackboard, ending with a flourish. "I don't hear my applause," he says, to which the students clap obediently. This is where he belongs, a paper-thin teacher in command of his subject matter and his students, pacing back and forth in front of a blacktop experiment counter with shiny chrome faucets, his natural habitat.

Mr. Teitel proved his stick-to-itiveness when he started as a full-time science teacher in 1971 at William Howard Taft High School, a public school in the Bronx so tough that administrators had warned him not to walk out of the building alone at the end of the day because teachers were getting mugged. At first he told his ninth-grade students at Taft that he was a substitute teacher so they wouldn't really bother him, figuring he was temporary. But when he kept showing up, a student eventually raised a hand to ask, "Weren't you only going to stay for a week?"

Only later did Mr. Teitel find out that he had been hired because a student had hit the previous teacher on the head with a garbage can— and that teacher had promptly quit. An assistant principal had been making book, taking bets that Mr. Teitel wouldn't last a week. "I'm sure he was giving good odds," Mr. Teitel says.

He lasted a dozen years at Taft.

As a teacher at Stuyvesant, he didn't harbor notions of greatness, allowing himself only to dream of one day becoming assistant principal, which happened, to his surprise. But when Ms. Perullo, the principal, unexpectedly announced her retirement in the winter of 1999, Mr. Teitel went home to talk to his wife about applying for the top job. He took a practical tack, considering the long, hot summers he had worked as a teacher for extra income. "I said, 'Look, I've worked summer school many, many years, you know, for the money, and if I become principal, I will make enough money so that I won't have to work summer school anymore, and we'll still be financially better off than we were.'" His wife, herself a schoolteacher, agreed, not giving the prospect too much credence since his was a long-shot candidacy. Mr. Teitel was up against formidable rivals, including two other assistant principals. But then one of them was physically removed from the building in a pair of handcuffs.

An assistant principal of biology was accused of molesting a fifteen-year-old student, a charge to which he ultimately pleaded guilty. His punishment: three years' probation and retirement. After a newly initiated background check, Mr. Teitel was rewarded with the title of principal, and no one was more surprised than he. "I never envisioned this job," he says. "That's the truth."

His wife was not exactly pleased with his promotion. Shortly after he took over, the school system changed Mr. Teitel's job description, making the principal's position a twelve-month-a-year job.

The accidental principal hasn't had a summer off since 1984.

Ms. Lee, the accidental student teacher, can't remember the last day she's had off. Between teaching history and Korean and Sunday school and taking pedagogical classes for her master's degree at Columbia, the days and evenings begin to blur together, including this blustery Tuesday, March 14.

She is always on the go, and much of her life dangles from a thread around her neck in a small black computer memory stick that contains all of her lessons, homework assignments, and grades. Inside her backpack is Rick Warren's *The Purpose-Driven Life.* Today, she reads this passage: "You never understand some commands until you obey them." There is little else to adorn Ms. Lee. She obscures her quiet beauty in a functional outfit, a brown V-neck sweater, gray slacks, and brown shoes, adding no jewelry other than a pair of simple silver hoop earrings and a matching necklace, a minimalist look meant to avoid distracting students while she stands in front of them in class.

It's just one trick she quickly learned as a student teacher. Other lessons of the trade have come harder. Early on, a student challenged the question that Ms. Lee wrote on the chalkboard: "Was Abraham Lincoln really a great man?" Though Ms. Lee's mentor, a teacher of nearly thirty years at Stuyvesant, had used the same question, it provoked a different reaction coming from such a young, inexperienced teacher as Ms. Lee. "I don't think it's appropriate to question his greatness," the student scolded the teacher. Another student threw a paper ball at Ms. Lee while she was passing out a class assignment. "Every day," she says of those first trials, "I was challenged."

The experience reminds her of when she was a high school student at Bronx Science, not so long ago, when she and her classmates would look up arcane facts and then question their teacher about them. So Ms. Lee accepts the challenge now that it comes from Stuyvesant students. "I don't try to be something I'm not," she says.

Ms. Lee tries to have faith, something she learned in class not as a student but as a teacher. When a boy comes to class late, she doesn't lecture him; she calls on him but not in an intrusive way, asking him a question for which there is no wrong answer, his opinion, to give him confidence. When another boy fails to bring in his homework, she pulls him aside and gently asks not for all of it but only yesterday's. He complies by bringing in a stack of overdue homework assignments. He doesn't participate in class but does surprisingly well on an exam. "You never want to give up," she says. In a recent class, while a faculty visitor from Columbia was observing Ms. Lee's history class at Stuyvesant, the boy laid his head on his desk and fell asleep. She let him do it, knowing that she'd be criticized. "There are times you want to let it go," she says.

"I took it that he's a boy that needs a little time." That he comes to class every day is, she believes, a small victory. "I could be losing him entirely," she says. Such compassion isn't always the accepted norm of teaching, but it comes naturally to Ms. Lee, who is acutely aware of the pressures on her students, having once been one of them at Bronx Science, where the burdens of grades and college applications can be overwhelming too. "Sometimes," she says, "the best way to go is moderation." It's a philosophy that stands in stark contrast to the harsh dicta of success preached by her own parents, but perhaps that's the point. "Maybe that's why I take a different approach with my students," she says.

In return, students now shower her with an unusual degree of respect, especially those in her Korean class. As she passes her students in the crowded hallways of Stuyvesant, they will bow to her in the traditional Asian style, ignoring how the act clashes with the regular dyspeptic high school posture of studied uninterest. After school, she will be surprised to find her students by her side, walking with her on her way to the No. 2 or 3 subway on Chambers Street, speaking with her in Korean. She takes pride in their rediscovery of their Korean heritage, thinking about her own high school experience, when students jeered her Korean ancestry, calling her "FOB"—fresh off the boat—even though she was born in Queens. She tells her students that it's nothing to be ashamed of, that it's an advantage to be bilingual, that it would be foolish to renounce where they come from, even in what she calls a "white-centered society," including a school like Stuyvesant, where few of the teachers are Asian despite a majority-Asian student body. An Asian student who for the first time stumbled into her at school couldn't believe it, never thinking he'd come across an Asian teacher in the social studies department. "Wow, that's so cool," he marveled. Her response: "I want them to get that inspiration." She is an example—and a bridge to the school's many Korean parents, who have for years felt detached from the goings-on at Stuyvesant if only because of the language barrier. She translates school documents for them; she takes phone calls to explain issues to them; she meets them outside school to give them guidance.

"Right now, I'm having the time of my life," she says. "This semester is an unbelievable adventure." Already, the student teacher feels like a full-time staffer. "I play a more conspicuous role here. I'm not simply in the shadows."

But that may not last. There are still no teaching openings at Stuyvesant, and she worries, "If I go to a regular school, am I in for a rude awakening?" Here, she says, "I was able to find this passion and joy." At another school, she fears, "it might not work."

A devout Christian, she prays for the opportunity to teach three periods of social studies and two periods of Korean at Stuyvesant when she graduates from Columbia and obtains her license as a social studies teacher in a matter of months. "I trust whatever path will be laid for me," she says.

She also trusts Mr. Jaye, who continues to work to find her a full-time job at Stuyvesant. But a day later, Wednesday, March 15, it seems that his own prayers are going unanswered. Sitting at his cluttered desk, he's absorbing the news that New Jersey denied his principal's license because he lacked one course in educational law and finance from his academic transcript. It's a technicality—he studied those issues in other classes—but it's slowing his courtship with Bergen County Academies.

Adding to his agita is another transcript snafu involving a student who has grades of 95 or above in all his classes except biology, in which he ended up with a lowly mark of 70. Mr. Jaye, ever the rabble-rouser, decided to investigate, even though the biology teacher did not fall under his purview as math chairman. What Mr. Jaye found confirmed his suspicions, that the teacher in question was a notoriously tough grader, to the point of being unfair, at least in the case of this otherwise straight-A student. Mr. Jaye took the matter to other administrators, asking whether they were aware of this biology teacher's aberrant grading policy, which could potentially damage the student's college prospects. Administrators were indeed aware. Mr. Jaye fumed, "You allow a teacher to grade outside the institutional standard? So I can give a hundred and five?" It was, to be sure, a rhetorical question, for there was no answer forthcoming.

But what's really galling Mr. Jaye today is the person he loves to hate: Ms. Damesek. In their latest dustup, Ms. Damesek told the principal that she didn't want Mr. Jaye attending the kitchen cabinet meetings, explaining that she thought it would be better if attendance were rotated among other school administrators. Mr. Jaye became livid, telling the principal, "You'll have to call security to get me out of the meeting." Still fulminating in his office hours later, Mr. Jaye relives the unpleasant episode with a neutral observer, Mr. Cocoros, the lawyer turned math teacher, who suggests that an appropriate solution would be to invite an advanced placement psychology class of students to mediate the kitchen cabinet meeting on the first floor. "Why do people downstairs make things so complicated?" Mr. Cocoros wants to know.

Again, a question with no answer.

In Mr. Jaye's outer office, Milo is sitting, head down, at a round wooden table, working out answers to questions for his homework in tomorrow's trigonometry class. He is also actively ignoring the three freshmen and one sophomore who are sitting at the table, talking about Milo as if he weren't present.

"Milo's, like, a junior," says one of the freshmen.

"He has the math mind of a junior," says another.

After a brief lull, Milo looks up and notes that the word *sophomore* actually means "clever fool," and it's unclear whether he just emitted a non sequitur or insulted those in attendance who might fall into that category. The boys around the table have no clue what Milo is talking about and begin laughing uncontrollably about nothing in particular.

Moments later, Milo clips his homework into his loose-leaf binder and removes himself to a quiet spot alone on the floor outside the math department. There Mr. Siwanowicz joins his kindred spirit. Without preface or pleasantries, Milo launches a math mind bender for Mr. Siwanowicz to solve on the spot: There are 13 pirates, 1 treasure chest, several locks and keys. For every lock, there can be more than 1 key. Every key fits only 1 lock. Any 6 pirates cannot open the treasure chest. Any 7 can. What is the least number of locks they need?

Within seconds, Mr. Siwanowicz computes an answer: 1,716. Milo douses the suspense by saying he doesn't know the answer; he just saw the question online. Suddenly, both man and boy look greatly fatigued, as if one is a reflection of the other, just at different points in the evolution of time.

Insomnia continues to afflict Mr. Siwanowicz. He can't fall asleep when he wants and he dozes at the most inopportune moments, like when he is standing in a subway car. "Several times," he says, "I nearly fell down."

If there's a silver lining, he says, his insomnia surmounts his depression. "I'm too tired to be sad."

He seems almost resigned to library duty during his free seventh and eighth periods, even though he'd rather be doing something more useful, like talking to students about math, which he views as his one unique talent. And he's come around to the idea that perhaps he should return to City College over the summer and finish his degree. But he's distracted from his own future by that of two troubled students in the math research class that he unofficially teaches. One is still failing to show up. The other shows up only sporadically. He wonders if he could be doing more. But he knows he won't reach every student. That is an unfortunate part of teaching, he admits, yet he says, "I worry about them. They're developing habits which will impede them later."

Mr. Siwanowicz knows something about being impeded.

After school, Alexa is feeling impeded too. The freshman coproducer of Sing! is seething backstage about dirty tactics being employed by the enemy just a week before opening night. The juniors have allegedly appropriated the equipment that the freshmen and sophomores had intended to use to hold up their scenery. "It's a horrible thing to do," Alexa says. But she takes comfort in what the reputed act of thievery seems to imply, that soph/frosh is looking good enough to worry the upperclassmen. Maybe the juniors should be concerned. Later that evening, it is almost impossible to hear the voices of juniors trying to sing above the cacophony of amplified instruments during rehearsal. Hunched in orchestra seating, codirector Ben Alter has trouble removing the frown from his face. "It's pretty hectic," he says, "but it'll come together." His codirector, Liam, is not his usual confident self either. "You never know," he says philosophically. "Sing! is like *Waiting for Godot*." His mood isn't helped by Xevion, who is openly fretting. After worrying that "Respect" is an octave too high, and then deciding it isn't, she now hears that her biggest competitor, Molly, the senior, is planning to sing the classic Patti LaBelle hit disco song "Lady Marmalade," which Xevion is sure will bring down the house. What Xevion doesn't know, though, is that Molly is worried about Xevion's singing too. Such are their prodigious talents that their stentorian voices make them stand out like two giants in an open field of Lilliputians. But Molly also has this to contend with: she is not only the Big Fish, she is the seniors' last, great hope to graduate with a victory in the grand musical competition. "If we don't win," Molly says, her face flushing, "I don't know."

The following day over lunch, Xevion is still obsessing, telling Romeo that her rival is singing one of her favorite songs. "I'm worried about everything," she says. So is Romeo, who is competing with his own rival, just in a different arena: academics. Who, he wants to know, will get the higher SAT score?

One of his Stuyvesant friends just achieved near perfection on a practice exam—without studying. And Romeo, approaching the field of academia with the same fierce determination he shows on the football field, intends to practice his way to a better score. "I want to beat him," he says.

When it comes to football, Romeo's sheer effort is paying off. He is getting bigger and stronger, sweating in the cramped weight room, pushing himself with bench presses, military presses, squats, pull-ups, and Romanian dead lifts, which sound as painful as they are. Yet even as he builds mass and muscle, Romeo knows what he is up against, opposing players from regular public schools who could give a hoot about academics, who focus all of their energies on getting even stronger. He conjures up the immovable force at the line of scrimmage, fit linemen with big stocky legs.

"When they take their stance," he says, "they take up a lot of space."

Over a tray of roasted chicken, Xevion tries to make amends for a joke she made about Stuyvesant's woeful football team. "I'm sorry about the wisecrack," she says.

The well-intended apology touches a sore spot. "I don't remember anything you say," Romeo says in a knee-jerk reaction.

Xevion is wounded too, and Romeo immediately regrets it, saying that he generally remembers what she says, although that doesn't last because what he's recalling now is how he received only a 4.5 out of 5— a high score that wasn't high enough, by his standards—on his autobiographical essay assignment in English class. "I didn't push the narrative form as much as I could've," he rues.

"Alexander, focus on what you did correctly," Xevion says; she calls Romeo by his last name when she's taking him to task. "You got a great score. Be happy."

Romeo tries to write off the less-than-perfect grade, saying he isn't worried about grades anymore. "I don't feel stress anymore," he says, as if he is trying to convince himself.

Xevion notes how two nights ago Romeo went to sleep earlier than she did. "It's a miracle," she says.

"I didn't go to bed," he corrects her. "I read."

So much for easing up. The bell rings. In passing, as they head out of the dining hall, Romeo mentions that he recently broke up with his first girlfriend. The relationship, it turns out, wasn't so great. Maybe it wasn't love. Maybe it was a chemical reaction in the brain, as he had read about in that issue of *National Geographic*. Down the hall, he catches sight of a pretty blond sophomore, who flashes a big smile at him. Without a farewell, he pursues the girl, weaving through a jostling hallway of students, evading them like so many blockers on the football field. Watching him disappear, Xevion says absently, "I think he needs more of an emotional attachment."

> *BUILD A SOCIALIST AMERICA*
>
> —desktop graffiti, Stuyvesant High School

CHAPTER THIRTEEN

Protests and Demands

THAT THURSDAY NIGHT, MARCH 16, FATHER AND daughter are pursuing opposite ends of an intractable debate that has plagued them ever since she began contemplating attending Stuyvesant:

Is the school a good idea?

No, Mr. Davis maintains.

Yes, insists his daughter, Katie Johnston-Davis.

"My thing was to keep Katie out of a gifted and talented program," he says while frying flounder in a sizzling pan as the Beatles' "Drive My Car" plays in the background of his Upper West Side co-op.

"Oh, that worked well," says Katie with a heavy dose of sarcasm.

She is a seventeen-year-old senior at Stuyvesant.

Mr. Davis, the parent who made an impassioned plea against attendance scanners at the School Leadership Team meeting last month, never liked the idea of a public school that admitted only students who passed a test. A math teacher for pregnant students in the Bronx, Mr. Davis even turned down an opportunity to send Katie to a gifted and talented program in middle school, sending her instead to a more progressive, alternative public school. He doesn't believe in segregating students by academic ability. He believes that high-achieving students can learn from low-achieving students—and vice versa—and that school diversity is a good thing. "Everybody has something to offer," he says. Tests, he argues, "devaluate social worth, human worth," failing to take into consideration what he calls "multidimensional personalities" and "multiple intelligences."

Besides, he adds, "the test only tests for certain qualities."

Katie barely studied for the Stuyvesant entrance exam, but when she aced it anyway, her father told her it wasn't the kind of school he would choose for her.

Mr. Davis had graduated from Stuyvesant.

So, of course, Katie defied her father by choosing to attend his alma mater. And she loves it.

"I've gained so much from being around people who are so gifted," she says. Katie has thrived—a picture-perfect teenager, wholesomely pretty and well-adjusted even as she pushes herself as the captain of the girls' soccer team—the city champs last year—while maintaining a 93 grade point average.

"There's never been any pressure on her to get high grades," her father says. "That's her issue."

If anything, he tries to give her a break. At midnight on a Sunday, as she's hunkered down studying, he's apt to poke his head in her room to see if he can excuse her from school. "Katie, are you going to school tomorrow, or should I write a note?" he'll ask lovingly. At the same time, he says proudly, "I encouraged her to be all she could be," to which Katie rolls her bright blue eyes and says, "You're so cheesy." All that Mr. Davis will grudgingly admit is, "The Stuyvesant she goes to is better than the Stuyvesant I went to."

It's true, the school wasn't always a class apart, filled with brainiacs like Katie.

In the beginning, when Stuyvesant opened in 1904, it called itself a manual training school for boys. Educators named the school after Peter Stuyvesant, the son of a Dutch Reformed church minister who was a college dropout. Rising through the ranks of the Dutch West India

Company, he served as the commander of Curaçao, where a cannon-fire tussle with a Portuguese-run Caribbean island left his right leg severely damaged, requiring amputation below the knee. Thus, the man's peg leg (and the football team's unseemly name).

Given a more prestigious appointment, the hobbled Stuyvesant arrived in New Amsterdam in 1647 as director-general of the unruly colony, commanding what later became Manhattan with a dictatorial style marked by unvarnished bigotry. He persecuted Quakers, Jews, and others, making him a curious selection for the namesake of a public high school filled with immigrants of various faiths more than two centuries later. But history is history, and back in Stuyvesant's day, the Lower East Side was a tremendous swamp until he purchased land there, building a chapel on what became known as Stuyvesant Town, site of the original high school.

A five-story beaux-arts-style limestone building, the original school cost what was then a princely sum—$1.5 million—a hundredth of the price of the new school built nearly a century later on the other side of town. In a ceremony to lay the cornerstone of the building at East Fifteenth Street, William H. Maxwell, then superintendent of the city's schools, boasted, "This school, so recently established, should become the greatest in the United States."

He couldn't have known then how those words would ring true one day.

At the time of Stuyvesant's founding, fewer than 7 percent of seventeen-year-old Americans graduated from high school, and there were just a handful of secondary schools in New York City. Most people with merely seven or eight years of schooling had little problem finding a job, whether as a farmer, a clerk, or an unskilled factory worker.

In the early 1900s, with the rise of the Industrial Age, when manufacturers were just beginning to mass-produce automobiles on the assembly line, high school enrollment was bulging and manual training was all the rage, especially popular among education reformers and business leaders who wanted to make school more practical, preparing students for the workforce and aiding the nation's budding commercialism, says Diane Ravitch, a research professor of education at NYU and noted education historian. "Now we are a nation of manufacturers and traders, and the army that we have to fear is not an army of any nation, equipped with guns, but a German army of skilled workmen with tools in their hands, directed by captains of industry educated in the matchless Prussian schools," said Thomas M. Balliet, NYU's dean of the School of Pedagogy, in an address at Stuyvesant in 1904. "No artificial protection of our markets will avail to guard our industries permanently against the invasion of that army. Our only abiding protection must be found in the training of our own workmen and in the education of our industrial and commercial leaders."

Also at the turn of the century, millions of new immigrants from Eastern and Southern Europe poured into urban centers—and public schools—giving even more urgency to the growth of manual training schools catering to a clientele for whom English was a second language. When Stuyvesant opened, more than 70 percent of students in the New York City schools were children of foreign-born fathers.

"The island was just bursting at the seams with humanity," said Philip M. Scandura, a Stuyvesant teacher of the history of New York City.

The island of Manhattan also teemed with overcrowded tenements on the Lower East Side, a neighborhood carnival of street peddlers and lines of clothes hanging out to dry, not far from docks and harbors packed with exotic ships from all over the world. From these tenements, many poor immigrant boys walked to their local high school, Stuyvesant, where traditional academics, like English, history, and science, were coupled with practical courses in carpentry, pattern making, and forging. Among the lowest priorities was preparing students for college.

"Although the courses of study in the new school afford complete preparation for college, neither this school nor any other high school should be administered mainly in the interests of college preparatory work," said the school's first yearbook, the *Indicator* of 1905. ". . . The new high school is to be a preparatory school in a new and unusually broad sense, and will give unusual emphasis to the idea that schools prepare hundreds for life while preparing a few for college."

Instead, that first yearbook touted the benefits of manual training: "The city boy is confined at home, restricted on the street, and necessarily repressed in the ordinary school till he aches to do something with the motor cells of his brain and nerves acting through his growing muscles; hence more than half the disorder and mischief of troublesome boys. Manual training gives the boy an opportunity to do proper and serviceable things instead of creating a disturbance."

With rising enrollment, educators after 1920 restricted admission to Stuyvesant to those with high academic records in elementary school as the high school moved away from manual training to an increasing emphasis on math and science, according to New York City Landmarks Preservation Commission documents. When the nation descended into the Great Depression, parents kept their children in school longer so that more of the scant remaining jobs would go to the adults, but that created overcrowded conditions at schools like Stuyvesant. To limit enrollment, the school introduced an entrance exam in 1934. Students needed at least an eighth-grade average of 78 and one letter of recommendation to qualify for the test. The first entrance exams drew from questions written by an assistant to the principal and the chairman of the math department.

Not until the social upheavals of the 1960s did activists begin to clamor against the idea of the test. Accusing Stuyvesant and the other specialized schools of being culturally biased against black and Hispanic students, activists demanded that such public exam schools in New York City be eliminated. They wanted to convert the exam schools into neighborhood schools open to any child in the community.

"It was a period of protests and demands," Dr. Ravitch says. "There was a great revolt against any form of elitism, privilege."

In response, Stuyvesant and the other two specialized schools—Bronx Science and Brooklyn Technical High School—then adopted the Discovery program, the affirmative action initiative to accept some minority students who barely missed the cutoff. That, however, did not allay criticism.

A few years later, some local educators joined activists in demanding the abolition of Stuyvesant and the other public exam schools, again charging that the test discriminated against black and Hispanic students. This time, the protesters gained more traction; the schools superintendent designated a commission to study the test, a move that alarmed supporters of the three specialized schools, especially those at Bronx

Science. Parents, alumni, and others mobilized quickly, garnering the political support of two little-known Bronx state lawmakers, who introduced a bill to preserve the admissions exam. The proposed legislation would ensure that a citywide standardized test would determine admissions, underscoring the notion that a meritocracy would prevail at these schools. As a compromise, lawmakers added the affirmative action Discovery program as a formal provision of the bill, even though it contradicted their promise to maintain a test-only admissions policy. Despite heated debate, lawmakers passed the Hecht-Calandra bill, named after the lawmakers.

Stuyvesant introduced the Math and Science Institute in 1995 to help disadvantaged students prepare for the test. But that did little to assuage critics as the proportion of black and Hispanic students continued to drop. The controversy flared up again in May 1997 when protesters barged into Stuyvesant, staging a demonstration in the school's lobby, accusing the school system of operating a "secret apartheid." The activists, known as the Association of Community Organizations for Reform Now, or ACORN, released a study charging that middle schools failed to adequately prepare many black and Hispanic students for the kind of material found on the admissions exam for Stuyvesant and the other specialized public schools.

"The current test for the specialized high schools must remain permanently suspect as the product of an institutional racism inappropriate to an educational system in a democracy," the report said.

In a statement, then schools chancellor Rudy Crew responded by saying it was "an unfortunate truth that African-American and Latino students traditionally have been underrepresented in the specialized high schools." He said he welcomed suggestions. The demonstrators called for the immediate suspension of the entrance exam. That suggestion went unheeded.

The debate continues to simmer.

Mr. Teitel, Stuyvesant's principal, is the first to come to the defense of his school—passionately. "There's a difference between a child who is gifted and talented and a child who simply works hard," he says, choosing his words carefully. "And we have lots of children in New York City who come to school every day and work hard, doing the right [thing]

and are successful in their schools. . . . Those are good kids. But they're
not gifted and talented kids, okay? Gifted and talented is a kid who sits
in a math team class and has the insight to see where this problem's
going. Gifted and talented is when I teach my physics class and I don't
have to go through every single algebraic step. I can jump to here to
there. I can go from step one to step four, and no one is going to raise
their hand and go, 'How'd you do that?' They can be with me. That's
gifted and talented."

Mr. Teitel is quick to point out that he doesn't include his own children among them. He is also quick to note that not only does
Stuyvesant draw from the same pool of teachers as any other city school
but that his school is like any other in another important respect:
Stuyvesant receives the same funding as all the other schools in the system. It's based on enrollment, not achievement. "In fact, if anything," he
asserts, "I'm getting underfunded" because Stuyvesant doesn't receive
the additional federal money given to schools that serve underprivileged
students. As a result, Stuyvesant administrators say, they frequently
scramble to meet the special needs of gifted students, scraping funds
together to cover extra costs of advanced math textbooks, for example,
or new literary works not found on the school's shelves.

"Gifted children are the most underrepresented class in the United
States," Mr. Jaye says.

He includes himself among them as a former student who went
unchallenged and bored in a regular school. "I know what happens when
you have a gifted student who isn't in a gifted program," he says. "It's
child abuse." That's why he finds himself ensnared in an argument with a
new administrator at City College, where he created a summer program
for gifted high school students to earn college credits. When the college
administrator looked at the sea of faces in the auditorium, she saw only a
handful of black students participating in the program. The administrator told him the program needed more diversity. Mr. Jaye said he wasn't
"compromising on the quality." While Mr. Jaye agrees that the program
hasn't "met its diversity target," he says admission is based on academic
credentials. "We don't have to apologize for being elite," he says.

Such exclusivity isn't always an advantage for Stuyvesant students.
For one, they are thrust in an environment where there is always some-

one better, which can be a rude awakening. "Where they came from, they may have been the star," says Ms. Archie, the assistant principal. " . . . And then they come here, and then they realize there are thirty-four kids [per class] that are stars."

Mr. Polazzo, coordinator of student affairs, goes as far as to say that, for the most selective colleges, "being at Stuy doesn't help you, in fact it probably hurts you." Students are vying for limited spots at the top colleges, he notes, and schools like Harvard will accept only so many students from Stuyvesant, no matter how gifted.

That's one reason Mariya, the Ukrainian immigrant, thinks she'd be better off at Edward R. Murrow High School, a public school that admits a mix of high- and low-achieving students not far from her home in Brooklyn. "With less pressure, I think I could do better there," says the Stuyvesant sophomore. It occurs to her too that she might "look better compared to some of the regular people." And there's the added benefit that her best friend, Natasha Borchakovskaia, another Ukrainian immigrant, is a junior at Murrow who likes the school. Unlike Stuyvesant, Natasha says, Murrow students have a social life, they have the freedom to make what they want of their education, grades are not as important, and while violence is an occasional problem—a stabbing took place Natasha's freshman year—somehow that seems more palatable to her than a school packed with nerds whose weapon of choice is a "pocket protector."

Still, there is a palpable sense among students that Stuyvesant is a privilege, whether it's a function of the rigorous admissions test, the $150 million building, or the students themselves. "Everyone here is brilliant," Xevion says. "We're like any other high school, except we have one thing in common. We are really bright. We have a lot of potential."

Many students at other city schools come to view their Stuyvesant peers differently as well. "Stuy kids, they are among the top," says junior Elaine Liu, herself a top student at Leon M. Goldstein High School for the Sciences, a well-respected public school in Brooklyn, where students are chosen based on a formula intended to ensure a balance of low and high achievers. Elaine had wanted to attend Stuyvesant, eyeing its wide range of advanced placement classes, some of which aren't offered at her school. "Another thing is reputation," she says. At Stuyvesant, "all they have is constant praise." By contrast, she says, "if I tell people what school I go to, they go, like, 'What? Where is the school?'" Stuyvesant's fame has a tangible benefit, she says, discounting the theory that it's a disadvantage to be a star among many stars. Colleges, scouting prospective students, are apt to take kindly to Stuyvesant students. "They look at them [in] a better light than other kids," Elaine says. "They would choose Stuy kids over normal kids."

Even students who make it into the public exam schools wrestle with the privilege accorded them. "I guess it's not fair for those people who didn't get in," says Bronx Science sophomore Rosabella Magat, a Filipino immigrant. But if educators abolished the exam schools, she says, only students whose parents could afford private school would obtain the kind of specialized education that many colleges are seeking. "If it's not a competition of skill, then it'd be a competition of who can afford it, and I don't think that's fair," Rosabella says.

Yet gaining admission to public schools like Bronx Science and Stuyvesant is, to an extent, a competition of who can afford the costly private courses to prepare students for the exam, say many students and parents. Sixteen-year-old Francisco Bencosme makes that argument, saying he suffered the consequences because his parents—a security guard and an assistant in a doctor's office—couldn't afford such a prep course. He borrowed a friend's used Kaplan test prep book, studied for a week, and narrowly missed the Stuyvesant cutoff. Now a Bronx Science sophomore, Francisco still wonders what would have happened if he had the opportunity to take a prep course. "In the back of my head, I always think I could've gone to Stuyvesant if I did a little better on the test," he says. "I feel there's an economic advantage for parents who can afford these courses, whereas my parents couldn't." Francisco, though, is hard-pressed to come up with a better way to select students for elite public schools, if they are to be. Admission can't be determined by middle school grades, he says, because there is too much variation inherent in them. That, he reckons, leaves a uniform entrance test as perhaps the least of all evils.

"It's as fair as it can be," he says.

Educators and policy makers are equally confounded. Some say public exam schools send the wrong message to students about their self-worth if they fail to gain admission. Another concern is that removing gifted students from regular schools deprives those places of "the yeast that makes the whole school rise," Dr. Ravitch says. Still others challenge whether taxpayers should fund public exam schools when so many other students at the other end of the spectrum are in need of remedial education or are at risk of dropping out. How, they say, can you justify a school like Stuyvesant?

"It's elitist," says Thomas Toch, cofounder and codirector of Education Sector, a policy think tank in Washington, D.C. "Should you be spending public dollars in that way? It's a fundamental question." The answer, he says, "is a tough call because those schools are truly elitist in both the best and the worst sense of the word."

Katie, for her part, is at peace with her decision to attend Stuyvesant, despite her father's protests. The seventeen-year-old, though, is not without her own concerns about educational elitism. In less than two weeks, she will be hearing from the colleges to which she applied. She's a little nervous. One place she won't be hearing from: the Ivy League. Despite her high grade point average and SAT scores, she didn't apply to any of those colleges.

"I've crossed them off," she says.

Katie has always been unimpressed with the Stuyvesant frenzy over such brand-name schools, especially among students who from the beginning of freshman year are set on attending an Ivy League college before they know anything about the schools—let alone about themselves. "In the end," says Mr. Davis, a proud papa, beaming about his daughter's decision, "it's a badge of courage." Who needs Harvard when you have Haverford College? That is where Katie will eventually be heading—happily.

CHAPTER FOURTEEN

Grief Virus

THEY ARE SO YOUNG, THEY KNOW SO LITTLE ABOUT themselves. But on the morning of March 17, they know this much: Fourteen-year-old April Lao is a small but spirited freshman, a gifted piano player and talented swimmer on the Stuyvesant team who loves brownies and other sweet things. Sixteen-year-old sophomore Kevin Kwan, also a promising member of Stuyvesant's swim team, has a way of making you smile with that infectious laugh of his, and if he insults you, please don't take it personally; it probably only means that he likes you.

At about 5:30 a.m., April kisses and hugs her father, saying, "Good-bye, Daddy."

Then she and Kevin, members of the Flushing Flyers, a private swim team in Queens, head to a YMCA swim meet in Buffalo. Both swimmers' mothers and Kevin's and April's ten-year-old brothers accompany them. At about 7 a.m., Kevin's mother pulls over their minivan to check a flat tire, stopping in the right traffic lane instead of pulling onto the shoulder of the New York State Thruway. Just behind and around a slight bend, out of sight, a tanker bears down in the same direction.

Another trucker, spotting the minivan stopped on the highway, desperately tries to radio the tanker to avoid it. "Get over!" the trucker screams into his CB radio. "Move over!" But the fifty-two-year-old tanker driver doesn't pick up the warning.

The trucker flashes his headlights to alert the tanker, but the driver remains unaware.

Kevin's mother climbs back in the minivan.

Barreling down the highway at sixty-five miles per hour, the tanker driver doesn't see the minivan until he is practically on top of it, and in the split second that he tries to swerve around it, his truck smashes into the back of the minivan, ripping off the car's roof and propelling the minivan about sixty feet down an embankment. In the sudden impact, Kevin is thrown from the demolished car. April lies nearby, bleeding, soundless.

Kevin dies there, as do his mother and his younger brother. A helicopter flies April to a nearby hospital, where hours later she cannot be saved. Her brother and mother survive.

"I have lost my beautiful daughter," April's father says. Kevin's father breaks down, inconsolable.

Police do not charge the distraught tanker driver, who is treated and released with a shoulder injury.

Word of the tragedy reaches school almost instantly. Students gather on the Tribeca Bridge outside the building and weep. Grief counselors arrive at Stuyvesant the following Monday. Students erect a garland-wreathed memorial at the second-floor entrance, spangled with helium balloons and photos of the dead children. Other impromptu memorials spring up throughout the building. R.I.P. APRIL AND KEVIN, announces one sign, showing two winged angels in flight. But the bereavement doesn't end. Instead, a grief virus spreads imperceptibly, a wrenching pall gripping even students like Namita, the senior, who never knew April or Kevin. Namita can't stop thinking about them, weeping quietly on a bench in the school lobby. On another bench, Alex Larsen, a freshman girl who did know April in biology class, also can't help but think of them.

"That could've been me," Alex says.

The fifteen-year-old sits, too stunned to show any emotion. "I couldn't imagine dying," she says sotto voce: "I have my agenda all planned out. I want to be a brain surgeon."

Alex also can't help thinking about her recent fight over a boy with another student, her best friend—ex-best friend. They haven't talked since. But April's and Kevin's deaths—the fragility of life—puts the squabble in a different light. What happened to April and Kevin gives a painful context and a blunt perspective to teenagers who, like Alex, feel that they're impervious, that they'll live forever, that every little thing counts. Now Alex is embarrassed about the fight with her good friend. "It wasn't even worth it," she says, and in that instant, she absolves her friend. "I forgive her," she says. Though Alex has trouble understanding the meaning of April's and Kevin's deaths, she finds certainty in thinking about her former best friend. One day, Alex knows, "we'll work things out."

The tragedy is hard for Mr. Teitel to fathom as well. In his nearly quarter century at Stuyvesant, the principal cannot recall a year when as many as two students died. For him, the only tragedy that compares occurred five years ago. No Stuyvesant student died then, but the entire school mourned.

Sitting at his desk on that morning, September 11, 2001, Mr. Teitel heard a blast, then noticed the lights flicker. "The whole building shook," he recalls. Looking out of his window, he could not believe the calamity he was witnessing only four blocks from Stuyvesant: the World Trade Center in a billowing haze of smoke and fire. In the chaos that ensued, FBI and Secret Service agents converged on the school. No one at Stuyvesant knew at first that terrorists had struck, and Mr. Teitel announced over the public address system that students were to remain in class. Then the first of the two towers came crashing down, sending reverberations throughout the school. Suddenly, it dawned on Mr. Teitel that the authorities did not know what was happening, and he ordered students to evacuate the building. Children in backpacks fled up the street, only turning back to witness debris and human remains descend like the mushroom cloud of an atomic bomb on Lower Manhattan.

"They saw this live, in living color," Mr. Teitel says, as if he still can't believe it.

Though no harm came to students that day, when Stuyvesant

reopened in October 2001, many students returned to school damaged, suffering from rashes, nosebleeds, and what many parents and others believed was a lingering case of post-traumatic stress disorder. The last class to witness the destruction of 9/11 graduated in 2005, with fewer laurels and prizes than usual for Stuyvesant, and an unsettling legacy remains for succeeding generations of students to ponder: a big gaping hole at the World Trade Center site.

With the pit full of cranes and hard hats and excavated dirt, time seems to have stood still since terrorists struck, leaving the site in a heap of construction delays and false starts blamed on political infighting and clashes about artistic visions over the new towers to rise again. It's enough of a morass to turn unspeakable tragedy into a distinctly American spectacle, one of the city's biggest tourist attractions, drawing a battalion of sightseeing buses and more than a million visitors a year.

But there's no way to recast the tragedy of two children lost in a car wreck. It is what it is.

"This was different," Mr. Teitel says.

At Stuyvesant, life sputters on. Five days after April's and Kevin's deaths, a sense of normalcy struggles to reemerge in Mr. Siwanowicz's fourth-period math research class. Several students straggle in late, as if it doesn't matter, the straggling or the lateness. "Stuff happens," Mr. Siwanowicz says, "but try to be on time in class." There's no venom in his voice. It's almost too perfunctory. The tardy students seem not to care. Nor does Mr. Siwanowicz. Maybe he's just too tired or too depressed or both. Mr. Jaye makes a cameo appearance in the room, attempting to inject more life into the class, exhorting the students to take this course seriously. "We really do want you to work," he says, and then he's gone. Taking his cue, Mr. Siwanowicz lumbers over to the whiteboard, a red marker in hand to make a point about Pascal's triangle, a mystery of math that seems to grab the attention of at least one student: Milo. Sitting in the first seat of the first row, the ten-year-old prodigy remains riveted by all things math at the same time that he continues to morph into something less childlike. He is wearing a horizontally striped sweater eerily reminiscent of that worn by the former prodigy, Mr. Siwanowicz. But Milo's jeans contain a feature lacking in his teacher's version—a well-placed hole in the right knee—which brings him a step closer to acceptable fashion in these teenage parts. Milo even wields a bottle of Poland Spring water, another standard Stuyvesant classroom accoutrement, except that he accidentally dumped most of it inside his backpack, soaking his papers in a soggy reminder that his transformation isn't complete.

"I can't teach how to ask questions," Mr. Siwanowicz is saying. "The key is to find one good question."

He's talking about how students need to ask questions to find a good math topic to research, but he might as well be asking questions about himself: Will he ever finish college? Will he ever obtain his teacher's license? Will he ever stop patrolling the library? But there are no answers to those questions, not on this day. It's his students' turn to ask questions. So Milo pairs with his Stuyvesant friend Daniel, the Cuban immigrant who went for ice cream with him that day not so long ago. Now the two boys huddle over a gray desk, searching for the right question.

Later, during seventh period, Mariya, the fifteen-year-old Ukrainian immigrant, is huddled over a gray desk of her own, listing to her left, head in hand, pondering the miseries of chemistry, which are adding to the woes of her failed petition drive to eradicate that scourge, homework over vacation. On the blackboard resides a riddle: "How do you calculate ksp values?" The teacher asks Mariya's friend, Mariana, for the variable of a certain "A." Mariana answers, "Um," letting the utterance draw out until it dies of its own accord with no discernible answer. Evidently, Mariana's mother is going to kill Mariya, who was supposed to rescue Mariana from the last chemistry test.

Mariana failed spectacularly.

Mariya, though, faces perhaps a worse fate than the ire of Mariana's mother. If Mariya's parents punished her for a report card that dipped slightly below 95, she hasn't begun to imagine the repercussions of a disreputable 84 on her latest chemistry test. But it seems that Mariya cares less and less about grades, that the moorings of parental censure are loosening. It could be because Mariya recently celebrated—survived, is more like it—her two-month anniversary with her inscrutable first love, Tom. But more likely, it's because of April and Kevin, whose deaths linger in Mariya's consciousness, though she knew neither. She feels bleak about her own future, worrying about becoming one of those people who take a job just for the money. She feels overweight even though she isn't, not nearly. She feels nostalgic, if that's possible for a fifteen-year-old, for the old days when she and her best friend, Natasha, stood on the concrete handball courts of the park in their Brooklyn neighborhood, in a kind of Rockwellian portrait, innocent and pure, simply spinning round and round, going nowhere, not hoping for tomorrow to come because today is all they need.

But then, it seems that everyone in school wishes this day, Wednesday, March 22, had never arrived. Mr. Teitel even offered to postpone it. The principal consulted with the swim team to see whether he should move back tonight's opening performance of Sing! He also approached freshmen and sophomore leaders, since it was they who had lost their own in April and Kevin. All agreed: Sing! must go on.

On a practical level, it has to. By eighth period, only 8 of the 840 tickets remain for tonight's performance, even though it's merely a dress rehearsal known as "New Haven," named after the Broadway tradition of tuning up a musical in the Connecticut locale. Tickets for the real performances on Friday and Saturday nights are scalping for a hundred dollars a pop, five times face value. Already, the Student Union has spent six thousand dollars on Sing! T-shirts and sweatshirts, expecting to double that in profit. And a stockpile lies in wait: eight hundred bottles of water, cases of Mountain Dew, boxes of strawberry Pop-Tarts, Starburst, and Reese's—teenage booty.

Everything is in place, except the performers, the sets, the props, and just about everything else. "We're not as ready as we should be," says senior hip-hop dancer Olga Safronova in quiet understatement. She's referring to the mayhem on the second floor, where students are scrambling to finish making black and green toxic-mutant-fish dance costumes, airing them with a blow dryer on a clothesline. Sitting nearby, Allie Caccamo, a member of the Indian dance number, raises the ghost of the dreaded curse that every six years the seniors are fated to lose Sing! "Oh my God," says a fellow senior who is playing the animated character SpongeBob in the play. "That's not even funny." Even less funny is the condition of Molly, the seniors' star singer, who approaches with cheeks flushed red. The singer can't sing. She has lost her voice to strep throat, or tonsillitis, or a disease as yet undiagnosed, such as overwhelming anxiety, and she's about to leave school to see a doctor. The early prognosis from her grandfather, an otorhinolaryngologist, a term Molly can't define (an ear, nose, and throat specialist), is appropriately dire. He says she might burst a blood vessel in her throat if she sings. "I'm so sick, I don't know what to do," Molly says.

"If it makes you feel better, I'm worried about my song," says Xevion, the juniors' singer, who has wandered into enemy territory.

It's a rare act of sympathy between junior and senior—bitter rivals—on the eve of Sing! But Xevion rises above the intense competition, showing pathos for a fellow diva, confiding that she's nervous about her Aretha Franklin cover, that she forgot some of the alternative lyrics in a run-through yesterday. Molly returns the compassion, showing admiration for the junior class's stage handiwork. "I was really intimidated by your set," she says.

Outside, a group of freshmen and sophomores is heading up Chambers Street to buy sandwiches—and to try to resolve the jarring disconnect between tonight's celebratory performance and the searing memory of April and Kevin. One sophomore singer can't. She shudders at the thought of the soph/frosh musical. "Our Sing! is about death and wanting people to die," she says. "I don't want to have Sing! because I'm the one who has to go up there and say all those things."

Taylor, the freshman codirector, changed some of the lyrics because a boy in the choir, a good friend of Kevin, who had also been in the choir, would break down whenever the song mentioned death.

The lyric "It's not all that bad to die" became "It isn't that bad down here."

"We all want to stay alive" transformed into "We all want to see the world."

Alexa, the freshman coproducer, wrote the play's dedication to Kevin and April, whom she knew from attending the same private Asian academy. Alexa kept typing the dedication over and over. Each time, she says, "It didn't seem right." Sometimes, she understands, words cannot suffice.

At 5:41, the thirty-fourth annual Sing! opens to a darkened auditorium of parents, teachers, and students, who hold a moment of silence in memory of April and Kevin. It's an appropriate forum. Few things at school other than Sing! bring together so many disparate factions of Stuyvesant, students who would otherwise never interact, whether it's Katherine, the Korean immigrant who somehow has time to serve as an usher tonight, or Jane, the senior struggling with a drug addiction, whose presence in the audience is startling in its own right because it means she's not in rehab, or Milo, who's here with his mother to see what the fuss is all about.

Then, a spotlight on two boys in front of the curtain, strumming a guitar. And the heavy black curtains separate, distending the air of mourning until it dissolves, like speckles of dust in a shaft of light, into the mercy of forgetfulness, into the make-believe playground arrayed on stage: a swing set in green and yellow, a seesaw in orange and yellow, and a playhouse in red and yellow. Coltish boys and girls prance on stage, breaking out in a carefree dance and song drowned out by the static buzz and blare of balky speakers. But it doesn't matter. It's soph/frosh. It's messy. It's confusing. It's perfect.

One sophomore vocalist, playing the role of Pandora, climbs a makeshift throne, overcoming her misgivings about the deaths of April and Kevin to sing majestically. Sammy, the putative troublemaker from French class, amazes in a hip-hop dance. Another student, decked out all in black like a dominatrix, does a rousing imitation of Ms. Damesek, the assistant principal of organization, in the thinly disguised role of "Ms. Ramesak." "I'm going to crush your bones," she howls onstage to the delight of the audience. The real version, Ms. Damesek, isn't around to appreciate it. She's patrolling the lobby. "I've seen enough of it," she says later. When Pandora is foiled in the end, and the curtain closes, the audience erupts in applause, and even a grizzled math teacher, Richard Geller, a notoriously tough grader, sits in the audience in quiet approval.

"Pretty smooth," he says grudgingly.

Mr. Geller is even more impressed when the juniors take the stage next, storming a gloriously rendered pirate's ship, and it's instantly clear that rumors notwithstanding, the juniors are taking nothing for granted. Wyndam, editor of the school newspaper, inspires big laughs as a patch-eyed pirate. The girl Romeo likes in his advanced math class does a beautiful dance step in a red dress, looking bookish no longer.

And then there is Romeo's lunch companion, Xevion, who plays Captain Hook. When she sings her variation of Aretha Franklin's "Respect," the microphone stalls but it can't obfuscate the ethereal sound of her voice, which draws one of the biggest applauses of the evening. When the juniors bow off stage, one thing is clear: they have a legitimate chance to win.

The seniors seem to sense the challenge, opening the final musical of the night with a tentative version of the Bee Gees' "Stayin' Alive." They look so much bigger than the underclassmen, almost world-weary by comparison, and the difference in age is reflected in the dark underside of their comedic script about an alcoholic father with an unwanted child. For the only time tonight in any of the three plays, a boy on stage tells a girl, "I love you." Jokes abound about the imminent arrival of the school's attendance scanners and, of course, about Ms. Damesek. As a whip-wielding queen, Molly parodies the assistant principal of organization, screaming, "There will be no stopping my evil reign," drawing laughs from the gallery, but not from Ms. Damesek, who is now standing alone in black stiletto boots, mirthless, by the auditorium door. But there is something critically missing from the seniors' performance: Molly's voice. On doctor's orders, she is saving her lungs for Friday and Saturday nights, when it counts, when anonymous alumni judge the performances. But during tonight's New Haven performance, her voice is sorely missed.

When it's over, Mr. Geller, the math teacher, abruptly rises to leave without giving a thumbs-up to the seniors. Mr. Polazzo gives voice to the murmurs circulating in the audience after the show. It looks like soph/frosh is out of the running, in spite of its valiant effort, but he says, "The juniors are going to give the seniors a run for their money." As for Ms. Damesek, she has no hard feelings, even if her image took a beating in two of the three Sing! plays. "Home, boys, home, go, go," she says softly, waving a group of students to the exit. "Be safe."

It's an invocation that finds an answer the next day, Thursday, March 23, when Milo arrives in the safe embrace of the ice-skating rink at Chelsea Piers, just north of Stuyvesant along the Hudson River. Protecting his sandy blond head is a baby blue helmet. Surrounding him is the cocoon of high-pitched squeals belonging to dozens of tiny people. For once, no child in attendance is older than Milo, and it's comforting on this crisp, bright afternoon. Here pimply-faced teenagers are replaced by freckle-faced kindergartners to fifth graders. Here, where Milo's parents regularly send him to be around kids his age, no one judges him, and his genius is so ignored that an adult ties the white laces of Milo's black skates, same as for the rest of the kids. Milo lets him. And then he scampers onto the ice rink, promptly careening into a Bud Light advertising sign on the wall. He's okay. He's alone, teetering forward and backward, zooming precariously on the ice until he's joined by another ten-year-old boy, a friend from P.S. 234 before Milo left for high school. Together, the two little boys crash purposely into each other, on the ice and against the walls in a mindless physical activity, which is just what Milo needs. Happiness is conveyed in his easy smile: there's something freeing about roaming the smooth surface of the ice under soaring rafters.

"Here, he's a kid," says Gil Rubin, who oversees the mayhem as head of the after-school program, Gilsports for Kids.

The other kids know Milo is different but accept him here. During a break, Milo and his fifth-grade friend order pizza with extra cheese and join a table with second and third graders, where the level of conversation barely rises above the complexities of what a burp sounds like, backed up by impressive demonstrations. Milo, though, quickly grows fatigued. Dark circles ring his big brown eyes. Last night, he fell asleep at 10 p.m., woke up at 1 a.m., and couldn't wrestle himself into slumber until 3:30, before waking up again at 7 for school. He has no idea why. "I'm going to go dunk my head in the freezer," he says.

Rising, Milo marches over to an icebox stocked with Häagen-Dazs ice cream and burrows his head in it. Refreshed, he rejoins the group, where a third grader welcomes him back by calling Milo "Pre-K," as in "pre-kindergarten," as if that's the most heinous epithet the younger boy could muster. "Quite the opposite," Milo retorts. His fifth-grade friend comes to his side, predicting that Milo will be a great math or science teacher one day. "None of the kids would be able to outsmart him," his friend boasts. Milo remains silent on that point; he doesn't know what he wants to be when he grows up, and that's okay here.

The boys run back to the rink to collect trophies. All get one. There are no losers here at Gilsports for Kids. Not like at Stuyvesant, where everything, it seems, is at stake. Straddling both worlds, of teenagers and elementary school friends, Milo finds it impossible to choose one over the other. "That'll keep me up tonight," he sighs. Then he decides, "I choose Pluto."

In Queens the following day, mourners pay their final respects, bowing in Asian custom as they file by the polished wooden coffins of sixteen-year-old Kevin, his brother, and his mother. A woman feeds gold-leaf scrolls into a stove, where they vanish in lashes of fire. The Stuyvesant choir sings. Classmates leave notes to Kevin, words wished for but not spoken.

The same day, the long-awaited attendance scanners arrive at school, unannounced, for a trial run. Scanning is voluntary. There is no protest.

Sing! reaches a crescendo the next evening, Saturday, March 25, when the curtains close on the final performance and hundreds of students cram into the lobby, awaiting the judges' scores. The gathering quickly deteriorates into a mosh pit, like a punk rock concert, where boys are pumping fists and pounding drums, girls are bouncing on boys' shoulders, and students are literally climbing the walls, screaming rival chants.

"Senior Sing! has got to go! Hey-hey, ho-ho!"

"Junior Sing! has got to go! Hey-hey, ho-ho!"

Emotions are running so high, they are almost primal, full of fury. Students storm back into the auditorium, climbing on top of the seats while several boys, including Romeo, rip off their shirts, whirling them overhead. Mr. Teitel, the principal, tries to restore order, taking center stage, a bullhorn in hand. "Get off the furniture!" he shouts, but the order is drowned out by visceral chants of "Senior-senior Sing!" The principal looks on, speechless. Almost instantly, though, the room falls silent for the reading of the judges' scores.

Third place . . . soph/frosh.

Then second place . . . the juniors. And the auditorium explodes in a deafening roar: the seniors have won. Hundreds rush the stage, as if it's the game-winning home run in the World Series, hugging and pointing index fingers skyward.

The six-year curse is denied another year.

Later, it comes out that the juniors almost captured a victory Friday night, only to be overtaken by a big senior surge on Saturday, aided no doubt by Molly's vocal recovery. Later, it also comes out that several judges almost marred the final results by showing up at Sing! drunk. One inebriated judge, hoping to be bribed, was disqualified. Other soused judges, rooting for the soph/frosh underdogs, shamelessly heckled the upperclassmen.

By the following Tuesday, all four of the attendance scanners are up and running. Scanning is now compulsory. Weeks ago, several students had e-mailed one another, planning to stage a "slowdown," to take as much time as possible to swipe through the machines as a form of protest and thereby demonstrate the futility of the new system. But there seems little fight left in students now. Almost everyone scans efficiently, each in less than a second. Quietly, it appears they have begun to accept this new reality.

CHAPTER FIFTEEN

Polazzo's Time

IN A CLUTTERED CUBBYHOLE OF AN OFFICE AT STUY-vesant two days later, March 30, at least one individual remains who is not willing to quietly accept the attendance scanners, a goateed rebel in cargo khakis who is talking about the possibility of students staging a march on City Hall and railing against the school system, even though he is part of it: Mr. Polazzo. He teaches advanced placement comparative government, which puts him in a position to know a thing or two about rebellions against an entrenched bureaucracy. At the age of thirty, he knows even more about being a teenager.

"He's a kid—he's a big kid!" exclaims a junior who sounds more like an exasperated mother talking about a wayward teenager, which in some ways makes Mr. Polazzo the perfect coordinator of student affairs, or in school lingo, the COSA. Teaching three classes instead of the regular five, he spends the rest of his days—and many of his evenings—overseeing the student government, dances, plays, and elections, not to mention the latest teenage cultural trends on MTV. No one at Stuyvesant cares about the kids more than Mr. Polazzo does. When he talks about students, he is apt to use the pronoun "we," before he catches

157

himself. He's actually one of "them," the adults, although the grown-ups aren't always persuaded.

"I'm trying to convince the administration I can kick ass," he says.

Mr. Polazzo might start with a makeover of his Student Union office on the second floor, a magnet for students because it resembles their own natural habitat—a teenager's eclectic hangout—where they check e-mail, eat candy, toss rubber balls. A sign on the wall reads, "If you touch this air conditioner, hose, or plug, I will track you down and kill you. Love, M. Polazzo." On another wall hangs a row of clocks with one supposedly telling the time in Beijing and another in "Ricoville," named after a former addled student. There are also clocks telling the time in New York, Madagascar, and Bronx Science, as if the latter were in a different time zone, not just uptown. None of the clocks works, although one dubbed "Polazzo's Time" shows the second hand twitching, as if it wants to move forward but can't quite get beyond 8:44.

It's just as well. Mr. Polazzo has no intention of growing up to become an intransigent adult, especially at the moment when he is bemoaning the crackdown on student freedoms, namely, the introduction of attendance scanners.

"The kids are really upset about it," he says.

Not all of them, including Jonathan Edelman, a senior who enters the cramped office ready to challenge Mr. Polazzo. "What liberties did they take?" Jonathan asks, siding with the school administration. Underscoring that he's a contrarian, Jonathan is wearing a blue T-shirt that reads, "Nuke a godless communist gay baby seal for Christ."

Mr. Polazzo, settling into the role reversal, defends the students, saying that Jonathan has become "institutionalized," like a prisoner who's fallen in love with his cell bars. Mr. Polazzo also blames student "apathy," and for good measure, he thinks students like Jonathan are "overthinking things."

Jonathan isn't convinced. "What right is being taken away by the scanners?"

"It's an issue of trust," Mr. Polazzo says, but perhaps sensing he's losing the argument, he also questions the merit of spending a hundred thousand dollars (actually, sixty thousand) on scanners in a school with nearly perfect attendance. Furthermore, he wants to know, what effect will the scanners have on the school environment?

"It feels fairly innocuous to me." Jonathan shrugs.

Mr. Polazzo persists: "Why bring in something that creates a further division between students and the administration?"

But Jonathan likes the scanner system. "Maybe because it's new," he says.

It's no use. Jonathan is unmoved. Besides, Mr. Polazzo has his own personal battle to wage. Despite his immense popularity with the students—or because of it—he is in jeopardy of losing his beloved job as COSA, which would force him back into teaching full-time. The principal has indicated that he may appoint a new coordinator of student affairs at semester's end, making the argument that Mr. Polazzo is about to finish his fourth year in the position, and if four years is enough for a president's term, it's enough for a COSA, ignoring that he himself is in his seventh year as principal.

The thought of being stripped of the student coordinator job pains Mr. Polazzo, but he hides it well, maintaining a stoic front in solidarity with the students who have little idea—yet—that their greatest advocate is feeling the pressure. It's a strange predicament for a teacher who never intended to be a teacher. He had briefly contemplated becoming a lawyer but couldn't muster the energy to pursue it. He had tried his hand at writing, publishing book reviews and blurbs for a nonprofit. Then he figured he'd try teaching, thinking it was an interlude, never planning to follow in the footsteps of his father, who taught history at a Stuyvesant rival, Brooklyn Tech. But Mr. Polazzo realizes this now: he loves the students. And he intends to reapply for the job, even if his prospects look dim.

"It's all about the students," he says. "That's who I serve."

Prospects look dire upstairs in the dining hall, where Xevion is not eating what looks like turkey, instead poring over a prep book for the SAT, which is a mere two days away.

"I'm freaking out," she says.

Romeo isn't. Sitting with her, the football captain is casually studying for a differential equations quiz today before he changes the subject
to resume a heated discussion between the two of them about the
nature of love.

"I bet Xevion I would fall in love in the next few weeks," Romeo
explains.

"I'm going to win this bet," Xevion says, already picturing collecting
her winnings—Romeo taking her out to dinner and a movie. Fueling her
confidence: Romeo isn't dating now.

"I'm hunting," he says defensively.

"He's playing," she corrects him, adding that he's nowhere close to
falling in love. "Can't you tell? He's too relaxed."

Xevion can't say the same. Yesterday, her nerves were so frayed she
almost screamed at her mother. Tomorrow, Friday, she plans to stay home
from school to calm herself before taking the SAT on Saturday. Romeo
plans a different pre-SAT ritual, catching up on sleep tomorrow. He'll
also be reviewing vocabulary words and writing a few practice essays.
One thing he won't bother reviewing: math, his specialty. But for the first
time, Romeo is giving in slightly to the possibility of falling short of near
perfection on the SAT. Lowering his expectations, he now expects to
score at least a 2200 instead of a 2300 out of 2400, which is still stratos-
pherically high. But he says he isn't sweating it.

"Romeo will take care of things," he says.

Xevion, rising from her chair in disbelief, says, "Did he just speak
about himself in the *third* person?"

Romeo calmly explains, "I've built this machine." Today, on the last
day of his SAT prep class, all he can do, he says, is "let this machine run."
By disconnecting himself from the imminent college exam, Romeo
doesn't need to say that he is compartmentalizing the pressure. Xevion
gets it. But the machine's left knee is shaking under the table.

Other students are feeling the pressure today, and it's not just the
SAT. College admissions—or rejection—letters are due to arrive in the
mailboxes of seniors on the same day that the juniors take the SAT:
April Fool's Day. This cruel joke of scheduling seems to be inducing a
stomach virus that's quickly making its rounds at Stuyvesant, a queasy
feeling compounded by another big worry on this Thursday: prom. Just

as the frenzy of Sing! has subsided, the specter of prom has begun to emerge, more than two months before the Big Night. Reyna Ramirez, for one, doesn't have a date yet. The senior is trying to avoid her former boyfriend, who she knows is lying in wait to ask her to the prom. All the while, she wants to go with another boy whom she hardly knows. "It's all about the photo op," she says, worried that one day she'll look at her prom pictures and wonder why she went with him, whoever he is. Now *that's* pressure. "Somehow," she says, speaking generically about Stuyvesant students, "I think we look for things to stress ourselves about."

Senior Danielle Fernandes isn't stressing, not anymore. She just found out that she gained entrance to Cornell, Dartmouth, and Tufts, and to top it off, she found a prom date too. Her friend, senior Richard Lo, surprised her with a clutch of pink roses and tulips, nervously asking her to the big dance. Danielle didn't hesitate. Richard saved her from the machinations of Mr. Polazzo, who gave new meaning to his title as coordinator of student affairs when he scoured his Delaney book in search of a prom date for Danielle. "I wasn't going to go with random kids in his class," she says, smiling broadly.

Mr. Siwanowicz is animated on the last day of March, even displaying what appears to be the wisps of a smile. Surrounded by eight teenagers, playing board games after school, he is one of them again, a kid. Like Milo at the ice rink, or Mr. Polazzo in the Student Union office, Mr. Siwanowicz finds comfort in the easy banter of teenagers, partaking of Teddy Grahams passed around like so many energy fixes, forgetting for the moment the pressures of finishing college and obtaining his teacher's license. Here, in the back of the math research room, all that matters is who becomes the Great Dalmuti, a game of strategy recommended for anyone eight or older. The object of the game is to run out of cards as quickly as possible. For Mr. Siwanowicz, always engaged in the battle against depression, the object of the game is to keep his mind honed, an aim that he will mention in passing, as if not realizing that he's thinking aloud. But there's no chance that he will lose his edge, not this afternoon, when he's having fun, explaining that if you win the game, you get to choose where you sit, which tends to be the most comfortable chair at the head of the table, the winner naturally being called the Great Dalmuti. Those who don't fare as well are called greater or lesser peons, with the least of them relegated to an uncomfortable stool. Mr. Siwanowicz is positioned somewhere in the middle, neither winning nor losing greatly, which seems to be just where he wants to be. Until he becomes a lesser peon. Then in a mock constipated voice, he practically genuflects, telling a student in the role of the Great Dalmuti, "There will always be a place in the stable for you, my lord." The other kids, gathered around the table, giggle in unison, unaware how true it is that Mr. Siwanowicz has just been reduced to a lower station at Stuyvesant.

It's no laughing matter to Mr. Jaye, in the office next door. He's ranting about the bane of his school existence, Ms. Damesek. Without notifying him, she recently reassigned Mr. Siwanowicz. He's no longer monitoring the library during his free seventh and eighth periods; now he's monitoring the newly installed attendance scanners, which particularly stings Mr. Jaye, not just because Mr. Siwanowicz is a math genius who should be teaching math, but because Mr. Jaye had opposed the scanners. He can't believe that Ms. Damesek first tried to banish holiday food and now is trying to banish his talented school aide. "She stole Christmas, then she stole Jan!" Mr. Jaye bellows. And he can't believe that the principal is allowing Ms. Damesek to get away with the maneuver; it's obvious to Mr. Jaye that she's using Mr. Siwanowicz as a pawn in a proxy fight with him. "I'm not going to let Stan live!" he yells, producing a copy of a letter from a student to the principal, expressing similar outrage over Mr. Siwanowicz's scanner duties. "I will tell you it clearly: This is completely and utterly stupid," the student writes. ". . . You're wasting some of the best talent on one of the most pointless jobs out there."

Mr. Jaye is also mad at Mr. Wong, the assistant principal of technology services, who recently accused a teacher close to Mr. Jaye of removing a letter, without authorization, that Mr. Wong wrote and posted on the Stuyvesant Web site. Mr. Wong had written an oddly lighthearted letter in support of the attendance scanners. "We're looking to hire [monitors] who are approximately 400 lbs with 25 inch biceps and 60 inch chest," he wrote, adding a cautionary note in support of Mr. Teitel,

the principal. "You should be aware that the school has a legal obligation to ensure the safety of all students and, therefore, you are not
allowed out of the building during a free period. Although this seems
unfair, we want to make sure that Mr. Teitel keeps his shirt (ugh!!)."

Mr. Jaye suspects that a student, not a teacher, removed the letter
from the Web site. To settle the matter, he storms out of his office, heading downstairs to find and confront the alleged perpetrator—only she is
nowhere to be found in school, leaving Mr. Jaye with nowhere to direct
his considerable energies except at his own increasingly complicated situation. Suddenly he isn't up for one principal's job. He's up for *two*. The
new entry is Midwood High School, a good public school in Brooklyn,
which has the added appeal of being the school where his younger
daughter is enrolled. Earlier this week, he went for a job interview there,
but not before he contacted officials at Bergen County Academies to let
them know that he had resolved his New Jersey licensing issue and,
more important, to see whether they were still interested in hiring him.
They are.

Suddenly, he is facing the burden of possibly two great choices:
heading a good public school in Brooklyn, where he can continue to
build his pension fund in the New York City school system, or moving
to New Jersey, where he can run another good public school, offsetting
his city retirement benefits with a sizable salary. Either way, the math
chairman knows his future is converging fast, and it doesn't look like
Stuyvesant is in it. Next week, on the same day, he is meeting again with
Brooklyn school officials, then heading to New Jersey to resume his
courtship with the schools superintendent there. If—when—he leaves
Stuyvesant, he vows to take Mr. Siwanowicz with him. Mr. Jaye knows
that Mr. Siwanowicz is wounded by the indignity of his monitoring
duties even though he accepts them in silence. There's no way Mr. Jaye
will leave him at Stuyvesant, unprotected.

And yet the present tugs at Mr. Jaye. When he explained that he may
be leaving Stuyvesant to Milo's mother, she broke down in tears, worried about what that may mean for her child. For the first time in his life,
Milo recently woke up to the prospect of going to school by enthusiastically chirping, "Yay, it's Monday!" Gone is the dread of a school that
doesn't challenge him. What will happen to Milo in Mr. Jaye's absence?

Will he be allowed to continue his education at Stuyvesant? How many other high school administrators would have welcomed a ten-year-old, no matter how gifted? Mr. Jaye himself worries about what his departure will mean. "I might be copping out 'cause what I should really do is stay [at Stuyvesant] to fix it," he says. It's not only about Milo. Mr. Jaye is helping Ms. Lee in her attempt to stay on at the school after she graduates from Columbia's Teachers College. But Mr. Jaye may not be able to see that through. Nor will he be able to fight the attendance scanners, which he considers the folly of the newfangled. "We have the technology to give every kid a CAT scan, but we don't do it!" he crows. Even more, he won't be at Stuyvesant to wage war against Ms. Damesek, who he worries will bully Mr. Teitel.

"Stan is so nice that he absorbs a lot of punches instead of just saying, 'This is the way it's going to be, you know, and deal with it,'" Mr. Jaye says.

And for all the tantalizing prospects of more money and more authority running schools elsewhere, when it comes down to it, Mr. Jaye doesn't want to leave his beloved Stuyvesant. But he doesn't feel that he has a choice because the principal isn't retiring, and Mr. Jaye believes that now is the time to seize his own opportunity to run a school. The decision, though, leaves him uneasy. "I feel like I'm deserting a sinking ship," Mr. Jaye says, "and the ship is sinking, trust me."

That Friday, a Buddhist monk presides over the funeral of fourteen-year-old April. Her father stands over her open coffin, touching her forehead, and the month of March comes to a merciful end.

CHAPTER SIXTEEN

Hell's Kitchen

ON THE FIRST OF APRIL, JANE IS PRESIDING OVER ROW upon row of white T-shirts and sparkly silver high heels and billowy dresses, the unwanted remnants of other people's lives, in a cavernous room under the harsh glare of fluorescent lighting. It's the unlikeliest of places to find Jane at nine on a Saturday morning: the used clothing section of the Salvation Army on Forty-sixth Street between Tenth and Eleventh avenues—Hell's Kitchen—a gritty neighborhood on the western edge of Manhattan known for its criminal element of yore and encroaching gentrification of today. But Jane isn't here by choice. She says she's here by court order, collecting plastic hangers, which constitutes community service for a public misconduct charge involving a fight that she doesn't want to talk about. Not that she's really here. She's withdrawn into a CD headset of grunge rock, courtesy of Kurt Cobain before he put a shotgun to his head and pulled the trigger.

Today is a gray contact lens day. Jane's eyes, though, are shrouded by the fog of marijuana, which she smoked before punching in for work. It's not enough. Later today, she plans to up the ante, plunging herself into the oblivion of angel dust. A recent drug test she took at rehab turned up a smorgasbord of cannabis, cocaine, and heroin. Jane says she's merely dabbling, that it's okay "as long as I don't get addicted." At the same time, she says bitterly, "I've been realizing that sobriety is a disappointment. Right now, there's no consolation. Tomorrow's going to suck too."

The other day wasn't so great either. In third-period gym, Jane argued with a girl who owed her money. The teacher kicked Jane out of class. Fifth period, a teacher caught Jane reading Toni Morrison's *Beloved*, her book from another class, Great Books, the only course she cares about. The teacher confiscated the novel. Jane promptly borrowed a library copy and, during sixth period, excused herself to the bathroom, where she broke a needle trying to shoot up. It was her last one. So seventh period, she skipped out of school to take the train to a nearby needle exchange just before it closed, grabbed three needles, and slipped into a restaurant bathroom, where she accidentally squirted out the last of her stash of heroin, lost forever.

"All my old stuff is coming back," she says. "I know drugs messed up my life, but guess what? I don't like my life." She says that all she has is the twin companionship of "depression and misery."

They, she says, are "my only muse," the fuel for her poetry:

> simple reduction
> if it really was that
> easy
> what the top and bottom have
> in common is deemed valueless
> simple compulsion
> if only it could be
> easy
> what I have is worthless
> that much we have in common
> so little
> mass and high
> density it's a blackhole
> I follow the scent of gravity and

simply sink, the pull keeps my world together
and drags me under
a concurrent current joint by
my free falling will.
I'm a blackhole
I turn
concrete to quicksand.

What solace she finds in her poetry, she can't find elsewhere, certainly not in rehab. "No one can answer my questions," she says. The foremost question is, "What do you do when the problem is when you're sober?" Her own answer: she decided to stop taking her medication about a week ago. "I hate the idea of antidepressants, which is ironic," she says. "I just hate the idea of swallowing pills every day." She's also decided that she can't countenance her mother, who gives Jane cash but demands that her daughter save every receipt or package to prove that she didn't spend the money on drugs. Suffice it to say, their short-lived truce is over. Jane is thinking of finding a part-time job to raise money so she can move out when she turns eighteen in less than two months, setting her free from her mother for good.

Jane's almost free of Stuyvesant, saying she's on track to graduate in June despite her mounting absences from classes this semester. But even as the end nears, she still wonders about the beginning, whether attending this school was a good idea in the first place, given how she tumbled into drugs here. Past and present, though, fall by the wayside as she reconsiders the future, the possibility of attending college next year. Ever so briefly, Jane lowers her hardened exterior to admit that "dealing with the whole thing," life after Stuyvesant, leaves her "scared."

Mr. Grossman, her Great Books teacher, intervened about a week ago, persuading other teachers to retroactively raise some of her grades from last semester to improve her college prospects. It's not a common practice, he says, but "I just don't think she should be penalized for grades that she received while she's in the throes of a debilitating addiction, and it doesn't reflect the work that she's capable of doing, or the work that she's done."

He's also spoken to one of the college counselors, who told him it's not too late for Jane to apply for September admission to some universities. Mr. Grossman believes there is a place for her. He's told Jane about the grade changes, and he's urged her to stop by Stuyvesant's college office to figure out the next step. But then she responded by not showing up to his class, and he's concerned that he pushed the idea of college too hard. "I wonder if the prospect of being close to doing it just sent her back the other way," he says. "With her, I always worry."

As English chairman, Mr. Grossman has much to worry about these days. That includes the prodigious work that his teachers assign to overloaded students, a frequent topic of debate in his department. He poses the question, "What's a fair and productive amount of work and at what point does it become simply a stress that is crushing?" There isn't unanimity on the faculty, but he is of the opinion that the teachers, himself included, must take responsibility for sometimes placing too much pressure on the students, to "catch them when they fall," and he's not just talking about the Janes of the world. One of his hardworking students, perhaps striving beyond her reach, found herself wait-listed at every college to which she applied, prompting Mr. Grossman to write an extra recommendation for her. Parents have called Mr. Teitel, complaining of their children's being in similar predicaments, and he has been working to use Stuyvesant's good name in the hopes of tipping the balance in favor of such students in college purgatory.

In the meantime, Mr. Grossman is still trying to help some of his English teachers, who are dangling in their own purgatory. Now it looks as though as many as four may lose their jobs, displaced when the school completes its search for a handful of new guidance counselors. He can at least find consolation in one development: the controversy over his firing of an English teacher is finally beginning to subside. "It's quieted down a lot," he says. "The routine of school has reasserted itself."

On Monday, April 3, school administrators scramble to douse another controversy: the attendance scanners. Just when it seemed that students had acquiesced to the new devices, several begin agitating behind the scenes, threatening to disrupt the school if the administration doesn't broker a compromise. It turns out that students are resurrecting the idea of a march on City Hall and staging a slowdown while passing through the scanners, creating a perfect storm on the same day, tomorrow.

Mindful of the administration's embarrassment over the cuddle puddle controversy, the media-savvy students are planning to notify the press to ensure local coverage of their City Hall protest. They also are e-mailing just about everyone over the head of Mr. Teitel, the principal, including his ultimate boss, the New York City schools chancellor. Apparently, Mr. Teitel gets the message just in time. This afternoon, less than twenty-four hours before the massive showdown, he invites student leaders to his office for a peace summit, and quickly, they reach a resolution. Students will be required to scan in only during their morning arrival; they will not have to scan out for lunch or at the end of the day. The administration also agrees to drop the one-dollar fee charged to students who lose their ID. Mr. Teitel can console himself that he gets to use scanners to take attendance, while the students exult in preserving their school freedoms.

"It seems like the bad atmosphere created by the scanners has been neutralized," says Nathan Buch, an official of the Student Union, on the renegade student Web site he operates, www.stuycom.net. In a flyer dispatched shortly after its powwow with the school administration, the Student Union writes, "All in all, the scanners do not seem anywhere close to a nightmare any longer."

Mariya, the fifteen-year-old Ukrainian immigrant, has her own nightmare. As she wades through a sea of students passing through the second-floor entrance, she tries to camouflage a look of sorrow under the lid of her army green cap. What seemed an inevitability now shocks. It's over with her first love, Tom, just after their two-month anniversary. "I don't know why," she says, almost devoid of emotion. But on this afternoon, on April 5, as the glum sophomore heads out of school, tromping across the Tribeca Bridge, there's little time to contemplate the loss of love, or the gain of cynicism, the rite of passage to adulthood, because she's instantly assaulted by a burst of sunshine, then by two junior boys who cajole her into heading over to Burritoville, a fast-food joint, their after-school ritual of late.

There they grab a bunch of white paper plates and pile them high with tortilla chips and salsa, all of which is free, and that is the point. Their only cost is a single soda, $1.61 after taxes, which they constantly refill, also for free, rotating among Dr Pepper, Pepsi, and Mariya's favorite, Sierra Mist.

One boy places an index finger on his nose, and so does Mariya, leaving the other boy the odd man out, the loser who has to fetch the next refill. And in the act, and the ritual, Mariya loses herself, creating a memory of life at the moment that, looking back, will seem to have been nothing more complicated than teenagers sitting in a red vinyl booth, holding index fingers to their noses.

But then, one boy skips off to run track and the other heads to driver's ed, and it all comes rushing back to Mariya as she sits, remaining at the Formica table. It's not just Tom. It's Mom.

Mariya wonders how her parents will react to her latest grades. She knows computer science may be a problem. The classwork is packed with complicated computer commands involving lots of parentheses and memorizing. But if anything is going to drag down her grade point average, it's chemistry, which continues to befuddle her. A test next week may determine whether she finishes with a grade above or below 90 for the term, which in turn may determine whether she can surpass last semester's overall average of 94.86. And there's little chance her mother won't find out. The father of another student, who monitors his son's every academic step, works with Mariya's mother and keeps her informed of her daughter's progress, or lack thereof, in school. But Mariya just doesn't seem to care as much as she used to about grades, even though she knows that if her parents punished her when her average dipped slightly last semester, another minor drop would surely spell more trouble. "My mom will give me the I'm-so-disappointed speech," she says. Worse, Mariya reckons, her mother might punish her by making her play with her nine-year-old brother. Or worst: "Probably what will happen is, my mother won't let me hang out after school," Mariya says with the same dead voice that she used to announce the end of her first love.

After school on the following day, April 6, hundreds of students crowd into the auditorium in a school memorial for April and Kevin. One after another, friends step to the podium to express what words can't.

"I don't believe it, I don't believe it at all," says one student. ". . . When I think about it now, my heart aches with pain."

Another student quivers as she says she hasn't been able to keep track of time since their deaths. "I'm still stuck," she says. ". . . I feel sick and angry and most of all confused. . . . I miss them, I miss them so much."

During a moment of personal reflection, the only sound is that of children quietly weeping.

A block away, the only sound is that of children laughing riotously in front of P.S. 234 on Friday, April 7, just as the rains of the day have given way to emerging spring buds. Finished with high school for the day, Milo reenters the red door of his former elementary school to work on the newspaper, the *234 Latte*, the umbilical cord to his otherwise departed fifth-grade life.

When Milo enters room 304, he is greeted by reminders of what drove him out: an education already surpassed. Above the blackboard reside the letters of the alphabet: *Aa Bb Cc Dd* . . . On the blackboard: "Factors of 100 . . . 1, 2, 4, 5, 10, 20, 25, 50, 100." A magnet pins a sheet of white paper to the board, touting "Writing with Interesting Language." Milo frowns as he begins reviewing an article that he wrote in the latest edition of the school paper. The topic: global warming, a serious concern of his. To his great consternation, the title, "What's With Winter," was changed to "What's With the Weather." It doesn't have quite the alliterative ring he had wanted. At least the editors didn't remove his reference to the Kyoto Global Warming Treaty, or his assessment of the worst-case scenario:

> Global warming may eventually cause sudden severe changes in temperature either up or down; so severe that it might cause the next ice age. A bit less severe but still catastrophic is that global warming may make large parts of the world uninhabitable. This may

lead to food and beverage shortages. This in turn may lead to migrations, which may lead into World War III.

A ponytailed girl musters the courage to sidle up to Milo, her face just inches from his, to say, "I liked your article on"—and hesitates before finding the right words—"global warming." Milo, deeply engrossed in ferreting out the editing flaws of his story, completely ignores his fan.

Moments later, he heads down the hall to pose for yearbook photographs for an elementary school he no longer attends. Making funny faces for the camera, including a raised brow, à la Clark Gable, he holds against his red sweater a white plaque that reads "MILO Beckman 72."

"That's how old I am," he says, poking fun at the number representing the school's system of organizing students for the portraits.

Against a muslin-draped backdrop, Milo proceeds to trot out a series of silly poses. Cross-eyed, *click*. Sleepy, *click*. His red shoes stacked on top of his head, *click*. And for a moment, Milo is a fifth grader again. He can put aside his struggles with sleep, forgetting that when he finally succumbs to a restless slumber, he unconsciously rotates 180 degrees so that his head is pointing north, like a compass drawn to an unseen beacon, when he awakes. He can also put aside his recent discomfort at Stuyvesant when he received the lowest grade in his life: a 77 on a trigonometry test. "Pretty horrible," he says. Milo is stunned by a new reality. Even he has to study sometimes. But not now.

When he returns to the fifth-grade classroom, he joins a group of other little boys at a table. One scrawls in pencil on loose-leaf paper, "Have you got a pet that costs a lot of cash?" Another is writing in an uneasy hand about a coyote found in Central Park. Milo, partaking in the writing exercise, decides to describe a major discovery of an extinct fish called the *Tiktaalik roseae*. "THE MISSING LINK," he entitles his paper, explaining to the boy to his right, "They found these bones yesterday. It's a huge thing. It was in the *New York Times*." The boy, scratching his forehead, is not sure what to make of that. The boy, however, is saved from his confusion when a little girl comes over to ask Milo for the correct spelling of a term.

"*Fire trucks* is one word, right?"

"No," Milo says.

His mother, helping out in the class, arrives a moment later to reconfirm. "It's not one word?"

"No," Milo repeats patiently.

His mother shrugs as if to acknowledge that her ten-year-old son isn't to be disputed on such matters.

Milo responds by ripping up his unfinished paper on the *Tiktaalik roseae*, an act that he relishes, each tear causing delight, before he turns his attention to art. He draws a ball with lines spinning off it, creating a sense of motion on paper. Milo, however, doesn't move an inch as the class comes to an end. Instead, he finds consolation in the solitary confines of his imagination, continuing to draw his picture even as other children place chairs upside down on tables, and the entire room clears out, empty except for him.

CHAPTER SEVENTEEN

The Contest

ON A DRIZZLING SATURDAY, APRIL 8, THE GYMNASIUM at Nyack High School in suburban New York lies empty before the big event, almost too quiet. The only sound is the hum of powerful beams of light projecting from the rafters, reflecting against the shiny wood floors below, moments before they are to be scuffed up in a rush of frenzied activity. On the wall, the scoreboard reads HOME OF THE INDIANS. And then the players begin to trickle in, carrying their gear: backpacks, tote bags, and . . . calculators. Unceremoniously, the star enters, a slouching Danny Zhu, last year's individual high scorer, a slight boy, remote and unsmiling, behind oval, black-rimmed glasses, decked out in blue jeans and a navy blue T-shirt, the front of which announces that he is a member of the vaunted New York City Math Team.

A Stuyvesant sophomore, Danny is here to defend his title as the best high school mathematician in the prestigious New York State Mathematics League annual contest, and his pose says it all: sitting in the first row, he holds up his head with his right hand; otherwise he might fall asleep. "I don't normally feel pressure about much," he says on another occasion. His dark hair stands up in different directions, as if it were static electrified when he woke up and he didn't bother to do anything about it. Perhaps the fifteen-year-old didn't get enough sleep. Minutes before the contest starts, he rests his head on his desk, as 409 of the best teenage mathematicians in New York State, mostly seniors, about thirty from Stuyvesant, take their seats. It's an incongruous sight, an army of pencil-wielding math assassins assembling in rows of little school desks arrayed across an echoing gym, not a bouncing ball in sight. And yet there is an athletic dimension to the spectacle as the students take on the personalities of rival baseball clubs, twenty-seven teams dressed in T-shirt uniforms of green, yellow, and other shades of allegiance.

On the sidelines, Mr. Teitel is wearing a baby blue Stuyvesant jersey—the Yankees pinstripe of high school math. He loosens the neck as if he is about to join the field of battle, carefree about today's outcome.

"I already have too many trophies in my office," he boasts.

It's true. But it's also true that this is a big event in the life of Stuyvesant competition. The Peglegs may stumble on the football field, but the young masters of math—the "mathletes," as they are known—bring greater glory to the school in its sport of choice, the bloodless, silent warfare of mathematics.

"This is football in Texas," says Mr. Jaye, here for the kickoff.

Danny removes his glasses and yawns. Math contests have become old hat for the academic sharpshooter. He entered his first math competition, sponsored by a Chinese newspaper in Queens, when he was a second grader, and finished in first place, getting every question right, even though he was the smallest child there. Other contests quickly followed. Like a gunslinger, Danny would show up, the outsider, at competitions sponsored by private Asian academies that he did not attend, and he'd win, taking home their trophies and their fifty-dollar checks.

One Chinese parent, desperate to learn the secret of Danny's success, did not ask permission when she photocopied the problem-solving examples that she found in his book bag. Other Chinese parents clamored to find out what Asian academy Danny attended to become such an incredible math machine, so fast, so efficient. But his parents didn't send him anywhere. He was a homegrown product.

Displaying curiosity and a long attention span at an early age, he learned the basics of math at the knee of his mother, a math teacher, and his father, a computer programmer, both from China. When he was four, Danny learned the meaning of positive and negative numbers from the example of cars rushing back and forth along the highway during a family trip to Washington, D.C. Before the third grade, Danny's mother introduced him to algebra, and at the age of nine, he took the statewide high school algebra test, finishing in a mere hour—two hours early—and easily posting a score of 94.

"That was the beginning of his acceleration," says his mother, Jie Zhang, now an administrator in the city school system.

In the fourth grade, Danny took tenth-grade geometry, earning a 100 on the statewide exam. The next year, he studied trigonometry and biology. In the sixth grade, precalculus and physics. As a seventh grader, he posted an amazing 1440 on the SAT, including a perfect math score.

Danny can't explain his academic wizardry, but what he loves about math is reminiscent of the pleasure that Romeo finds in it—that it has a specific formula, a right and a wrong, unlike people, who, Danny says, are "more fuzzy."

By the time he arrived at Stuyvesant as a freshman, Danny had little to learn from high school math. "He came in almost done," Mr. Jaye says. Last year, Danny took calculus. This semester, he's taking a graduate-level class at NYU in linear algebra, even though he has never taken the required undergraduate course leading up to it. And for the first time in his life, Danny finds himself struggling in math.

But not today. At 11:19 a.m., head down, feet tucked under chair, he begins the statewide contest of elimination, a test of skill, pressure, and speed involving math up to and including precalculus. Danny and his peers have exactly ten minutes to answer the first two questions, one of which asks them to "compute the sum of all the positive integer factors of 2006." Five minutes later, he scratches the back of his head. At 11:28, a contest organizer announces, "One minute." Then, "Fifteen seconds." Finally, "Stop." Proctors collect the answer sheets. When the organizer announces the solution to the first question, he asks those who answered correctly to raise their hands. Danny does so, as do scores of other students. When the organizer announces the answer to the second question, Danny raises his hand again.

Perfect, so far.

Proctors hand out a slip of paper for questions three and four. Ten minutes later, he raises his hand again. He's four for four. The questions become increasingly difficult, and when the organizer announces the answers to questions five and six, an immediate buzz races around the gym as one student screams out a euphoric, "Yes!" Danny simply raises his left hand, still alive. Six for six. He is now one of fewer than twenty remaining who have answered all questions correctly.

Questions seven and eight will determine who wins or faces off in a tiebreaker. With eight minutes left on the clock, Danny waggles his head side to side, as if to loosen his brain. Three minutes later, he shakes out a stiff right arm. Then time's up. Danny raises his head, weaving his fingers together before him, at eye level, like a mandarin in quiet repose. Other students murmur about the test, awaiting the answers. Question seven: Danny raises his left hand. Question eight: up goes the hand. Danny, the defending champ, is back in the final round—one of six students left.

"In its own sick way, it's exciting," Mr. Jaye says.

Danny and the other finalists retire to the auditorium, which is packed like opening night at the opera with hundreds of students, teachers, and parents, and take seats in the front row for the tiebreaker. They have five minutes to solve the following problem:

Compute the number of ordered pairs of positive integers (m, n) that solve

$$2m + 6n = 2006$$

and for which $m + n$ is a multiple of 13.

Danny tilts his head toward the green ceiling. He mouths words. He frowns. He stops writing. Then drops his head—something registers— and he nods, furiously beginning to scribble. Stops. Raises his head again. One minute to go. He seems confused. Fifteen seconds. Just before time expires, he hands in his answer. Adults confer at the front of the auditorium until one breaks off to shake Danny's hand. It's not the expected outcome. Not entirely. Danny answered correctly—but so did one other student, not from rival Bronx Science or Hunter or Brooklyn Tech but from Benjamin N. Cardozo High School, a neighborhood school in Queens that also selectively admits some students into specialized programs. There will be another tiebreaker. Whoever answers the question first within five minutes will be crowned champion. The two boys shake hands before the resumption of hostilities.

Go.

Danny glances at the question, then dashes off an answer in a single minute, and in the second after he submits it, he buries his head in his hands, immediately realizing he botched it. The other boy, noting Danny's blunder, calmly continues to work on the problem, knowing he can take the full five minutes to reach the right answer. Danny betrays a rare human emotion, banging a fist into his thigh. The other boy submits his answer. It should be over, but it isn't. Neither answered correctly. A third tiebreaker falls by the wayside with the same result. Danny actually chuckles. They move to a fourth tiebreaker, and this time, Danny instantly grasps the dimensions of the problem, racing to an answer. His head pops up; he's ready to hand in his paper. But he takes one last look, then, with two hands, he reaches out to submit his answer, like an offering to the math deities, while the other boy continues to work the problem.

The adults confer, and then the organizer announces finally, "We have a first-place winner."

Danny.

He is utterly expressionless. He lowers his head, appearing to work on another math problem, though there are none left. The two-time winner of the statewide math contest wins a sweatshirt and a $150 check. When asked how he feels, he distills his reaction into a one-word computation: "Tired."

It happens with little notice on the following day that Danny's fellow prodigy, ten-year-old Milo, wins a medal in the citywide high school math fair, along with several other students, including his friend, Daniel, the Cuban immigrant.

That night, Mr. Teitel receives a call that Stuyvesant biology teacher Susan Biering—known to her students for her fun classes and her free associations that bump into memories like her first kiss—has passed away after a bout with emphysema.

When Ms. Biering, an inveterate cigarette smoker, took ill in February, Mr. Teitel always thought she would return to school, but he says, "She just never gave up smoking even when she became sick. She used to stand in front of the building and smoke. This was a *biology* teacher, so the rest of us used to look at her and go, 'How do you not understand what's going on here?'" And yet, Mr. Teitel does understand. He himself began smoking when he was thirteen and continued—at one point smoking two packs a day of Marlboro—until he was thirty-one, and he learned that his wife was pregnant. Then, after consulting with his doctor, he promptly gave up the habit. But he knows, more than a quarter century later, "If somebody developed a cigarette tomorrow in which there was a guarantee that there would be no adverse effect to my health"—and here he snaps his fingers—"I'd be in the store tomorrow morning. I loved it."

Ms. Biering is buried on Tuesday, April 11, at Mount Ararat Cemetery just east of New York City.

On the same day, miles from the mourning, Ms. Lee is in a state of sorrow sitting in room 365 at Columbia's Teachers College. Today, she isn't a student teacher at Stuyvesant with limited prospects of staying on as a full-time faculty member; rather, she is a graduate student in a course about alternative models for a social studies curriculum. Stuyvesant seems a distant place as the student who would teach is shunted into an old-fashioned wooden school chair attached to a small, arm-length writing surface. Surrounding Ms. Lee are rickety, exposed radiators painted the same off-white color as the cracked walls, which complement worn wooden floors and the musty scent of age wafting to the high ceilings. Now the class is discussing the assigned reading, *Putting the Actors Back on Stage: Oral History in the Secondary School Classroom*, by Margaret Smith Crocco. Now they're talking about incorporating oral history—and family history—in a classroom exercise in social studies. Now Ms. Lee is paired with a late-arriving student. They ask each other why they want to be teachers.

"It was by chance I stumbled upon this career, but I found the right career," she begins.

"What is your inspiration?" the other student asks.

But before Ms. Lee can explain it all—the disappointments of a father, the demands of a mother—she runs out of time as the teacher resumes the lecture.

Ms. Lee feels like she is running out of time at Stuyvesant. With little more than two months left in the semester, there are still no openings in the social studies department. It's another curious feature of the system that teachers need not give early notice to the principal if they intend to retire, meaning that Ms. Lee may be forced to wait until the last minute to learn if there's an opening. While she waits, Mr. Jaye continues to plot. In his latest scheme, he suggested that she create an independent study curriculum in Korean, then persuade one of the city colleges to sponsor it, so that she can be licensed as a Korean-language teacher. But it's a gamble—a big gamble. She'd be accumulating more school debt, and there's no guarantee that Stuyvesant would hire her anyway. In a recent meeting with Mr. Teitel, the principal assumed the paternal role, telling her, "I won't let you do this."

In a testament to her effectiveness as a teacher, parents of Korean students have offered to pay to send Ms. Lee to Los Angeles to take a Korean proficiency exam that could bolster her chances of staying on at Stuyvesant. But she doesn't feel right about accepting the largesse, especially when it may come to naught.

"I need to ask myself how badly I want to stay at Stuyvesant," she says.

The alternative—teaching students in a regular urban public high school—is difficult for her to accept. "Could I be challenging them in a way that's impossible for them?" At a regular school, she worries that history lessons may be reduced to the simplest terms. She worries that it would be difficult to ask nuanced questions about, say, the Holocaust, such as, "Were the Americans liberators, or were they collaborators?" That, she says, you can't do in many urban schools.

"They're going to say, 'What? What was the Holocaust?' I mean, you have to teach them the basics."

But her younger sister, an undergraduate student at Barnard College, challenges that assumption, arguing that it is precisely these kids—the regular students—who need the better teachers, who need someone like Ms. Lee. "You never know," her sister says. "You can change these kids' lives. They need inspiration."

Ms. Lee isn't prepared to cede that point. She holds on dearly to those Stuyvesant students whom she has come to adore. Her Korean students expect to take her class next year. A history student asked whether she would write a college recommendation next year. The common denominator: next year. A place for her to be. "If it weren't for them," she says, "I wouldn't be able to test my limits." Besides, she doesn't think that with her tiny frame—a mere ninety pounds—she could hold her own in some of the notoriously tough urban schools, a fear that her sister would concede.

"She knows deep down I wouldn't be able to survive in a place like that," Ms. Lee says.

Yet that knowledge doesn't comfort her. She is troubled, confused, unsure. "This is the worst state I have been in," she says. Today she takes a ten-minute stroll through a career fair at Columbia without bringing her résumé. "That's how disinterested I am in regard to other schools," she says. All she can do, she says, is pray, letting go of her attempt to control life: "I'm going to surrender."

Romeo is surrendering as well. He's giving up on his bet with Xevion that he would fall in love in a matter of weeks. Under a crush of upcoming tests, he simply doesn't have the time for matters of the heart. He needs to postpone them until he can shoehorn them into his frenetic schedule.

"In the middle of all this schoolwork," he says, "I can't fall in love until June."

Xevion isn't at lunch in the dining room on April 12 to gloat over her victory. And perhaps that's for the best. Romeo has his hands full with a history test today, three advanced placement exams in about two weeks, followed by three SAT II tests in June, the same month he faces a series of statewide subject exams. Adding to his load is an even weightier subject lately: his mother. "My mom gets on my back," he says. She's particularly concerned about his performance in French, her native tongue. Last semester, Romeo posted a 95 in French, but this term, he slipped on one test, earning a 78, bracketed between two high grades, endangering his overall grade point average because he didn't know one grammatical rule. And now, Romeo's mother is assigning him homework on top of his homework: French articles to read and transcribe to improve his comprehension. The problem is, it was eleven o'clock the other night, and Romeo was studying history when she insisted that he do his French dictation. He said no. She persisted. He relented but made several mistakes because he wasn't paying close attention. She stormed off, slamming a door behind her and refusing to talk to her son until the next day. Romeo forgives her.

"I mean a lot to her," he acknowledges.

Even at sixteen, Romeo has the wisdom to understand where she is coming from: that his mother once was a rebel in her French family, that she defied her demanding father by wandering off to America, where, he notes, she "married a black musician." And now, Romeo surmises, "it would make her feel more worthy if she felt like she produced a son who is productive."

That's another way of saying, "She wants me to go to Harvard." In another setting, when she imagines her son at the historic American college, her eyes lift to the heavens, and she says reverentially, "There's this myth . . ."

But now, seated alone with his chicken-patty lunch, Romeo says, "I've always felt isolated," though it's unclear whether it's because he imposes so many expectations on himself, or because he's black and white, not quite at home in either world. But from his freshman year, he has erected what he calls a "coping mechanism," an ideology of himself as invincible. His role model is Odysseus. Romeo pledges he will not fail. He will not go out. He will not rest. Sometimes, though, reality intrudes. Because sometimes, he says, "I feel like I'm burning out."

Like now.

Yesterday, after weight lifting at football practice, Romeo arrived home to study but dozed off. When he awoke, he made another run at his schoolwork but ended up listening to Internet radio, a desultory mix of Prince, Jimi Hendrix, Devo, Duran Duran, and David Bowie. It was as if he needed a rest from his mind, from the words of exhortation that remain on his walls, beckoning, "The world is yours." Those words, he says, have "lost [their] effect." Next week is a welcome spring break. It's also a crucial moment in time when Romeo will find out how he fared on the SAT and whether the world he wants—that his mother wants too—is still within his grasp.

PART THREE: SENIORITIS

Late April–Late June

CHAPTER EIGHTEEN

Zero Tolerance

A RATTY BROWN COUCH, OF INDETERMINATE HYGIENE, resides in the outer chamber of the Student Union, site of untold numbers of despondent, confused, enamored, foolish, frolicking, studious, slumbering, dreamy teenagers. But today, Wednesday, April 26, the ratty brown couch is serving as a psychiatrist's ratty brown couch, where two of the sanest teachers in the school are commiserating about the end of spring break and probing the inner psyche of an academic asylum that they are beginning to suspect is going, quite simply, batty.

At one end sits Mr. Grossman, right ankle over left knee, hugging a pillow, bemoaning the school's selection of committee members who are drawn from the faculty to hire guidance counselors, key personnel who will help steer students to their college of choice, the ultimate Stuyvesant coda. "I think it's important to point out how corrupt the process is," he says. By corrupt, he really means *daft*, noting that the selection committee includes no English teachers, himself included, even though guidance counselors' jobs are largely to write secondary school reports for seniors applying to college, essays that give a litany of students' unique talents but, in the wrong hands, can start to sound to admissions officers like blah, blah, blah.

The whole thing seems particularly daft to Kristen, the Student Union president, a representative on the selection committee. On another occasion, she had noted that a school administrator crossed out a specific word from the panel's written description of the kind of educational consultant who will assist in training the hired guidance counselors in writing college reports. The deleted word: "qualified."

"Only in school would you have such incompetence," agrees Mr. Polazzo, sitting at the other end of the couch, arms folded against his chest. Mr. Polazzo then wonders about an even more inscrutable issue: whether he can save his own job. Other faculty members are now angling to find a replacement for Mr. Polazzo as coordinator of student affairs while student leaders have met privately with Mr. Teitel to express their support for Mr. Polazzo.

"It's all a war of shadows," Mr. Polazzo says.

But the real target of Mr. Polazzo's and Mr. Grossman's discontent today lurks beyond the school in the form of New York City mayor Michael R. Bloomberg.

The mayor introduced a major new policy on the first day of spring break, when no one was around to protest it, like a stealth rider to a bill in Congress. With no warning, police will bring mobile metal detectors—akin to those used to screen airline passengers—to random middle and high schools as a way to ferret out dangerous weapons.

"This will be a systemwide deterrent," the mayor said at a news conference outside an empty Abraham Lincoln High School, one of the most dangerous public schools in Brooklyn. "Our reasons for doing this couldn't be clearer or more compelling: we have zero tolerance for weapons of any kind in city schools."

About 20 percent of the city's high schools already are equipped with metal detectors, but the mayor said he wanted to assure the safety of the remaining 80 percent. The number of illegal weapons confiscated in city schools this year has increased by 5 percent to 307, including 20 guns. But the mayor was quick to cite general gains in school safety. Since the 2003–2004 school year, violent crime has dropped by 27 percent.

That decline reflects the broader national trend. The rate of violent crime in public and private schools across the country has dropped by about 50 percent since 1992, according to the most recent joint study of the Justice and Education departments. There were about 740,000 violent crimes in schools in 2003, with an estimated 150,000 reports of rape, sexual assault, robbery, or aggravated assault. Students reported feeling less fear in school and getting involved in fewer school fights.

As the National Education Association observed, students are more likely to be victims of violent crimes outside school. "In fact," the education association said, "this study shows that school is still the safest place for kids—more so than any place they go all day, including their homes."

Stuyvesant is among the safest havens of all. The school reported zero "crimes against persons" and only three property crimes in 2005, the most recent year for which data are available. Which explains why Mr. Polazzo is sitting on the ratty brown couch, dumbfounded. "We don't have a security problem," he says. "We are the showpiece school." Adds an equally perplexed Mr. Grossman, "They all know we are different." And yet the school did not elude the mayor's new city-wide metal detector edict. In a follow-up letter to parents, Mr. Teitel dutifully wrote that the detectors, when and if they arrive at Stuyvesant, "will identify not only weapons but other objects that are never permitted in our building and will help us to keep everyone safe in our school."

Those other forbidden objects, he noted, "include blades, knives, other sharp metal instruments"—and then he lowered the boom—"cell phones, beepers, iPods, MP3 players, etc."

Cell phones?

Beepers?

iPods?

Those are merely among the most common items found on a typical Stuyvesant student, second only to that other teenage accessory, insecurity. Suddenly, the students' challenge of the *attendance* scanners seems like a hollow victory. Even Mr. Teitel had attempted to forestall the introduction of security metal detectors at the school after the September 11, 2001, terrorist attacks, when some parents began clamoring for them. "I resisted," he recalls, "saying I did not feel that that would be an educationally sound thing for our school. . . . It will only give [students] the feeling that this is not a school anymore." Now Mr. Teitel pales at the thought of the metal detectors randomly finding their way to Stuyvesant and the herculean logistics of confiscating somewhere in the vicinity of three thousand cell phones, a student's lifeline to parents who, at Stuyvesant, use wireless devices as a kind of radar to track in real time the whereabouts of their children.

"My parents, of course, are going nuts," Mr. Teitel says.

Already, he is conceding a major loss should the metal detectors arrive: an entire school day, wiped out. "Here's what's going to happen," he says. "I went out and bought three thousand zip-lock freezer bags, and should these scanners show up, I will hand out the bags, tell the children to put their cell phones and their iPods in the bags." Then, later in the day, students would line up—in the line from hell—to gather their belongings.

Already, students are posting signs of rebellion around the school building:

THEY WILL
TAKE YOUR
CELLPHONE AND iPOD.
WILL YOU
SIT BACK
AND LET THEM?
IF THE METAL DETECTORS ARE INSTALLED,
DON'T GO TO CLASS THAT DAY,
PROTEST!

Battling signs with signs, a formal warning is soon posted on the first-floor entrance:

ALL STUDENTS AND VISITORS ENTERING THIS BUILD-ING MAY BE REQUIRED TO SUBMIT TO A METAL DETEC-TOR SCAN AND A PERSONAL SEARCH, IF NECESSARY, TO ENSURE THAT WEAPONS ARE NOT BROUGHT INTO THIS BUILDING. BAGS AND PARCELS MAY ALSO BE

SEARCHED BY MEANS OF METAL DETECTING DEVICES, BY HAND OR OTHERWISE.

Miffed students abound, including Nathan, the senior who runs the renegade stuycom.net Web site. He doesn't understand the security threat that cell phones and music players pose. "You're going to stab someone with an antenna?" he wonders. "I don't really see someone getting hurt with an MP3 player." Adds Molly, the senior singer, "Of all the schools to be checking, why would they check ours?"

It's a question almost as mystical in nature as the existential wanderings of Mr. Polazzo, who is now preoccupied with thoughts on the meaning of life and death and love and desire and his dog, Norton, may he rest in peace, none of which has anything to do with the arrival of metal detectors, or with his possible demise as coordinator of student affairs, but all of which perhaps serve as a close proxy for that which he can't fathom. "It's the questing that really, I think, ultimately is the essence of living and life," he says, ruminating aloud before a small gathering of students in his cramped second-floor Student Union office. "I mean, even though it's great to reach the end point and making the discovery, I mean, it's like Alexander the Great, you know. They say that when he completed his conquest of Persia, he wept, and the general said, 'Why are you weeping?' And he said, 'There's nothing left to conquer.'"

Mr. Polazzo is just warming up.

"I think you should let your desire flourish, but you have to be careful because if you ever get your desire—I mean, the Buddhist philosophy is that death is death," he says. ". . . It may well be true that desire is a bottomless vessel, but it's a beautiful vessel, you know? That's what keeps us going, keeps us moving. Like there was an interesting NPR special about this guy who had this condition where something happened to his body and he stopped producing testosterone, and I thought it was going to be interesting because he was going to talk about, like, the bizarre side effects, which would have been kind of neat, but instead it turned into this weird discourse. Apparently women have testosterone too, less than men, but it's what makes you desire. Testosterone is the chemical synthesis of desire, and he said, like, when he stopped manufacturing testosterone, he stopped wanting to do anything. He would just, like, sit there in his room. He didn't know he had this condition until a while later, but he would just sit there, like stare. He didn't know what was going on, what was wrong with him. He didn't want to do anything at all. And I think that's, like, what desire is, it's kind of like testosterone in that sense. It drives you forward, and you know, yes, it's . . . all consuming. But it's what gets you out of bed in the morning, you know what I mean?"

He doesn't wait for an answer from his audience of pupils.

"I mean, I bought a lottery ticket the other day," he continues. "I knew there was no chance I was going to win, but there was a need to buy the idea that I might possibly win. Too much of that, and you're gambling. But you know, a little bit is okay. . . . I'd like to believe in an afterlife. I mean, look, I can't prove it. I was in a philosophy of religion class in college, and we spent all day arguing about God and this and that, but one thing I took out of the class. I don't think you can either prove or disprove God's existence. It's a matter of faith, and faith is a very personal thing. I mean, like being religious is like being in love. When you fall in love, you have this deep emotional attachment to somebody, and it might be right and it might be wrong, you know, like it might be somebody who's going to be bad, wrong for you, but your friends aren't going to be able to talk you out of it, but neither will you be able to talk your friends into feeling that same way. I guess religion is a little different because with religion, you really can inspire that fervor among people if you do it well enough, but I don't know, I think it's a very personal thing."

The students, as if sitting in a fascinating college lecture, remain rapt in attention.

"For me, I just don't see it," he says, ". . . although I do have a very bizarre, like, ontological philosophy that makes me feel better about it. Okay, so here it is, this is how I feel better about oblivion. It's kind of crazy but bear with me for a second. What I was thinking about is the nature of time and existence, and if you think about time—and I'm sure there are, like, physicists, quantum physicists who'd, like, slap me in the face for all of this, but just my layman's knowledge, if you think about it, if you think about time as the fourth dimension, right, it's something we move through, it's something that impacts us, yet we lack the ability to step outside of it and perceive it. Think for a second about a being that's flat, that cannot perceive depth, right, it, like, lives on the surface of this piece of paper. Now that being might interact with something that has depth, but he or she or it would never be able to really understand what they were dealing with. The best analogy is, imagine that you are treading water in a swimming pool and your eyes are at water level but all you can see is that waterline, nothing above it, nothing below it, and now let's say a three-dimensional object intersects that. Let's say someone drops this Snapple bottle into the water." He gestures at a bottle on his desk. "Well, what would you see? You would see a line that stays the same shape and then it would get smaller and smaller and then bigger and then it would disappear. So after the event had occurred, you could say, 'Oh, maybe a Snapple bottle passed through,' or something shaped like this, but at the time of the event, you had no idea. For all you knew, right over here it was going to start zigging and zagging; you didn't know until it was done. In that way, depth affects a flat creature the way that time affects us. An event occurs. As it's occurring, we don't know exactly what's going to happen, but when the event is over, we can say, 'Oh, that event occurred.' So now the interesting thing is, as the event is occurring, it seems to us that anything possibly could happen, you know, like this plane could crash, that basketball could go in or could go out, but after it was done, that was it. To me, each event is like the Snapple bottle. It's already fully formed. It's just that we are passing through time."

Total silence.

"I have no basis to believe any of this stuff," he adds. ". . . I mean, the most likely thing is probably just that you die. . . . But to me, anything is better than this bleak idea of oblivion, even though if you were oblivious, you wouldn't know . . . but still, I like existence."

Here he laughs.

"I hope I'm wrong," he says. "I hope that, like, after I die, I'm surrounded in a field of loved ones, and my dog. I'd love to see my dog."

Upstairs, in room 401, Mr. Siwanowicz is feeling breezy, and it's not only the caress of spring wafting through the crack of a window. There's an aura about him. The depressed, sleep-deprived school aide is neither depressed nor sleep-deprived.

There's something indescribably leavened about his mood, such that the lumbering figure is almost sprightly in his response to a small boy who approaches him during his lunch break, asking for help on a math problem from a class taught by another teacher.

"I don't understand anything," the boy confesses. "Could you write it out?"

Mr. Siwanowicz obliges, instantly comprehending the mathematical hieroglyphics even though the problem fills an entire pencil-written page of the boy's loose-leaf binder. With a red pen, Mr. Siwanowicz fills the back side of a sheet of paper with another series of computations— something to do with $x^2 - 3x + 2$—to which the boy nods wordlessly, peering over Mr. Siwanowicz's hulking shoulder.

"Do you get it?" the unofficial teacher asks.

"Yes, I'm good," the boy responds, and he disappears without so much as a thank-you. Not that it would've made a difference. Mr. Siwanowicz is not to be shaken, not today, not even as he races downstairs to man the second-floor landing by the Tribeca Bridge entrance, standing behind a single red rope, linked on either end by a silver metallic stand, the kind used at movie theaters to cordon off ticket buyers. Nothing is being bought here, except a new attendance scanning system to which he is attached as a monitor, observing the comings and goings of students.

"Why are you so late?" he berates a group of students lollygagging back from lunch. "Where were you? Connecticut?"

The students ignore him. Mr. Siwanowicz doesn't care. He's kidding anyway. Suddenly, it doesn't matter anymore, not the indignity of monitoring duties, not the inability to get a college degree, not the lack of a teacher's license. Heck, bring on the broken photocopiers! There's no rebellion in Mr. Siwanowicz's peaceful posture. He could not care less— all because of one new, solitary fact.

He has a girlfriend.

To recall the last time he had such a companion, he squeezes his eyes shut in deep concentration, thinking back until he computes the math: *five* years ago. Perhaps it was a mathematical probability that it would eventually happen, the intersection of two people at a board game center in midtown, a hole-in-the-wall place Mr. Siwanowicz frequents late into the evenings. And perhaps it was an inevitability too that he would encounter someone who could match wits with him, was faster than him, could beat him, even at what he calls "full capacity," which is precisely what she did in a game of pattern matching and recognition when they first met.

"She kicked my butt," he says. "I was impressed."

Mr. Siwanowicz was a goner. They started e-mailing each other. She is a PhD who teaches music history at NYU, which turns out to be a good match for a college dropout who teaches math at Stuyvesant. They met. They took a stroll that became a journey across practically the whole city, ending up at Penn Station.

Kate. Dear Kate.

She's meeting him after tenth period today, a lifetime from now as Mr. Siwanowicz lurches back to room 401 to grade papers. A ponytailed girl approaches him there, almost on tiptoes, trembling.

"I have a question," says the nervous junior. "It's not about math." She pulls up a chair and whispers confidentially, as if she's about to confess to a major felony. "I want to take calculus," she says, already thinking of her course load next year, "but will I survive?"

Mr. Siwanowicz, showing tender mercies, assures her that she can handle calculus, that in some ways it's easier than precalculus.

"I just don't want to die," the girl says.

"You won't die," he volleys.

"I've been wanting to take calculus all my life," she says, still not convinced.

"Once you get past the first month, it gets easier," he insists.

The girl takes a deep breath and rises to leave, girding herself for the rigors of calculus. She turns back one last time, for one last reassurance. "So I won't have a nervous breakdown, right?"

The bell rings before he can commit. Instead, Mr. Siwanowicz offers a wordless wave of his left hand, a gesture of carefree hope, and that does the trick as the girl, nervous no more, recedes into the crowded hallway.

> *MCDONALDS RULES*
>
> —desktop graffiti, Stuyvesant High School

CHAPTER NINETEEN

College Night

ROMEO ISN'T QUITE READY TO FACE THE CROWDS. Which is why he's perched alone atop the Wall a block from school on the evening of April 27, draped in his Sean John black jeans and Sean John black jacket, less than an hour from the official onset of his future, an annual rite of passage at Stuyvesant when more than 150 colleges converge on the school, setting up recruiting booths throughout the building in what devolves into a frenzied courtship over higher education.

They call it "College Night."

But Romeo isn't thinking of what is to come when he enters the school. He's thinking of what has already transpired, long before his time, how John F. Kennedy won the Navy and Marine Corps Medal for his courage in World War II and how his elder brother, Joe, immediately signed up for a dangerous military mission in an attempt to outshine John—only to perish when his plane, packed with explosives, accidentally exploded shortly after takeoff.

"Competition," Romeo says, "can kill you."

There is time to ponder other pitfalls. Like today's math test. He made a careless mistake that may have cost him five points, and he begins to scold himself, as if he's internalized what a parent might say in such a circumstance, telling himself that he can't afford to make such slipups in the real world and how he doesn't know what he'll do if the troubling trend "keeps up."

Then again, Romeo, always driving, always pushing, is rarely satisfied with his own performance. The other day, he logged onto the computer to find out how he did on the SAT. He left the score up on the monitor for his mother to see for herself: 2200. A hundred points below his goal—but stellar nonetheless. To Romeo's surprise, he scored slightly higher in reading, 750, and writing, 730, than he did in his favored subject of math, 720. His mother was thrilled. He was moderately pleased. "Realistically, it's good," he says. "My id and ego are satisfied, my superego isn't." He can't help but think of two other juniors who achieved nearly perfect scores, identical 2340s. It stings until he ponders the vagaries of chance and circumstance, the accidents of birth, where they were raised, and the infinitesimal difference those early years of academic training may have made, a slight advantage, no matter how hard he strives to catch up.

But here's the thing: with his SAT scores and outstanding grades, Harvard is well within his grasp.

Romeo already has a plan for tonight. "I'll do the whole tour of the Ivies," he says. Princeton, Brown, Columbia. A guidance counselor suggested he visit the University of Chicago as well. "It's like dating," he says. "You try to get their attention. Then once they like you, they try to get your attention."

Senior Deke Hill has been through the courtship already. He won the hand of Cornell, but he's not ready to commit because he's still trying to grab the attention of Harvard, which wait-listed him.

That's why he's standing outside school. His mother called a Harvard admissions officer, who suggested that Deke stop by at Stuyvesant's College Night. He dressed for the occasion in a brown leather jacket, black jeans, a pink polo shirt, and a simple gold hoop earring in his left ear, an accessory that he says his mother thought would tell Harvard, "This is not your average Stuyvesant student."

The seventeen-year-old has managed to distinguish himself but not in the way he meant. While Deke maintained a 94.8 overall average through last semester, he has been struck by an early bout of a debilitating high school disease known as senioritis. Last term, he slacked off, at least by his standards, barely pulling a 90 average, which he thinks ruined any chance he had of early admission to Harvard. This semester, the slackening has worsened. Deke is particularly worried about his class in differential equations. "Every time I come out of that class," he says, he asks himself, " 'What just happened?' "

What's happening so far is that he's in jeopardy of landing a low grade. "If they see one grade of eighty, that can be a killer," he says.

But it gets worse. "The gym grade is not going to be good," Deke admits. "At the moment, I'm in danger of failing, which would not be the best thing." The problem is that gym is his first class of the day, which happens to be third period, not exactly the crack of dawn, but early enough that he's made a habit of arriving late. None of which he intends to share with Harvard tonight.

"The key," Deke says, "is to make an impression."

At 6:59, a minute before his date with Harvard, he wades in.

They're all here. All the great and good colleges, from Adelphi University to Yale University, filling classrooms with expectant herds of juniors—as well as an inordinate number of freshmen and sophomores planning ahead—and their parents, many of whom have brought pen and pad for obsessive note taking of the relevant particulars, any shred of intelligence to get a leg up on the competition: Is a college looking for anything in particular other than a high SAT score and a robust grade point average? A gifted flutist? A record of charity work? An expertise in the classics? And just how important are teacher recommendations? Is financial aid a factor in admissions? And how many advanced placement credits can be racked up? Yet it goes the other way too, with the colleges not just fielding questions but showing off their best features: small classes, leafy campuses, notable professors. So packed is the school tonight—a potluck soup of students and parents bubbling throughout the building—that there is hardly room to fit everyone in. Fifty-four colleges are squeezed together in the dining hall alone. "Throughout the night, the number of people in rooms 739 (Harvard), 735 (Yale) and

327 (Princeton) grew considerably past the fire-hazard limitation," writes a student in a follow-up opinion piece in the *Spectator*.

A boy who evidently doesn't want to be here is garbed in a T-shirt that announces, COLLEGE IS OVERRATED. On arrival, a mother is instantly mapping strategy, circling in red pen the colleges she wants to visit—not necessarily those her child prefers—which include the usual suspects: Yale, Princeton, Stanford. Another parent flips on his cell phone, communicating like a member of a SWAT team with his child, who is located elsewhere in the building. "Which school do you want to start with?" the father asks urgently. "You want to start with Brown?"

The mania is par for the course at Stuyvesant, despite the spiraling cost of a college education. The average tuition and fee charges at four-year private colleges, the target of most Stuyvesant students, amount to $22,218 in 2006–07, up 5.9 percent over the previous year. It gets worse when room and board charges are thrown in. Then the average total cost is a whopping $30,367. The expense is even higher for many of the elite private universities. But as the College Board notes, college can pay off down the road. The gap in earning widens over time between those who graduate from college and those who don't. In 2005, women between the ages of twenty-five and thirty-four with a bachelor's degree earned 70 percent more than those with only a high school diploma; for men, the gap was nearly as wide at 63 percent. Not surprisingly, enrollment in degree-granting institutions is increasing rapidly in the United States. Between 1984 and 1994, enrollment rose by 17 percent, and it jumped 21 percent from 1994 to 2004, when more than 17 million students crowded into the nation's burgeoning colleges and universities.

At Stuyvesant, the Gold Rush remains the attainment of the Ivy League, that select handful of northeastern colleges, where about a quarter of the Stuyvesant senior class will end up. This fact may help explain why room 511 is virtually empty tonight. In one corner is the University of Aberdeen, all the way from Scotland. In another corner is Babson College, a fine institution in Wellesley, Massachusetts, not far from Harvard, represented by a hip twenty-four-year-old recruiter with a small gold stud lodged in her left nostril. On her green tablecloth, a neat stack of Babson pamphlets sits virtually untouched. "You know you're about to make one of the most important decisions of your life," the school says in its literature. "You want the best education you can get. You want a career that will take you wherever you want to go. You're proud of your achievements and you want a new challenge." Then in bigger letters: "You know what," followed by, "IT'S POSSIBLE. AT BABSON." The pamphlet seems to speak directly to the typical Stuyvesant student, but it's not what draws three stragglers, finally, to the display table. One boy comes right out with it, saying he has no intention of applying to Babson. He and his buddies simply want the green pens. That's what Babson is giving away. Taken aback, the recruiter hesitates, and the boy amends his rejection of Babson, saying that he may want to teach economics there one day. It's unlikely. But it's a start. The pens go. The recruiter knows it's a small price to pay if it might help ever so slightly raise her small school's profile.

"We'd love to get students from here," the recruiter says. "It's a great school."

Two floors above and a million miles away, Harvard isn't giving away anything except the legend of its weighty reputation before a rapt crowd of more than forty students, nearly half sophomores, and their parents—all that this biology demonstration classroom can hold. The blackboard isn't just erased clean, it's *sponged* clean, a meticulous measure stating what is unstated, that this is a special gathering. In front of the blackboard, behind a lab counter, is the equally meticulous Harvard recruiter, a well-preserved middle-aged woman with a carefully coiffed blond bob and a massive, glittering rock the size of an eyeball on her ring finger. She takes notice of a parent carrying a bag with MIT's logo.

"MIT's outdone us—they've given away *bags*?" she cries playfully in falsetto.

The recruiter recovers quickly, beginning by saying that Harvard is the oldest college in the nation, founded in 1636, a fact that is causing a fury of scribbling from a stable of parents in the classroom stadium seating. She notes that Harvard offers more than 3,500 classes from which students can choose. She dispels what she calls myths, that Harvard is "inaccessible, snobby, students don't have any fun." And she mentions that Harvard did go to the Rose Bowl—in 1928—which draws stiff guffaws from the gallery. Just as students are here to sell themselves, Harvard is making a pitch, which it states in a glossy handout: "The pursuit of excellence has long been a hallmark of Harvard."

"We know Stuyvesant is a great school," the recruiter says, mentioning the "long, long history" of association between the great college and the great high school, which results in the admission of many students every year to Harvard. "We're not worried about the level of preparation you're going to experience here," she says, adding that Harvard isn't only looking at applicants' grades and test scores. "We're looking at you as a whole person," she says.

Sitting in the front row, Romeo has stopped taking notes to absorb what the recruiter is saying, as if trying to unlock the secrets of the Rosetta stone. But there's little wisdom to glean from the presentation other than the implicit message that Harvard is really special. When the thirteen-minute presentation ends, Romeo rises and makes his way over to one of the admissions officers in attendance, saying he'd like to speak with the Harvard football coach. It's a perfunctory exchange, one of countless tonight, but necessary, and Romeo seems to know it as soon as he steps out. "It was nothing new," he says, as he heads next door to another packed encounter with an Ivy, Brown.

Deke, the senior, leaves Harvard unimpressed as well. In the few minutes he spoke with the Harvard recruiter, he had the distinct impression that she was maintaining a "fake smile" the whole time that he tried to make his case to be admitted from the waiting list. Deke's not convinced she was moved by the idea that he put forward, that he could take a year off before attending college. He even offered to send his upcoming grades, a risky tactic given the state of his academic affairs. She simply told him to send the grades if he wants. So Deke shrugs.

"It's a very murky process," he says.

It's okay, though, because Deke is thinking of the magic of spring washing over his final days at Stuyvesant and the riverside park behind the school where he and his friends hang out. Now the idea of waiting to hear from Harvard doesn't seem so onerous after all.

"It can be worse," he says, reminded of the Langston Hughes poem "A Dream Deferred."

"What happens to a dream deferred?" he asks. "Answer: It gets wait-listed in April." While Deke makes light of the situation, his brow darkens ever so minutely as he begins to resign himself to the inevitable. Harvard isn't going to happen. It's not over but it's over. He will have to settle for the consolation prize of merely another prestigious Ivy League school. Look out, Cornell, here he comes.

CHAPTER TWENTY

Peter Pan Tilts

MILO, THE LITTLE MAN-CHILD, ENTERS HIS EMPTY bedroom after school on an overcast Tuesday, May 2, and his visage darkens at the wreck before him. "It's not usually like this," says the embarrassed ten-year-old. His room, which he shares with his three-year-old brother, Romy, is too tidy. "It's *never* clean," he says, explaining that it's his mother's fault since she had the *nerve* to straighten things up before a couple came over for one of her birthing classes. But he gets over the infraction, moving to his desk, over which is taped a picture he drew of George W. Bush. The president has a set of fierce horns, red beady eyes, and a pierced earring. In a bubble of dialogue, Milo, the political cartoonist, has Bush saying, "More bombs." A pile of books lies on the little sophisticate's desk, including *To Kill a Mockingbird* and *A Short History of Nearly Everything*. On the nearby windowsill stands a gathering of trophies, profits of the prodigy, including his first-place finish in the "3rd Annual Youth Chess Tournament." Milo trounced a bunch of kids in Central Park. They never had a chance. He knows the Sicilian defense. He toys with the English opening. He pummels adult wannabes. Years ago, he beat his older sister, Willa, taunting her that he would checkmate her in four moves as he proceeded to checkmate her in four moves. She hasn't played him since. Then there's the gold medal from the math fair. And that trophy from Gilsports for Kids, the award given to all the children. It's a hint of his life outside high school, a segue along his baby blue walls to a series of shelves displaying the remnants of a childhood, artifacts like the board games Othello and Operation and Mouse Trap. *Peter Pan* tilts on a shelf. But the tale of a little boy who wouldn't grow up gives way to the ruminations of a little boy who can't help but grow up, so unbridled is his vast intellect.

"I always have trouble sleeping," he says.

The scenario is always the same. He flips. He rolls over. Eventually, his eyes flutter shut. And still Milo can't explain the insomnia. He's running out of ideas. Things are actually good at Stuyvesant—better. Sure, he misses his elementary school friends, but trigonometry is going well, although the class still requires an hour of homework a night. He's even made a second friend in high school, another smart boy in his math research class, which is captivating his attention as he prepares a research paper on the predictability of the climate. "It's not really about the weather," he says. "It's about chaos."

Plus, he loves his teacher, Mr. Siwanowicz. "We think alike," Milo says, though he can't explain how. But more than anything, deep into this semester, he has reached a new plateau in his career at Stuyvesant, an elusive step that also is difficult to define, and there's nothing tangible to point to, other than when he says, almost surprised himself, "I sort of feel like a freshman."

Emboldened, the unofficial freshman wanders over to the door of his sister's room, where a sticker hints at the grave risk involved in disturbing the girl who lies beyond it: WHAT PART OF NO DON'T YOU UNDERSTAND. But when Willa emerges, she's in a charitable mood. "Milo knows everything," says the seventh grader. She notes, however, that she has more common sense, recalling when he was seven and "putting on his pants backwards." When she adds, "*Smart* is something he has going for him," the remark seems laden with an undertone of resentment as dark as a Slavic novel. It turns out that, even though Willa is incredibly bright, a whiz in school who doesn't have to work hard to maintain a 95 average, being two years older than a prodigy has its pitfalls. Willa isn't shy about explaining why: if they take the Stuyvesant entrance exam at the same time this year, they'd end up in the same grade next year. "I won't go to Stuyvesant because he'll be there," she says, referring to the boy the top of whose head doesn't yet reach the bottom of her chin. "We'd be in the same year, and he'd probably take some classes ahead of me."

By now, Milo has retreated behind the half-closed door of his parents' adjoining bedroom.

"There's the whole sibling competition," Willa says.

Milo peeks out from behind the door. "How would we be competing?"

If an answer is forthcoming, it's lost in the tumult that ensues as Milo launches a sneak attack, whacking his sister with a stuffed elephant, and she orders him to get away. And just like that, the natural balance of things has been restored, the younger brother yielding to the older sister.

The following morning, things begin to fall into place for Mr. Jaye. He's offered the principal's job at Brooklyn's Midwood High School. And he promptly rejects it. That's because he's on the cusp of taking the job at Bergen County Academies, the New Jersey school he really wants. They've come to terms on a salary of $130,000, which doesn't include the pension he'll earn when he retires from the New York City school system. There's only one sticking point—his title. The school already has a principal. For now, he doesn't know what title he'd hold. Mr. Jaye can live with that because he knows this: he has taken less money in the hopes that he can bring Mr. Siwanowicz with him to Bergen County.

"I negotiated—are you ready for this?—a thirty-three-thousand-dollar increase in his salary," Mr. Jaye says, proud of his wheeling and dealing on behalf of Mr. Siwanowicz. As an added bonus, if the deal goes through, the school aide won't be manning attendance scanners; for that matter, the school aide wouldn't be a school aide. At the New Jersey school, Mr. Siwanowicz would be a technology staff developer who'd also help teach the math team. With the new job all but a certainty, Mr. Jaye urges Mr. Siwanowicz to think about moving out of his parents' apartment, maybe move in with his new girlfriend, who lives uptown, where it would be easier for Mr. Siwanowicz to commute to Bergen County.

"It's time to grow up," Mr. Jaye tells him. "It's time to get a real job, make real money, take the next step up in terms of responsibility."

"I'm ready, let's go," Mr. Siwanowicz says.

Mr. Jaye is already figuring out how Mr. Siwanowicz can finish his college degree, if not at City College, then at Fairleigh Dickinson University in New Jersey. "I don't care if he does it through a correspondence school," he says.

Oddly enough, Mr. Jaye can indirectly thank Ms. Damesek for all this good fortune; after all, he blames her for foisting the scanning duties on Mr. Siwanowicz. "It got me so soured on the way things are run here that I can't take living in a place where someone like Jan would be asked to scan," Mr. Jaye says.

When the math chairman informs the principal of his impending departure, Mr. Teitel doesn't try to persuade him to stay at Stuyvesant. The principal knows that Mr. Jaye aspires to be a principal himself. Mr. Teitel simply wishes him good luck. "It'll be a big loss for us, a tremendous loss," he says. Though they argue like brothers, they are close like brothers too. Mr. Teitel says he will miss Mr. Jaye, who says the same. And Mr. Jaye means it because, in light of his new job, he comes to see something different about the principal, that while he always criticized Mr. Teitel for being too nice, for giving his people too much latitude, Mr. Jaye now understands that the principal also gave him the freedom to grow, even while allowing Ms. Damesek to grow too. "His inability to control her might also be a willingness to allow people to be themselves," Mr. Jaye says. Forgiveness comes with knowing that his time at Stuyvesant is almost up. Which prompts him to think of all the people he has come to know here, making him the unofficial mayor of Stuyvesant.

"I walk in this building, I know everyone," he says, "from the guy who sweeps the cafeteria to the cops on the street to every kid, every parent, every merchant, every person who has anything to do with the school. . . . It's real tough." He thinks about what he must leave behind, the math department he built, the teachers he hired, a family to him. Mr.

Jaye almost thought of staying at Stuyvesant. But then his wife gave him a nudge. "When I was waffling, I said, 'Why don't I just stay at Stuy?' And she said, 'No, go to Bergen, the money's too good.'"

Mr. Jaye always thought that he would retire from Stuyvesant, hoping for a plaque erected in his honor. But the school bestows such an honor only on teachers who have passed away. "It's probably not going to happen," he says. ". . . I'm not dead." He's just tempted enough to "buy my own plaque." After thirty-four years at Stuyvesant, he reasons, "if you walk out under your own power, or [are] carried out [in] an ambulance, what is the difference?"

But Mr. Jaye is getting ahead of himself. He hasn't signed a contract with Bergen County yet. His departure from Stuyvesant is to remain a closely held secret until then. It will be hard to keep to himself the knowledge that his time is quickly running out. When the phone rings, Mr. Jaye picks it up and, after a beat, says into the receiver, "No, I'm not here. This is an apparition, but a goddamn good-looking one." The apparition, decked out in a conservative blue button-down shirt, dark slacks, and a navy tie, then adds, "I'm totally naked."

That afternoon, Mariya, the fifteen-year-old Ukrainian immigrant, is a bundle of unarticulated emotions as she comes home, near the end of the subway line in a working-class Russian section of Brooklyn not far from Midwood, the high school Mr. Jaye just rejected. Hers is a nondescript tenement where graffiti has migrated to the edges of the red-brick exterior. The elevator is the old-fashioned kind; when it arrives, she has to open the door to enter it, and it's impossible not to be assaulted by the stench of Clorox swabbed on the elevator floor. Her bedroom assaults the senses too, beginning with the door, on which there is an excerpt from Dante's *Inferno*: "Through me the way into the suffering city, Through me the way to the eternal pain, Through me the way that runs among the lost. Justice urged on my high artificer; My maker was divine authority, The highest wisdom, and the primal love. Before me nothing but eternal things were made, And I endure eternally. Abandon every hope, ye who enter here."

It's not a commentary on her state of mind, notwithstanding the

failed petition drive to eradicate homework over vacation, despite the
end of her first love, regardless of the parental pressure she faces. The
excerpt is just, as she says, "really cool." As is the sign on the inside of the
door, which announces, MEAN PEOPLE SUCK. This, after all, is the natural
habitat of a high school sophomore. Which is why there's a poster of her
favorite band, Disturbed. On her computer thumps the techno-rock
beat of Celldweller. By her bed rest chunky textbooks, including the
dreaded *Chemistry: Connections to Our Changing World*. And then it all
comes rushing back: school. Things are getting worse. Not that her
mother has an inkling. Mariya has evaded detection through a new tech-
nique.

"I haven't been telling her my grades lately because they've been
eighty-seven-ish," she says. "When it's ninety or above, I'll tell her
about it."

That means the indelicate issue of grades won't be coming up over
dinner tonight. Instead, over Ukrainian borscht at the small kitchen
table, talk turns to the more digestible topic of Mariya's transformation
into a great student years ago, while the present tense gets a merciful
bye.

Mrs. Goldman, marveling at her daughter as if she were an unexpected gift, can't think of anything that she did to help her daughter
academically. "Nothing, nothing special," she says in her staccato Eastern
European accent.

Mariya corrects her. "My mother always helped me with my homework," she says.

Mrs. Goldman corrects her in turn, saying that her English was so
limited that she could do little to help her daughter after the first grade,
when Mrs. Goldman could no longer understand the books that Mariya
was reading in school. "Then," her mother says, "she started to know
more than me."

Neither she nor Mariya spoke much English when they arrived in
the United States in 1995. But what language couldn't convey, a
parent's love did. From Mariya's earliest days, her mother impressed
upon her the importance of education and how Mrs. Goldman had herself been a good student in school, a potent combination that left a deep
impression on young Mariya. "I wanted to be like my mom," she says.

At parent-teacher conferences, Mrs. Goldman always showed up, even though she invariably heard the same refrain, that her daughter was a wonderful student, which actually was why Mrs. Goldman came. She just wanted to hear that, and who could have blamed her? "I thought she is smart girl, but I am mother," she says, dismissing her own bias.

Mariya discounted her own talent too. A few years ago, when she was passing by Stuyvesant, she pointed it out to her mother, who had no idea what the place signified, until Mariya explained. "This is a school for very smart kids," she told her. "I can't even dream about this school." Mariya didn't bother studying for the entrance exam—what was the use?—which made her acceptance all the more shocking.

"I was happy and proud," Mrs. Goldman says with restraint. Then she quietly rises from the kitchen table and gently kisses the top of her daughter's head, where all that magnificent intelligence resides.

Still, Mrs. Goldman is perplexed by her daughter's academic success. She wonders if it has to do with the magic potion of mixing parents of widely different ages, as she is sixteen years younger than her husband. But she doesn't wonder about all those times when she pushed Mariya to work harder. That pressure goes unstated even while it persists. Mariya lets it go too, at least for tonight.

"If I can be similar to her and her parenting," Mariya says, "that would be really cool."

The next day, Thursday, May 4, the new issue of the *Spectator* hits the stands by the second-floor entrance. On the front page blares the headline: "COSA Up for Reappointment." The plight of Mr. Polazzo, the beloved coordinator of student affairs, has finally come to light for all the students to see, and the news doesn't bode well for the school administration. In an accompanying editorial, the newspaper says, "It is our duty as the student body to join this fight to protect Polazzo in his time of need. As a student advocate in the face of the administration, Polazzo has been an ally of the student body and has always fought for its best interests. Now it is time for us all to return the favor."

Meanwhile, around the corner from the hustle and bustle of the newspaper stand, somber students are gathering to protect the memory of two of their own. They are selling blue plastic bracelets at two dollars apiece to raise funds for a memorial to Kevin and April. The bracelets carry a simple message, that they haven't been forgotten, that the day of the crash is remembered: "April & Kevin 03-17-06."

CHAPTER TWENTY-ONE

Neutral Ground

MR. SIWANOWICZ SEEMS TO FLOAT ABOVE THE BUSTLE of Chambers Street as he makes his way to the subway station after school on the evening of Thursday, May 4, oblivious to the blare of traffic, ignoring the congestion of humanity, disregarding his own screeching depression, which isn't screeching today. Not even remotely. Across the street from Stuyvesant, he takes note of the block where the day before Tom Cruise had made a cameo appearance at a gala premiere of his latest blockbuster, *Mission Impossible III*. A crush of adoring fans swarmed the movie star, a spectacle at which Mr. Siwanowicz scoffs. "I wouldn't trade places with him," he says. "I have a better job." And it's about to get better yet. When he joins Mr. Jaye at Bergen County Academies next year—and it's all but a certainty—Mr. Siwanowicz expects he'll be doing what he loves, teaching math, without the distractions of monitoring attendance scanners or fixing photocopiers. Still, he says, "I'll miss the kids" at Stuyvesant. And still, he has trouble sleeping. While Milo rotates 180 degrees in his sleep, Mr. Siwanowicz rises, walks a few steps to his alarm clock, and turns it off without waking up, without remembering a thing. But why let it get him down? It's springtime, and as he notes, "Sunlight chemically produces stuff that makes us feel better. That's why people move to Florida."

Mr. Siwanowicz has no intentions of moving south; he is thinking of moving uptown into an apartment with his girlfriend, Kate. "I don't know what the future holds," he says, "but it's going great." His parents think so too. They met Kate and instantly adored her, and now it's on his "to-do list" to meet her parents. His parents also think it'd be a good idea if he moved out of his room in their apartment and found his own place. He's almost thirty years old; it's time. "It's the natural order of things," he says.

On the No. 1 train heading uptown, Mr. Siwanowicz can't help but muse about Kate, admiring her natural abilities, her keen mind, which, while lacking the knowledge of such minutiae as multivariable calculus that packs his brain, nonetheless still implicitly understands math, a close kin to her expertise in music, another language of symbols that in the right sequence produces a specific and beautiful outcome.

So he better be ready.

At precisely 6:30 p.m., Mr. Siwanowicz arrives at the entrance of Neutral Ground on Twenty-sixth Street, where, he explains, "People beat the crap out of each other." Relishing the challenge, he takes the elevator to the fourth floor and enters a large, musty room that could pass for a poker parlor, except for the dearth of cigar smoke, the substitute for which is the waft of nuked popcorn and the whiff of fantasy, of hobbits and dungeons and dragons and abnormally muscular superheroes. The rattle of dice pierces the stale air as he wends his way over scuffed wood floors, under exposed red-painted piping, past a fire-escape door left open and massive windows painted shut and covered with steel bars. People are hunched in red vinyl chairs busted open with the innards of yellow fluff oozing out; the place is a repository for boys in backward baseball caps, bearded men in yarmulkes, ghetto gangstas in skullcaps, blacks, Asians, Hispanics, and one pregnant woman.

For one dollar, the price of admission, they do here what they could just as easily do at home: play board games. But Neutral Ground isn't just a place to play games. It's a community, a subculture of smart people—a Web designer, a Columbia University fellow, a 401(k) pension consultant, a brilliant school aide—who are looking for a fix of intellectual stimulation in the form of a game.

And then there's Kate, a revelation, playing against type. She's not just a brainiac, she's a beautiful brainiac, out of the Michelle Pfeiffer mold, petite, doe-eyed, a startling contrast to the hulking, bedraggled figure of Mr. Siwanowicz. Kate lights up as soon as she sees him approach, pausing from the throes of a board game, the Cities & Knights of Catan, which she's playing with three others. But her greeting is a blip on the screen. She resumes her game as he takes a seat at the table in front of her and plunges into a card game called Jambo. He can't see what she's doing. Maybe that's the way he wants it. Maybe it's so perfect, watching her would be too scary. Or maybe, even with his back to her, he doesn't need to see because he knows she's here with him and that's enough.

Nothing is ever enough, not two nights later, a warm Saturday evening, when Jane plunges into a frenzied crowd milling about at Union Square along Fourteenth Street. She's pumped. She's jazzed. She's power walking. Dragging behind her is an angular twenty-year-old named Mike whom she met a couple of days ago. They strike an odd contrast, she in fashionable sandals, jeans, and a pink halter top, he in a gangsta's getup, a New York Yankees cap and jersey of a baseball team he doesn't follow, his baggy jeans drooping far below his waist, a puddle at his ankles. On his sloped back is a black backpack, although he's not in school anymore. He did a month or so of community college, like a prison sentence, before he became gainfully employed selling what he calls "blue haze," potent marijuana. It turns out shoplifting didn't pay. Jane isn't listening. She's pounding pavement until she submerges into Sahara East, a hookah bar on First Avenue, where they pile into the back, under a dark red tent, to a corner table pockmarked with burn holes in the tablecloth. As soon as she sits, Jane begins to reach into her white Coach handbag, and almost immediately, Mike says, "Just save it. You told me not to let you."

Reminded of her own admonition, Jane complies, letting go of whatever she was about to remove, instead pulling out of the little handbag an unexpected accessory, a novel, *The Feast of Love*, like a rabbit out of a magician's hat. Required reading in her Great Books class. A life raft. Her English teacher, Mr. Grossman, would be proud.

Except that he's scared.

One day she's in class, the next she's not. When she returned to class on a recent day, she casually apologized by saying, "I'm sorry I wasn't around. I was kind of on suicide watch." It's a feeling she can't shake and can't explain. She can only respond to it, alternately smoking marijuana and watching endless episodes of mindless Japanese anime online, gaining ten pounds, then losing ten pounds in a span of two weeks. Mr. Grossman responded as a teacher would: with a lesson. He gave her the example of a farmer who every day feeds a chicken, so that the chicken comes to associate the farmer with food, a logical assumption until the farmer, one day, picks up the chicken and twists its neck, killing it. The farmer had only been fattening the chicken for slaughter. The chicken couldn't have known this; it had only a limited experience on which to base its assumptions, just as Jane, at the tender age of seventeen, has limited experience about life, about things not getting better, about things getting worse. Jane liked the parable, especially the way he worked in a chicken, as if Mr. Grossman were sending a subtle message that she was herself a chicken, threatening to opt out of life, which was indeed part of the point.

"The world's a much happier place for me with a little freak like you in it, so don't be selfish," he told her, making her laugh, which was the point too.

The point now, though, is to choose a hookah flavor to inhale, and Jane selects the Tony Montana flavor, which is apropos given that it's named after a movie character with a major drug addiction. It's perhaps the only thing that makes sense, as her mind is a disjointed caravan, ricocheting from one thought to another about how "anarchy rules" and "democracy is one step closer to anarchy."

Her new friend, Mike, plays it safe and remains silent until Jane says, "I don't think it's possible to live life without breaking the law."

Now he gets it. "That's true," he says.

Jane has a particular vantage point because she was recently arrested. The last time she checked in at rehab, she again tested dirty—registering marijuana, cocaine, and heroin in her system—prompting a search of her bag, which turned up two dime bags of marijuana. Police arrived, handcuffed her, and took her down to the precinct, where she was placed in a small holding cell along with several other women, one charged with shoplifting, another with child neglect. From about 6 p.m. to 2 a.m., Jane lost herself in the role of nursemaid, consoling the women for their misfortune. Then police officers took her to central booking, where she was shoved into another cell, which held little more than a toilet seat. She was robbed in her sleep. Awake, her mind kept churning in an endless loop, telling her, "This is my limit. This is my limit. This is my limit." When she was finally released—facing another sentence of community service—she began to think it was time to change. She began thinking about the future. About graduation. About prom. About a boy whom she barely knew who asked her to go as his date. And she began thinking more seriously about applying to college for next fall. She screamed, "Hell, no," when her estranged father recently called, asking to see her either for her eighteenth birthday later this month or for graduation in June, but still, Jane seemed to be in a better mood. Until now.

"I mean, what do you think the point of life is?" she asks in the darkened hookah bar.

"Be happy, be successful, help out your family," says Mike, her companion for the evening.

"How do you define success?" she wants to know.

"I don't need to be rich," he says, "but I want shelter."

She's unimpressed. "That's pretty basic."

He doesn't know how to respond to that. So Jane picks up the thread of conversation, gives it a different stitch. "Do you know that addiction can be genetic?" she asks.

"Alcoholism runs in my family," says Mike, who has a stomachache from drinking today.

"Everybody's addicted to something—food, television, even religion," Jane says. "I mean, we all need something to define us." She thinks of her past. "I used to be so against drinking and drugs. Why are there so many ironies in life?"

Another question Mike can't answer. Instead, his eyes flit about as he checks his cell phone repeatedly, finally saying he needs to get home before his mother does. That's their cue. They charge out of the hookah bar to catch the L train to head to his house, but just before Jane ducks into the subway station, she's caught by a final, stray thought. "I think life is so much better if you don't believe in God," she says. "We're personally responsible for what happens in our lives. There's no fate."

On Wednesday, May 10, Mr. Polazzo is wondering about his own fate, appealing to a higher power: the principal.

Even though his prospects remain dim, Mr. Polazzo has just reapplied as the coordinator of student affairs, submitting an application enumerating his accomplishments over the past four years.

"I kind of took credit for what the kids did," he confesses from his usual perch in the Student Union office, "but it happened on my watch."

"Like when the president takes credit for job creation?" queries one of the SU regulars, Nathan, the renegade Web master, who's off to Princeton next year.

It's a regular Stuyvesant occurrence: a future Ivy Leaguer keeping a teacher in check. Though, in truth, Mr. Polazzo didn't really take all the credit. "Ever since I arrived at Stuyvesant in November 2000, I have been consistently amazed at the brilliance, dedication, and excellence of the student body," he wrote in his application for the job. And each time he listed an accomplishment, he diminished his own role as student coordinator by naming the students who deserved credit, whether it was automating the sale and distribution of Sing! tickets or organizing a massive school blood drive.

"This is the worst job in the building," Nathan says.

Mr. Polazzo has at least one thing going for him: no one else has applied to be coordinator of student affairs, despite the behind-the-scenes efforts of some school administrators to prop up a rival candidate, and the deadline expires in two days. He would disavow his regular cracked-pepper-turkey-on-a-roll lunch forever for the chance to be reappointed, but he readily agrees that the job stinks. "Whenever a student does something wrong, I'm the first person they come to," he says of *them*, the adults. As exhibit A, Mr. Polazzo refers to what he calls the "chaperone's dilemma." At a dance, which he oversees, what do you do if a student is caught imbibing alcohol? Option one, he says, is to let the kid go. Option two is to call the parents, "but that kind of ruins the kid's life," he notes. Or option three, if the student is already drunk, call an ambulance "in loco parentis," he says. He doesn't particularly relish any of the options, though he's been forced to resort to option three, visiting a hospital, at least eight times.

Just then, Mr. Teitel barges into Mr. Polazzo's office, a rare sighting in this student hangout. It seems almost too good to be true. Has the principal already made a decision about the job?

"Did I win the lottery?" Mr. Polazzo asks.

Mr. Teitel leans in, excited. Then he breaks the news: a television news show wants to do a live shot at Stuyvesant, hoping to enlist more than eight hundred students to create a Guinness-record human wave. Mr. Polazzo hasn't won the lottery. He has won the task of getting the word out to students. The news segment will be heralding the upcoming flick *Poseidon*. It was too good to be true.

It may be too good to be true, but on Friday, May 12, it appears that Ms. Lee, the student teacher, may have found a permanent job. Not at Stuyvesant, however. She just returned from an interview at Syosset High School, a regular public school on Long Island. It all happened so quickly. Her mentor, Stuyvesant history teacher Warren Donin, had been offered the chance to apply for the job at Syosset, but he wasn't interested, so he suggested that she try. She didn't want to. She still wanted Stuyvesant. Besides, Syosset didn't want to hire a student teacher; the school wanted a veteran. But Mr. Donin kept pestering Ms. Lee, telling her there were no openings at Stuyvesant, that this was a chance for her to land at another good school with a full-time job and *benefits*. Then Ms. Lee learned that the Syosset teacher who had tried to recruit Mr. Donin was the daughter of Ms. Lee's mother's calligraphy teacher, and the coincidence seemed like a good omen.

Finally, Ms. Lee relented, though not enthusiastically. "What's the worst that can happen?" she asked herself.

The worst that could happen was that she could apply to Syosset and find out that she liked it, which is exactly what happened. She met with the head of the social studies department and instantly hit it off with him. The interview was supposed to be merely a courtesy. But the

department head especially liked how she responded to a tough interview question: What do you do if a student is failing? Her answer: Think
A-Rod. She was watching the Yankees on television the other night, she
explained. Alex Rodriguez, the slugger, was mired in a slump when
he crushed a mighty home run, and with one sweet stroke of the bat, he
was back on track. Similarly, Ms. Lee told the Syosset administrator, she
wants her students to know that they can always come back if they are
failing. "I want them to be perceived by me as all potential A-plus students," she explained. The Syosset administrator, not expecting a baseball analogy from the diminutive Asian woman, was impressed.

Ms. Lee had hit a home run.

The job, though, isn't a lock. Far from it. Next week, she will return
for round two of the interview process, when she meets with a six-
teacher committee and conducts a demonstration history lesson in front
of a live classroom. If she makes it through those hoops, she still faces
interviews with the school principal and other officials.

"Everything will be decided in the next two weeks," she says.

It may be scary to contemplate, but for the first time, Ms. Lee has
come to understand that she has no choice, that it's time to move on. "I
was so focused, if it's not Stuy, it's nowhere," she says, echoing her high
school experience when she fell short of Stuyvesant, settling for Bronx
Science. Now, she realizes, "There are other schools out there." And perhaps she is willing to believe there is life outside Stuyvesant. "Maybe,"
she says, "I won't hate teaching at another place."

> *I love you*
> *I always have*
>
> —desktop graffiti, Stuyvesant High School

CHAPTER TWENTY-TWO

Love Notes

OUTSIDE, ON A QUIET PATCH OF MIDTOWN PAVEMENT, there is no sign of the pulsating, primal, hip-grinding bedlam that is about to bust out here on the evening of Saturday, May 13. In fact, there is no sign at all. T New York, a chic nightclub, sits incognito, an anonymous front of maroon stucco walls, its identity betrayed only by three stone-faced, burly bouncers standing sentry by a strip of felt rope cordoning off the entrance. But the momentary tranquility is disrupted at four minutes to six when Mr. Polazzo, the coordinator of student affairs, blows in, wielding a weapon of mass deterrence.

"Hopefully, we'll keep it clean," he tells the proprietor. "I have a Breathalyzer."

It's the calm before the soph/frosh semiformal.

It's been a harried few days for Mr. Polazzo. He found out just the other day that at least two rival teachers are now vying for the student coordinator job—unexpected candidates who've emerged at the last minute, just as his reappointment seemed assured. Then a girl who goes around school posing as a boy named "Max" was playing Hacky Sack when she fell, hit her head, and suffered a seizure, forcing Mr.

Polazzo to take the student on his umpteenth trip to a hospital emergency room.

And now, tonight.

A gaggle of girls begins to clatter inside, teetering on high heels, looking as uncomfortable as circus performers wobbling on precarious stilts. A battalion of boys tramples in, hair spiked toward the ceiling like shards of stalagmites in a cave. What follows is a kaleidoscope of white T-shirts and powerful cologne and purses and flip-flops and denim miniskirts over dark leggings and ankle bracelets. The freshmen and sophomores look either ten years old or twenty-five, depending on the angle of the lighting.

In they go, all of them, a crush of bodies piling into a tiled room, through a darkened hall, and out into an empty chamber, where they come to a halt at the edge of the dance floor, as if avoiding an invisible force field. The only dancing is that of the flashing lights glinting off the walls, a lonely Morse code of blue, green, and red. Two girls probe the perimeter, and two other girls join in, but the dancing fizzles out like the last pop of popcorn in the pan. It's too early. It's not too early, though, for Mr. Polazzo to worry and strategize, as he hits upon the idea to foil would-be imbibers by checking students' water bottles because such containers are commonly used to disguise alcoholic contents. Then, suddenly, like a herd of buffalo stampeding an open plain, about thirty girls storm the dance floor, because they're teenagers and there's comfort in numbers, and all hell breaks loose: random screams, the emergence of the first hip-grinding couple, and by 6:39 p.m., there's a critical mass on the dance floor as stereo speakers shake the ground, blasting out the lyrics, "Don't cha wish your girlfriend was hot like me," and it's degrees hotter and the air is thick, and manufactured smoke begins to spew out, and now more than three hundred boys and girls madly bounce off each other while bolder dancers climb on raised cube platforms, the better for unobstructed exhibitionism, gyrating wildly, hair flying, minds evidently blank.

Thus have they descended into a primitive state, an unleashing of anarchy, and *Lord of the Flies* comes to mind. But for this: on closer inspection, the faces retain the innocence of youth. The eyes cast uncertain glances, as if asking, *Do I look stupid? Am I dancing in rhythm? Am I cool?* On the balcony, a smattering of shy observers watches the frenzied spectacle below, outcasts in high school, loners here too. When the DJ flips on a slow song, dancers howl in protest, with most retreating to the sidelines, waiting to dance to a song less intimate. Still out there is a boy kissing a girl, and it's just that, a gentle, little peck. With practiced casualness, boys and girls lean against the wooden edge of the bar, ordering nothing harder than a Shirley Temple with a cherry on top.

But Mr. Polazzo, the mother hen, knows better. A bouncer caught a chaperone slipping a drink to a student. The chaperone insisted the student grabbed the drink out of his hand. The video camera says otherwise. The chaperone won't be chaperoning next year. It could've been worse.

"Last year, a lot of my chaperones got drunk," Mr. Polazzo says.

When it's dark, and it's a Saturday night, and there's a room packed with fourteen- and fifteen-year-olds dancing their heads off, drama inevitably follows. A girl weeps in the hallway near the men's bathroom. A brave boy makes a doomed dance request of a girl who responds by pinching her nose, a hand signal, like a third base coach calling a steal sign, which prompts another girl to slide to her rescue, to save the girl from the fate of a dance with a boy that can never, ever happen. Another boy observes on the sidelines, holding up a look of disdain because he doesn't intend to ask a girl to dance. "You can usually judge the situation if they mind," he notes sagely. How? "Experience," he says, and a period can almost be heard at the end of the one-word sentence.

It's a strange phenomenon but absolutely true here: girls mature faster than boys, and not just intellectually. Even in the dancing shadows and the flashing lights, many of the boys simply look younger—an awkward assemblage of skin and bones, a mass of puzzle pieces that don't quite fit together yet—than many of the girls who are the same age. But the girls show uncanny forbearance.

"I can't wait until the freshmen boys grow," giggles Taylor, herself a freshman.

By 9:01, they are growing up faster. On the dance floor, the grinding becomes a little more unstructured, sweatier, soupier. Girls are pounding the floor in bare feet in a kind of tribal drumbeat. Boys are knocking into each other with more force, threatening violence. Upstairs becomes a tangle of bodies in various wrestling poses that, in the light of day and direct supervision, would elicit appalled parental disapproval. But before a major infraction occurs, at precisely 10 p.m., the music snaps off, and just like that, the mood shuts off like a light switch. Boys and girls blink in the rising lights, becoming themselves. Mr. Polazzo, relieved, takes the mike to announce the dance is over. He's booed. It's time for them to go home, children once again.

Back at Stuyvesant, another transmutation has occurred, and an ineffable quality permeates the air. The hallways are emptier, almost bereft, as students are drawn, like sun worshippers, to the magnetic pull of the riverside park behind school to bathe in the warmth of springtime. In the crevices of school, the Hudson staircase among them, an unusual number of boys and girls nestle in embraces, discovering first loves. Students continue to trudge to class but, for many, their thoughts have fled to the not-so-distant future, to the end of the semester, just weeks away, to the end of school, to the beginning of summer, and, for seniors, to the beginning of college next year.

"Ultimately, what it's about is starting the process of disengaging, you know, and saying good-bye," says Mr. Grossman, the English chairman, who, with a hint of sadness, sees the same cycle play out every year. ". . . It's a mood and an energy rather than a specific set of activities and behaviors."

There is, however, a name for it: senioritis.

Wikipedia, the online encyclopedia popular with students, defines the dreaded affliction as

The decreased motivation towards studies displayed by students who are nearing the end of their high school or college careers. It is typically said to include slowness, procrastination, apathy regarding school work, and a tendency towards truancy.

At Stuyvesant, senioritis is defined by a cautionary note taped to the wall outside the second-floor guidance office:

Seniors—Read it and Weep Or—Try Going to Class . . .

What follows are letters to two seniors saddled with senioritis whose names have been whited out so as not to embarrass them. From Virginia Tech: "Dear [blank] . . . Because we are concerned about your desire to succeed here, the committee is considering withdrawing your offer of admission. . . ." And from the University of Delaware: "We were therefore surprised to see such a marked decline in your grades during your senior year."

Around the corner, signs of another kind herald on Friday, May 19, the definitive arrival of senioritis. Hundreds of love notes cover the entire gray tiled wall—about thirty feet long and ten feet high—bridging the white senior bar and the Asian senior bar like a rainbow of long-held truths. Here, in the twilight of their final year of high school, boys and girls have placed their names on the wall in a remarkable display of honesty—a frankness born of the imminent parting of ways—confessing their love and affection for those who never knew. They call them "Senior Crush Lists."

School lore has it that Peter Stuyvesant, the ornery Dutch commander, instigated the tradition by tacking up a list of people he wanted to kill, followed by a list of women he found attractive. No doubt wildly apocryphal, the legend finds more authenticity in the recent version of the story, which pegs the crush lists to about a decade ago when students faced insurmountable problems finding dates for the prom.

Whatever the origins, the annual tradition has become so entrenched that even in this arena, students engage in heated competition, going to great lengths to outdo one another with the most creative, over-the-top crush lists. This year, that includes a heart-shaped list that, when flipped open to reveal the names of the loved ones, automatically plays the love ballads of Barry White. Leave it to Stuyvesant's tech wonders. Or to one of the more literary types, whose crush list includes the author Robert Penn Warren because she loves his classic novel *All the King's Men*.

This, though, is serious business as clusters of students slowly shuffle along, examining love notes. The confessions even draw out teachers, like Mr. Polazzo, who's made it onto a handful of crush lists. "There's no accounting for taste," he kids.

But the truth is, many of the students do adore the coordinator of student affairs. Which is why, here at the wall, they are gathering to launch "Operation SPJ"—Saving Polazzo's Job. "It's a cause I whole-heartedly support," says Jonathan, the senior who had backed the attendance scanners, despite Mr. Polazzo's opposition to them. Jonathan overlooks their disagreement, worrying what will happen if Mr. Polazzo is replaced. So after school today, several student leaders from the Student Union, the Big Sibling program, the Arista honors society, and the *Spectator* are meeting with Mr. Teitel in a rare demonstration of student unity to register their support for Mr. Polazzo. The principal has no idea what he's in for.

Jane has no idea what she just missed. The troubled senior walks into the auditorium about five minutes too late. A friend, senior Elisa Lee, has just finished performing a monologue for her "Women's Voices" class to which she had invited Jane. The assignment called for Elisa to find a woman's story that has been silenced in some way. She chose Jane's story of drug addiction, wearing pink baggy UFO pants and a pacifier necklace in her subject's honor. The monologue, entitled "Once Is Too Much, A Thousand Never Enough," borrowed from snatches of Jane's own disjointed words, which Elisa recorded earlier in an interview but read like a haiku to the inexorable pull of narcotics:

> *Going to detox was mah own decision*
> *Cuz*
> *I was just sick of*
> *Just all the things I had to do*
> *I was sick of*
> *Having*
> *Like*
> *Waking up in the morning*
> *And needing something or*
> *Being sick when I don't have it*
> *And I was sick just thinking about it*
> *So I decided to stop*
> *And well*
> *I didn't really have a choice*

Because
By that time it was just time for me to stop.

But Jane hasn't stopped. She's resumed. She's consumed. And what she's been waiting for has finally happened, a way to escape from her mother, their fights, the distrust. Jane just celebrated a birthday. She's eighteen. She's an adult, legally. No one can tell her what to do anymore. No one can stop her. Not even she herself.

CHAPTER TWENTY-THREE

The Players

NO ONE CAN STOP ROMEO. THE JUNIOR IS THE TALLEST, strongest, fittest player on the field, with an upper torso cut in the shape of a heroic V, as he glides effortlessly across the green expanse toward an imaginary goal. Football is still months away. But practice is in full swing on the afternoon of May 24 on the rooftop of Pier 40, about a mile from Stuyvesant, which looms like a glistening mirage in the distance. It's peaceful, the sound of Manhattan traffic muffled by the three flights separating the Astroturf from the concrete sidewalk below. Only the high rises, like mountain peaks, come into view up here, including the Mount Everest of the Empire State Building, making it possible to forget the crush of pedestrians at ground level.

It's almost too beautiful a day for boys to be practicing the art of bone-crushing tackles. A chalky blue sky stretches to infinity above, almost pastel in hue and dappled with little white clouds, as if rendered by an Impressionist painter, so perfect is the vista. One imperfection, though, mars the landscape. The football field is not a football field. It's a soccer field. But it's not even that either. It's a *miniature* soccer field. A nearby aluminum bench serves as a kind of open-air locker with sneakers and backpacks strewn about haphazardly. A sign at the field's entrance warns NO DOGS ALLOWED ON LAWNS. It's a stark reminder that despite the massive expense of Stuyvesant's building, the school was constructed for brains, not brawn.

Romeo climbs into a harness. Two boys on either side of him pull down on straps, trying to hold him down. But it's no use. When he coils and jumps, his powerful legs propel him skyward, threatening to uproot the two boys and take them with him. "Explode up!" exhorts the new head coach, Brian Sacks. "Good! Fifteen seconds!" When the boys move to the next drill, one doughy player collapses in the middle of the field, unable to crawl any further. He tries to pick himself up but crumbles again until Romeo and the others gather around, urging him on, clapping politely, as only civilized Stuyvesant students are wont to do, as the wheezing boy musters just enough energy to grasp and claw his way, on all fours, to the finish line.

"Team's looking great," the coach pronounces after practice ends. But the prognosis becomes grimmer as Romeo and the other boys walk back to school, aching and dirty and pessimistic. One player bemoans the lack of fans. Another says he mistook Mr. Teitel, the principal, for the team mascot, thinking the bearded man was the peg-legged Peter Stuyvesant. Their first game in September is against a regular public school that crushed them last year sixty-four to zero. "They're bigger, blacker, stronger, and faster," says a Stuyvesant running back who is Asian.

Romeo says nothing. He's used to black kids on opposing teams coming up to him, picking him out as one of *them*, asking him how it feels, being a solitary figure in a sea of white and Asian faces framed in the Pegleg helmets. And yet Romeo is one of the Stuyvesant regulars too—a brainiac—and as the boys slump back to school together in the twilight of the day, talk turns to ways of using their biggest muscle—their minds—to come up with better schemes to beat physically superior opponents. The coach has already made one significant adjustment, shifting Romeo from tight end and defensive end to running back and receiver so that his best player will be in a better position to score more touchdowns. Romeo has made an adjustment of his own, switching to jersey number thirty-seven, reflecting his new role on the team. Meanwhile, he recently met a Harvard football coach, who asked to see more of Romeo's football tapes. His father had sent them. His PR man. His dad. Romeo had stayed with him recently, up in Harlem. It had been the first time in a month or so, and Romeo realized he needed to make the trip more often. His father in Harlem gave him something that his mother on the Lower East Side couldn't. Romeo felt that his mother worried too much. When he did the same, his father quickly told him to stop, as if he couldn't stand the sight of insecurity, weakness of any kind, in his son. It was always that way with the two of them. Once, Romeo had complained that he couldn't draw well, and his father shot back, "That's the attitude I hate," ordering his son to teach himself, to *will* himself to become good at it. Romeo complied, buying a bunch of books on the craft, including *Drawing for Dummies*. Now his dad may be leaving. He's been offered a full-time teaching job at the prestigious Berklee College of Music in Boston, his hometown. His father doesn't want to leave. He already teaches at NYU and the Institute of Audio Research. But it's not that. It's that he, like his son, wants to make it big, and there's nowhere to make it bigger as a musician than in New York. Romeo sees the parallel and yet can't help but feel their differences, son to father. His father is always telling him about the importance of selling his personality. He's always talking to him about presentation and style, but Romeo looks at himself as too serious, not funny enough. His father is always saying that Romeo is trying to break away from his past, from his blackness. "He likes to see it as a reverence for the struggle of our ancestors," Romeo says. The reverence is there. The son doesn't forget. But for Romeo, there's more to his striving, although it's so complicated that sometimes he says he feels he's "losing a sense of identity." The feeling came to a head recently when he flubbed a test—at least by his standards—with an 82 in math. When he arrived home, he remedied the situation by taping up on his wall an old album cover of his dad's band, Prinz Charles & the City Beat Band. Under the title "I'LL BE THERE FOR YOU," a photo of his father stares back at Romeo, a picture of a confident, dashing man with a dare-me look and a pair of large sunglasses resting on his forehead. Romeo also taped up a postcard of the idyllic seaside town of Arradon in France, home of his mother's family.

Little sailboats dot the indigo, picturesque waters along the coast. And between his father's photo and his mother's hometown, there's just enough room on the wall for a mirror where Romeo can contemplate where he fits in.

Mr. Polazzo, the embattled coordinator of student affairs, is hunched in his usual perch in the Student Union, chomping on his usual cracked-pepper-turkey sandwich, but on this Thursday, May 25, he finds himself contemplating an unusual problem: is a free hug okay? It isn't a metaphysical question. It's a campaign question. A senior running for class president wants to post a flyer offering the affectionate freebie. And Jamie Paul, cochair of the student elections, waits patiently for an answer.

"That's up to you," Mr. Polazzo decides.

Jamie decides it's okay. It's not like the candidate is offering a hug in return for a vote. But, she wants to know, is it also okay for candidates to play music from their boom boxes to draw attention? That's okay too, Mr. Polazzo determines. Just about everything is okay with the easygoing Mr. Polazzo but his own fate as coordinator of student affairs, which continues to dangle uncertainly. For the moment, however, he tables his own worries as he wades into these student elections, a remote facsimile of democracy in action. What isn't okay is "profanity, defamation, sex, or drugs" in campaign literature, according to the official rules and regulations of the Stuyvesant Board of Elections. What also isn't okay is for students to make signs except those that are eight and a half by eleven inches in size. The school doesn't want candidates with deep pockets, or too much time on their hands, to start employing billboards, neon, and other outsized campaign paraphernalia, which would be a distinct possibility in a school as hypercompetitive as Stuyvesant.

"It's to level out the playing field," Jamie explains.

But it's almost impossible to level the playing field, at least in a school where racial politics predominate. With an electorate that's more than 50 percent Asian, candidates of the same background typically prevail in student elections. "The Asians are the silent majority," Mr. Polazzo says.

One factor can upset the equation: if several Asian candidates run for the same office, they can effectively split the vote, which is not uncommon in the primaries, the first round, before the candidates with the highest vote totals go head-to-head in the general elections. Therefore, the white vote, a bloc consisting of about 40 percent of the student body, can't be ignored, especially since candidates for president and vice president of the Student Union are required to run as a joint ticket. That's why the conventional wisdom is that an "Asian-white pair" is a winning combination, says Harvard-bound senior Amanda Wallace, a Student Union regular who is black. The proof is in last year's election: the Student Union president is Asian, the vice president, white. Race is "definitely a factor but an unstated factor," Mr. Polazzo says. Sophomore Marta Bralic, who is running for Student Union vice president on an all-white ticket, is well aware of how past precedent doesn't bode well for her and her running mate. "We're two white kids," she says. "These are disadvantages."

Nonetheless, Mr. Polazzo is going against the grain in handicapping the players in this year's election. He reckons the front-runner is the all-white ticket of Marta, the Student Union special events director, and would-be president Michael Zaytsev, the Student Union chief financial officer, because of their vast experience in school government. But not to be overlooked is the pairing of a presidential candidate who is a white junior and Student Union chief of staff and his vice presidential hopeful, the sophomore president, who is half Thai and half Filipino. And then there's the dark horse candidacy of a white junior and cheerleading captain for president and her running mate, the sophomore vice president, who is half Asian. Each ticket offers a slew of reforms concerning hot-button topics like the need for more school dances and better food at the school convenience store. An even more common refrain among the candidates is the idea of recapturing students' rights against an encroaching school administration. Or as Mike and Marta note nostalgically in their campaign pamphlet, "IN THE PAST . . . Students were allowed many freedoms and Stuy was generally a good place to be. Students had many rights and fun and happiness had not been forbidden yet. However, the administration has been slowly but surely taking away rights that every student should be able to enjoy."

Cited as an example was students' former right to laugh. An accompanying stick-figure drawing in the campaign literature shows an individual, unshaven and unsmiling, locked behind bars.

Just as grim is the way the students reflect the grown-ups in their general apathy about elections. Not even a third of the school votes. "In a true democracy, voting is a right," intones a *Spectator* editorial. "Yet our student body does not seem to value it." Others find evident value in the process. Veteran filmmakers Caroline Suh and Erika Frankel have just arrived at Stuyvesant to chronicle the race for Student Union president and vice president in a documentary called *The Ticket*. In written handouts to students, they describe Stuyvesant as "arguably the best public high school in the city (if not the country)," saying they intend to explore "how democracy works—specifically, how young adults engage in the democratic process" and how the student elections serve "as a sort of microcosm of a national election." Among Stuyvesant's famous alumni, they hope to interview Dick Morris, the noted Bill Clinton campaign strategist. According to school legend, and his own accounts, the political adviser cut his teeth as a behind-the-scenes operative during high school campaigns in the sixties.

So far this year, electioneering is decidedly genteel. Indeed, it's difficult to detect an election in the offing at all, except for a smattering of posters that have begun to elbow their way onto crowded school bulletin boards, one of the most provocative of which proclaims, "The struggle endures, 'til proletarian rule." But it's early. There's still time for the fireworks of perfectly illegitimate campaign skulduggery and voter fraud.

It's early, but it's there, lurking somewhere in Mariya's expression of world-weariness, beneath the gothic layers of leather and studs, apart from the parental pressure, eons away from failed petition drives. There. Right there. A restrained smile, not even a complete smile, it's so ephemeral that it vanishes in the lunchtime shadows of Cafe Amore's, a block from school. Mariya nibbles on a slice of pizza, almost unaware of what she's eating. Because it's happened: Mariya met a boy in school. His name is Jarek Lupinski. They kissed. And just like that, because she's a sophomore in high school, and he's a junior, and things can be as sublimely simple as that, she's his first real girlfriend, and he's her first true love on this Friday, May 26. Which is why Mariya didn't even try to hide her latest report card from her mother. Mariya knew she had slacked off in English. She was well aware that she hadn't done all her homework. She was fully cognizant of the consequences of not studying hard for a variety of tests. But she says, "I sort of stopped caring as much." Her mother didn't stop caring, not even close. When she absorbed the shock of her daughter's grades, "she blew up," Mariya says. "She told me I was throwing my life away." She told Mariya that no college would want her. She stormed off, then returned twenty minutes later and started yelling at Mariya again before doling out a new edict: Mariya is not allowed to hang out after school for the rest of the school year. She is to come home immediately. This was the sentence Mariya received for coming home with a grade point average of 93.5.

The grades don't count toward Mariya's overall average. They're a kind of midterm indicator of her progress before the real grades are meted out at semester's end. But that, to her mother, is just an insignificant detail in the big picture, which is that her daughter's average dropped just over a point from 94.86 last term.

"It's a *point*, and it's not even the final grade," Mariya rails.

A point, though, takes on larger meaning in the context of a struggling family that uprooted its life in Ukraine in the hopes of grasping a piece of the American Dream—a dream made vivid by Mariya's dazzling academic potential. "To me, if I don't do as well, it's not as big of a deal to myself," she says. "To my mother, it's a different story." As for the future, Mariya says, "That's so far off. I still feel like a kid."

The future, however, continues to tug at her. Already, several colleges, noticing the same potential in Mariya, particularly her high score on the Preliminary SAT (for which she didn't study), have come beckoning, sending the sophomore flattering notes, two years before she is to apply to college, like football recruiters getting an early jump on a brawny young high school prospect.

"Dear Mariya, Mount Holyoke is a remarkable place—and one of the nation's top liberal arts colleges," begins an e-mail from the dean of admissions. ". . . I'd love to meet you, have our tour guides show you our stunning campus, and talk about how Mount Holyoke can help you achieve your goals."

From Marist College: "Dear Mariya, I am writing you today to invite you to become a part of a new, exclusive web-based program designed for a select group of high school students like yourself."

And another: "Dear Mariya, Welcome to Oxford College of Emory University! . . . Take a look at Emory's academic majors, and browse its Career Center website anytime. Maybe Oxford College will be your next step to a successful future!"

The letters keep coming. "Every week, I throw out a stack that tall," she says, spreading her hands about a foot apart.

Mariya can't think about college yet; she can barely think beyond tomorrow, her sweet-sixteen birthday. It's hard to keep up. She feels the innate contradiction of being a teenager, for whom things can't move fast enough while things are happening too fast. She doesn't hang out with her two friends at Burritoville anymore. She's drifted away from Mariana, her good friend from chemistry class. High school friendships are like amoebas, having no definite form. And then there's the constant of Jarek, her new beau, a strapping, blond junior who tells her he's the last living heir of the last Polish knight, and chivalry isn't dead. Her mother blames him, and the player before him, Tom, for distracting Mariya from her academic mission. But Mariya sees it differently. "It's not anyone's fault," she says. Actually, Jarek's had a good influence, at least in one respect. Mariya wakes up thirty minutes earlier than usual, at 5:50 a.m., just so she can meet Jarek, who lives two stops away on the local Q train, on the way to school. "It's really nice," she says, "because no matter what goes wrong, I have this to fall back on." It's true, though, that he's not exactly a stellar student and that he's persuaded her to cut school after lunch today. "He wouldn't let me go to class," she says, as if she has no choice in the matter. Mariya worries about missing gym class. She frets about being caught. She doesn't know what she and Jarek will do today. There's no plan, no pressure, no expectations. Maybe they'll board a train to Hoboken and sit on a park bench and do nothing but hold hands. That, all of sudden, sounds gloriously unproductive.

CHAPTER TWENTY-FOUR

The Human Element

IT'S 8:58 A.M. ON A LAZY SATURDAY, MAY 27, AND while his classmates are fast asleep, Romeo is already cutting a wide swath over the gray, empty pavement of Grand Street, a ghost town at this hour on the Lower East Side, his mind racing over a series of plans, pressures, and expectations. A glimpse: Romeo at Harvard. He's envisioning the day when he's in Cambridge, Massachusetts, out to dinner with his father, who will be in the neighborhood because he's taking that job teaching music in Boston after all. But almost as quickly as that pleasing thought materializes, it collides with the reality that Romeo's behind in his work on his Intel science project, which is why he's heading to NYU now. He's meeting his adviser, a professor who's dying of prostate cancer but who, in his final days, is attempting, with Romeo, to discover a novel model to unlock the power of nuclear fusion. "Nobody's listening to him," Romeo grumbles, turning right on Lafayette Street, sounding like an old man himself. Romeo could have ignored the seventy-eight-year-old professor too, coasting this semester by taking ceramics or a class in video production. But he didn't. He felt an obligation—there's always an obligation, a responsibility—to tackle an imposing Intel project. It's part of a pact he struck with his ambitious friends, dating back to their freshman year together at Stuyvesant. "We told ourselves we are the next generation," says the striving junior.

Romeo didn't want to take the easy road. He kept telling himself happiness didn't matter. He disdained students in school who lived only for the present. "I started to forget the human element," he says, turning right on Greene Street. Even now, he can't help but scold himself for making a few sloppy errors on a recent math test. "The mistakes I'm making are stupid, on the level of typos," he says, now sounding like a parent. And by his reckoning, little mistakes are just as unforgivable as big mistakes because if he's building a bridge, a slight miscalculation in its construction can lead to its eventual collapse. Never mind that he's nearly perfect, still maintaining a 96 grade point average, on a righteous path to Harvard.

Romeo makes a left on Houston Street, thinking he needs to practice the piano more, reminding himself that he has to rehearse for a salsa dance show next week. But then the noise of thoughts halts when Romeo is confronted by the impatient, stooped, sagging figure of Paul Garabedian in the lobby of NYU's Courant Institute of Mathematical Sciences. It's as if the aged professor, defying his chemotherapy treatment, couldn't wait for Romeo to arrive, so he took the elevator from his office down to the lobby, the quicker to get started with his sixteen-year-old charge.

"Of course, I have to bear down on him because he has a lot of obligations," Dr. Garabedian says, as if Romeo isn't present.

But then the professor seems to become aware, asking Romeo what time he went to sleep last night. Romeo says midnight. The professor chuckles, saying Romeo must've been on a poor date to arrive home so early in the evening. Though they have been working together on these quiet Saturdays for about three months, only now does the curmudgeonly mathematician think to ask Romeo a serious question about his future.

"What are your plans?"

Without hesitation, Romeo says, "Applying early to Harvard."

The professor and the student could hardly be more unlike, one so near the end he can almost see it, the other so close to the beginning that the future seems like an infinite highway; one so frail it looks as though a gentle breeze could knock him over, the other so powerful in his jersey number thirty-seven that he looks as if he could plow right through the professor's office walls. And yet, they share uncommon traits. Like Romeo, Dr. Garabedian as a boy taught himself calculus simply by reading a book. He too aspired to Harvard, receiving his PhD there in mathematics. And both of his daughters graduated from Stuyvesant. But neither mentor nor acolyte seems terribly interested in finding the common bond, the human element. There are mysteries of fusion to unravel, and who cares about cancer or chemo? "The point is to keep working on the project," the professor says. He doesn't say it, but it seems that this project with Romeo helps to sustain the professor, to wrap him in what he calls a "cocoon" of work. For Romeo, there's a benefit left unsaid as well in the study of fusion. These Saturdays bring him one step closer to that unceasing goal of his, to save the world.

Milo has just dashed off an article on fusion, writing it not with any visions of rescuing the world but simply to fill a page of his elementary school newspaper, the *234 Latte*. It's the least he can do since he dropped out of the fifth grade, leaving his little friends behind for the challenge of high school. He won't be donning a cap and gown at the upcoming fifth-grade graduation ceremony, though he plans to sit in the audience, like a proud parent, watching the giddy kids on stage. "I'm going to go there, but I'm not going through it because I'm not officially in the fifth grade," he says clinically, all facts, no sentiment. And yet something seems to be bothering him on this balmy, hazy Sunday, May 28. Milo's waiting on an undulating dock near Stuyvesant for a water taxi to take him on a leisurely excursion to the New Jersey side of the Hudson. But he's not all there. Whatever preoccupies him, he's keeping it hidden under the lid of his strawberry-colored baseball hat, which is pushed down low and tight on his forehead, as if that'll preserve the secrets contained therein. All that he gives away is on the front of the cap, a green patch with white lettering:

MILE
0

It's a riddle wrapped in a math equation: MILE – E + O = MILO. An inside joke, except he's not laughing. He's thinking of the other day when his mom packed a bologna sandwich for him, and he ate it in the park with his old fifth-grade pals. He saw them the next day when he joined them on a field trip, where they played kickball and nobody won or lost, an ambiguous result that he says "was really stupid." He's not sure what he likes about hanging out with other ten-year-olds. Suddenly he is acting his age: monosyllabic, nearly mute. He can't decide which he likes better, his fifth grade or Stuyvesant; he shrugs and waves his arms in surrender. He doesn't know why, but he's beginning to sleep more restfully, even if he still wakes up with his head pointing north. Milo knows this, though: in his trigonometry class, there's still a lot of homework, but he's scoring well on the tests with grades of 85, 90, and 92, and he plans to take the statewide high school math exam at year's end because, he says, "How could math not be fun?" Milo knows this too: he plans to take the Stuyvesant entrance exam in the fall so that he can officially enroll next year. He doesn't seem worried about the test, unlike his older sister, who's changed her mind and decided to apply too, as long as she doesn't have to compare scores with Milo.

And then, there he is, on the New Jersey shore. The whole trip— boarding the water taxi, navigating the Hudson, and debarking—practically happened in his absence. But now that he's here, he remembers. "I noticed something that's really weird," he begins, becoming present in the moment, freed from the confines of the other side of the river, where it all takes place, high school, math, restless nights, all of it. But now Manhattan might as well be on the other side of the planet.

"I read everything I see, and it gets stored in the back of my head," he says as if he's confessing a terrible truth, like seeing monsters in his closets.

On the back of his home keys, Milo can't help but notice the words "Corbin Russwin." It's impossible to forget the slogan of Lay's potato chips: "Betcha can't eat just one." Heading out of his speaker-building class on the second floor, he'll pass a classroom where a string spins in the vortex of a blowing fan. He'll then pass a poster in the hallway, black against red letters: "RU?" He doesn't know what it means. It just sticks. Just as it stuck when he was five years old, sitting in the back of a Volvo, reading license plates. He doesn't remember where the family was heading. But he can't shake the license plates from memory. One of them: ACE 1092. "It's just weird," he says. Then he clams up. It's time to catch a water taxi back to the other side.

On Tuesday, May 30, there is no sign of Jane in school. The eighteen-year-old senior has returned to the other side, the vortex, the oblivion, the needle. Mr. Grossman knows without knowing. He notices her absence in his Great Books class today. It's impossible to miss the absence of a supernova even in a room full of superstars. After class, he wanders across the street to the Pan Latin Café, a quiet refuge that isn't so quiet today. An infant is wailing uncontrollably at a nearby table, but Mr. Grossman doesn't take notice. He too is feeling inconsolable. He's now certain to lose two of his teachers to budget cuts, possibly three. And then there's the loss of Jane.

"I have all these great, successful students, all of whom I love and adore and respect and admire, and Jane takes up so much of my mental energy because she's so lost, and I'm so scared for her," he says.

A recent memory almost makes him laugh in sadness. Jane had missed a few days of school. When she returned, she paraphrased Oscar Wilde, telling Mr. Grossman that her excuse was merely, "I can resist everything but temptation," and he immediately understood what she was trying to convey to him. "She basically said, 'This is who I am. These are the choices I've made. I'm miserable when I'm using. I'm miserable when I'm not. It's a whole lot easier to be using, and I know what this means.'"

Mr. Grossman doesn't know that Jane has been carrying around his current required reading—*The Feast of Love*—to the forbidding places she frequents, but he knows what she has told him. "If it weren't for your class, I would've stopped coming to school ages ago." But now that slender lifeline has snapped too. Their last conversation frightens him. "She seemed to be divesting herself of those kind of moorings," he says. "She doesn't care about graduating. She doesn't care about going to college. In other discussions, she's at least been ambivalent, acknowledged there was probably some good in doing those things, and she seemed to be committed to a course of action."

No more. It makes him feel helpless, leaving him grasping for a way to find Jane's salvation until he reaches the point of absurdity. "There are those people who you can hire, like, to kidnap someone in jeopardy and, like, tie them to a chair in a room in the Midwest for nine months, and, like, for a whole lot of reasons, I can't really do that, although that's really what I want to do," he says, unconsciously mimicking the fragmented sentence pattern of the teenager. "You know, guidance knows about her. Her mother knows about her." And still, he worries, one day she'll turn up dead.

Already, she's left her mark, not just on him but on her classmates in Great Books, who constantly quote the words raging from Jane about literature and life. "I can't tell you how many papers I've read that allude to something she said in class," Mr. Grossman says. ". . . She's really real, and when she has things to say, there's no veneer of, like, 'I just want to hear myself talk.' . . . People are responding to her because there's something at stake in every comment. . . . When she participates, there's genuinely something on the line. She's trying to work something essential for her survival out."

He tries not to fathom the unspeakable ways in which she supports an expensive drug habit. "Just thinking about what her life outside of school is gives me such shivers," he says, recalling a recent conversation when she confided to him that she felt compromised, that it was too late for her.

"Look, I'm just bad," she told him.

"Of course you're not bad," he said. "You're smart and you're interesting and you're literate."

"I didn't say I don't have good qualities," she said.

Even now, he marvels at the girl's undeniable spunk. "How can you not adore that?" he wonders. He knows he'll never see her kind again. From her freshman year, Jane recognized something in Mr. Grossman, he in her, and it galvanized student and teacher in a bond that not even the hammer of heroin could break in the intervening time. "That's my heartbreak for the year," he says.

Ms. Lee, the student teacher, is feeling her own heartbreak. She's running a marathon but can never reach the finish line. It's all work, no reward. And she's beginning to question her faith. "I haven't been relying and seeking God as much as I had," she says after another exhausting day at Stuyvesant. "I know I have to get out of this. It's like a slump. I have to snap out of it." It's hard, though. Just when it seemed like the teaching job at Syosset was a lock, it's slipping away.

After her promising first interview at the Long Island high school, Ms. Lee had returned to Syosset for round two, where she sat at an imposing conference table, facing a committee of six teachers, who grilled her with such intensity that she barely had time to answer one question before they aimed another one. None were softballs.

What was the last book you read?

"The Juggler—"

Where do you see yourself in five years?

"I see students coming back and thanking me for the great influence and impact that I had made—"

What course do you want to teach in the social studies department here?

"It would be one where I could contribute as an Asian American—"

Round three: Ms. Lee returned to Syosset a couple of days later to teach social studies—a "demo" lesson—having no idea that she was being given one of the most disruptive classes in the school. Administrators wanted to see how the petite, young teacher could handle what they politely refer to as a classroom management problem. What unfolded in the class shocked them: utter silence.

Ms. Lee had made a crucial strategic decision, placing name tags in front of each student so that she could call on them by name. There was no hiding. They were known. And accountable. Before the students could recover to lob a grenade of mischief at Ms. Lee, she stunned them with a battery of provocative statements about the Cold War, her prepared lesson of the day.

The McCarthy era was the Salem witch trials revisited. Agree or disagree?

What?

They didn't expect this. Where was the regurgitation of historical fact? What happened to the litany of notable dates to dutifully record?

The Truman Doctrine and the Marshall Plan were excuses to expand American imperialism. Debate.

Huh?

That wasn't a high school question. This was something more. Ms. Lee was implicitly demanding a sophisticated level of thought, higher reasoning, something akin to an answer from a *college* student.

The high school students got it. They began to make connections. It wasn't just a history lesson anymore. McCarthyism was about the here and now and the question of privacy in the war against terrorism today. When class ended, several students walked up to Ms. Lee and thanked her.

Later that day, the school called her, asking her to return the next day for an interview with the principal. Round four. Things couldn't have looked any better—until Ms. Lee gave the wrong answer. During the interview, she told the principal how she would foster the kind of relationship where students would trust her as a confidante, which she would use as a lure to engage them in class. Fair enough. But, the principal asked, how far are you willing to go to be a student's confidante? What, he burrowed ahead, would you do if a student confides that she's pregnant?

Oh no.

Ms. Lee hadn't foreseen that. She couldn't imagine it. She wasn't prepared to answer. But she did, saying she would keep the student's trust until the end, holding the girl's pregnancy confidential. It wasn't the answer the principal was looking for. The right answer, he explained, is that if a student's general welfare is in danger or compromised—and that includes a pregnancy—the teacher must report it.

"I thought I blew it right there," Ms. Lee says.

But things only got worse when she returned to meet the school system's deputy superintendent. Round five: would you, he asked, be interested in teaching middle school? It seemed like a throwaway query, a casual thought tossed out there. But in fact, it was a targeted question. The middle school had a potential opening. But to Ms. Lee, the question was horrific. She had wanted nothing more than to teach at Stuyvesant. She had done everything in her power to make that happen. But she had been forced to give up that hope. She had then doggedly worked her way to this moment to teach at another high school. And now they wanted her to teach *middle school?*

No.

She let it be known that she wasn't interested, politely saying middle school wouldn't present a teaching challenge for her, that the classroom material would be less extensive. Whether the school official didn't comprehend what she was saying or simply chose to ignore it was unclear, but he responded by telling her to give him a call if she wanted to come in to do another demo lesson for the middle school job.

She hasn't called.

The school hasn't called her either.

It's been more than a week.

The silence is suffocating.

Now all that Ms. Lee can think about are the dwindling odds at Syosset. Two teaching positions. Two hundred applications. One out of a hundred. She'd have a better chance at the roulette table. And yet, she's made an all-or-nothing bet on the Long Island high school. She has no other options. Stuyvesant is effectively out. She's pursued no other schools. When the semester ends, she'll be out of a job—a student teaching job, at that. "I should not have all my eggs in one basket," she says, "but I do."

It's like a form of paralysis. Ms. Lee just started taking her summer courses to finish her master's degree at Columbia, but she completely forgot about the existence of one of her classes, missing a major assignment. In the history class she teaches at Stuyvesant, she's so behind that she hasn't returned to students their grades on an exam that they took about a month ago. And a strange feeling has come over her: indifference. "Maybe it's because I feel there's not one thing I'm looking forward to," she says. "I don't know." What she does know is "I can't breathe right now."

> *The ghost of you is all that I have left*
> —desktop graffiti, Stuyvesant High School

CHAPTER TWENTY-FIVE

The Last Dance

IT'S A STRANGE FEELING: IT'S JUNE 8, LESS THAN A week before the last day of classes, and yet it already feels like the semester is over, summer's come and gone and the school's fast forwarded into a new year. Maybe it has to do with its being a vacation day on a Thursday, and the building's crawling with students who look young enough to be next year's incoming ninth and tenth graders. Which is what they are. In an otherwise empty building, scores of students who passed the Stuy test are milling about—smaller, shorter, and higher-pitched than the usual crowd—with some dressed for the occasion in appropriate Stuyvesant attire, announcing their lofty aspirations in Harvard T-shirts.

They call this day "Camp Stuy."

It's a chance for next year's fresh batch of students to have a look-see at what's in store for them come next September. It's also a chance for them to audition for band or chorus, or to take placement tests in math and foreign languages. And it's a chance for overprotective parents to be reduced to an emotional meltdown when they practically refuse to leave the school after dropping off their children at Stuyvesant for the one-day visit. "They're attached by crazy glue," says Harvey Blumm, Stuyvesant's empathic parent coordinator. It's even more nerve-racking for many incoming students because today they have to take the dreaded swim test. "It's always traumatic for them," Mr. Blumm says. "They don't want to show their bodies."

That includes two thirteen-year-old girls who are standing in line, holding hands in solidarity, as they wait to dive into the pool. "I'm a good swimmer, but I'm not a good bathing suit wearer," says one of the girls. "So we're all nervous about it."

Michael, the eleventh grader who's running for Student Union president, tries to distract jittery swimmers. A Big Sibling volunteer, he's playing a child's singing game with a group of eighth graders who are sitting Indian style in a circle on the floor of the school lobby, waiting their turn for the swim test. But even for an old Stuyvesant hand like Michael, the gathering of next year's incoming class is a little strange. "Some of them are really small," he says in wonder.

One of the smaller ones stands in line on the second floor, unaware that she is treading in the senior Asian bar—forbidden territory on any other day—as she moves to sit for a photo ID. The thirteen-year-old is told to smile. She does so stiffly, clutching both sides of the metal chair as if holding on for dear life on a roller coaster in a swan dive. For the eighth grader, who took a private prep course for two grueling years to prepare for the entrance exam, there's no way to describe the feeling now that she's here—now that she's one of them. But then she blurts out, "Excited, nervous."

Upstairs in his office, Mr. Jaye is anything but. The firebrand is almost subdued, a sight as rare as Halley's comet. He's supposed to be overseeing the math placement test for incoming students, but his team is in place, and the machinery is operating on automatic, so he can preoccupy himself with the perusal of an e-mail from a parent congratulating him on his new job at Bergen County Academies. Borrowing from Mark Twain, Mr. Jaye fires back in an e-mail, "Rumors of my death are greatly exaggerated." The job still isn't quite his.

School officials have requested his academic transcripts. They've taken his fingerprints. They've even concocted a title for him, the nebulous "director of academy programs." The school board hasn't voted to make it official yet. Mr. Jaye, though, isn't one to wait. Now he's composing another e-mail, this one to Bergen school officials, negotiating on behalf of a gifted math teacher from Brooklyn whom he'd like to recruit to the New Jersey school that he himself doesn't work for yet. "I want to get her a decent salary package," he says resolutely. He's trying to do the same for Mr. Siwanowicz. That's not a done deal, either. "I'm working on that too," he says. But Mr. Jaye's wheeling and dealing are interrupted when his brother, Gary, also a math teacher at Stuyvesant, pokes his head in to ask a question about where to store some things for his brother. Mr. Jaye, still engrossed in his negotiations, absently tells him to have Mr. Siwanowicz "lock them up in the sex closet."

"In the sex closet?" his brother asks casually.

"Yes," Mr. Jaye says flatly.

They could be talking about the weather, so neutral is their tone, and yet, the sex closet is called the sex closet because it's a secret place to which not even the school custodians have a key. Only Mr. Jaye and Mr. Siwanowicz possess that level of security clearance. The most tantalizing thing in there is Mr. Jaye's bike. But the off-the-cuff remark is a reminder that this domain—the math department—belongs to Mr. Jaye in a personal, private way, if only for a short while longer.

"The fourth floor is my floor," he still insists.

Perhaps the most telling sign that it won't be for long is the number of yellow stickies populating the surface of his desk: two. That's all that's left. He's down to two last remaining to-dos, little slips of square yellow paper that can be peeled away all too quickly. Mr. Jaye doesn't even seem to have much reserve of anger left for Ms. Damesek, the assistant principal of organization. "I've spent a little too much time fighting with people," he says. After thirty-four years at Stuyvesant, he's finally beginning to think it may be the right time to let go. "I've gotten stale here," he says. ". . . All I do is come in and fight Randi." And even the fighting has lost its luster. After vying for the top job at Stuyvesant—the principal's blue chair—the position doesn't seem worth it anymore. Not financially, anyway, given the better deal he's negotiated with Bergen. But it's more than that. "You know what?" he says. "I'll sit in another chair."

Mr. Polazzo is in his familiar pose in the Student Union office, gobbling his cracked-pepper-turkey sandwich, but on this Friday, June 9, it looks like his days in this chair are numbered.

Operation SPJ—Saving Polazzo's Job—did not have the intended effect.

It started off well enough. Several student leaders met with Mr. Teitel, urging the principal to reappoint Mr. Polazzo as the coordinator of student affairs, questioning the experience of the other two candidates, neither of whom has worked with students to the extent that Mr. Polazzo has. The *Spectator* newspaper ran a page-one story above the fold with the banner headline: "Student Leaders Oppose New COSA Applicants." In a subsequent editorial, the newspaper wrote, "If it ain't broke, don't fix it. Matthew Polazzo, the current coordinator of student affairs (COSA), has succeeded in championing student rights and is respected by the entire student body. Despite this, the administration has chosen to consider other candidates for a position that does not need to be replaced." And the junior class president posted news of the students' meeting with the principal on his Web site, www.stuy07.org, including their criticism that the teachers vying for Mr. Polazzo's job aren't as qualified. But the uprising backfired, enraging and embarrassing Mr. Polazzo's two rivals and prompting Mr. Teitel to rush to their defense by taking the unusual step of ordering the editors of the school newspaper to insert a letter he dashed off at the last minute to address the burgeoning controversy. Such was the urgency that Andrew, the managing editor, says he was pulled out of his classroom to stuff issues of the newspaper with the principal's letter.

"I am sorry if the fact that I asked to hear students' concerns about the candidates played some part, however inadvertent, in creating an environment in which students felt that it was valid to criticize faculty publicly," the principal wrote in his June 9 letter. "While Stuyvesant is not a democracy, it should reflect the values of a democratic society, and I believe that the free and open exchange of ideas is vital to the healthy functioning of the community. I understand, too, that some conflict is inevitable."

Now in full retreat, the junior class president offered an abject mea culpa on his Web site for reporting news of the meeting in which students criticized Mr. Polazzo's rivals. "I formally and sincerely apologize to any people that may have been offended, including the applicants for COSA," he wrote. "Please let it be known that I did not mean to slander or disparage, nor attempt to influence anyone, but simply inform my fellow juniors as I usually do." The junior class president tried to clarify, like a product disclaimer, that Mr. Polazzo had nothing to do with any of the "aforesaid." But the growing perception, at least among some administrators, was that the coordinator of student affairs had orchestrated the student rebellion to save his job because—come on—how many students would really go out of their way for any adult, let alone a high school teacher?

Now all that Mr. Polazzo can do is wait in the bunker of the Student Union for the principal to decide his fate.

"Is not Mr. Teitel going to make a decision?" asks an impatient Kristen, the Student Union president.

"Maybe you can ask him," Mr. Polazzo says delicately.

Kristen, who makes a habit of challenging the principal, bolts out of the Student Union office determined to do just that.

Another senior, Alex Schleider, stays behind to offer moral support, saying that if the principal selects one of the other candidates, the Student Union "would fall apart."

"The SU would cease to exist," Mr. Polazzo agrees placidly.

"Maybe that's what they want," Alex speculates.

"What can I do?" Mr. Polazzo wonders.

The only thing he can do is change the subject. So Mr. Polazzo turns his attention to the other campaign—for student government—which is well under way and just as uncertain as his own campaign to save his job. Mike and Marta, the favorites despite their all-white pairing, lost in an upset in the primary. "It was pretty shocking," Mr. Polazzo says. But he reckons that "racial politics" played a role in a school where a white-Asian pairing presents a more effective demographic one-two punch. Indeed, the white junior who made it through to the general election as a presidential candidate did have an Asian vice presidential candidate on her ticket, as did the other slate, which also made it to the general election. But before Mr. Polazzo can proffer his latest election prognostication, Kristen, the lame-duck Student

Union president, barges back into his office to report on her just-ended tête-à-tête with the principal.

"He's a very weird man," Kristen begins, then recounts the conversation: She asked to know the choice for coordinator of student affairs before she graduates in two weeks. Mr. Teitel told her that he didn't want to lie to her. So don't, she retorted. Then the principal promised to make a decision by the end of June—after which he steered the conversation to the prom, which is tomorrow night, saying how Kristen will always remember it and how he doesn't expect students today to listen to music from the 1950s. At this point in the tale, Mr. Polazzo can't resist interjecting, "He's big into 'Hey Ya!'" The students instantly get the joke. It's funny to picture Mr. Teitel, a straitlaced man of nearly sixty, crooning to the hip-hop single from OutKast.

It's hard to imagine, but four intense, grinding, insane, mordant, ridiculous, laughable, sublime, pressurized years of high school culminate here, on Saturday, June 10, at the historic Waldorf-Astoria, one of the world's grand hotels, the luxurious Park Avenue site of Stuyvesant's prom.

"It's so gorgeous, oh my God," marvels senior Siyu "Daisy" Duan, entering the first-floor reception, gazing wide-eyed at the vaulted gilded ceiling, the massive stone pillars, the antique clock peaked with a gold replica of the Statue of Liberty. But Daisy could just as well be gawking at herself and her fellow seniors, boys looking dashing, like James Bond in tuxedos, girls done up like movie stars in flowing gowns of every hue, from midnight blue to blood red. In the muted lighting, playing tricks on the eye, they all look like grown-ups. Perhaps tonight they are.

Upstairs, in the three-tiered Grand Ball Room, Senior Class Adviser James Lonardo, a faculty member, is keeping close watch over final preparations as tuxedoed waiters lay down flatware on numbered tables. Mr. Lonardo missed his own prom but he's been to sixteen since coming to Stuyvesant. He knows the drill. There will be 662 kids tonight. "There'll be a lot of energy out there," he says knowingly, if apprehensively.

Momentum builds in the next-door East Foyer, where small clusters of students begin to coalesce, like cloud formations, nibbling on vegetable dip and small conversation. NYU-bound Nameeta Kamath sits stiffly at a corner table with friends, as if she doesn't want to upset her beautiful raven updo. And for good reason. It took three hours to assemble it at the salon this morning. "My mom forbid me from moving," she says, apparently still heeding the edict. "She refused to let me pick up even a single thing." After spending most of the day confined to her room, Nameeta escaped in a white Lincoln Town Car with her friends, the first limo ride of her life. A glorious thirty-five minutes, too short. No New York traffic.

Of all the days.

Mr. Teitel cleans up well in a white tuxedo as he stands at the threshold of the Grand Ball Room, trying in vain to make sense of the throbbing drumbeat pounding from the giant stereo speakers. Amid a kaleidoscope of flashing lights, seniors begin to hit the parquet dance floor, gyrating in a synchronized coolness that is as mysterious and baroque to the principal as a distant African tribal ritual.

"I don't understand this music at all," he says, grimacing.

For Mr. Teitel, though, the rest of the evening is old hat. Seniors may laugh. Seniors may cry. Seniors may make out. But one thing is for sure. This year, seniors will not streak naked across the ballroom. One boy did that several years ago, eluding capture because Mr. Teitel was seated at a table on the ballroom's first level, where it was impossible for the principal to track the boy's movements as he melted anonymously into the crowd of seniors. Not a chance now. Mr. Teitel has moved his table to the center of the second-level balcony, the kind of spot where kings might hold court at a fancy shindig like this, but which for the principal only serves to give him a bird's-eye view of potential mischief below on the dance floor.

"I'm here to supervise," he says resolutely.

If Mr. Teitel takes joy in the prom, it stems from the secret knowledge that he carries—the seniors think they know it all—that at 11:30 p.m., waiters will roll out an elaborate ice cream bar. Or maybe the principal is just looking forward to the ice cream himself.

Deke, for his part, isn't sure what to look forward to. The senior, who is going to Cornell after falling short of Harvard, looks as debonair in evening attire as Cary Grant. But he appears afflicted with a general malaise as he sits with his girlfriend on a quiet bench in the foyer just beyond the growing madness of the ballroom. The prom feels to him like his tenth-year high school reunion, only ten years earlier. People are friendlier than they are in school, even if you don't know them. Boys and girls have already taken a smoke break on the curb outside the Waldorf, shedding the artifice of hats and high heels in a moment of unvarnished friendship built over four long years of shared experience. "It's the end of high school," Deke says, chalking the feeling up to sentimentality. "So we're letting it all go anyway." Deke, though, isn't quite ready to let go. He vows to report to gym first thing Monday morning, lest he fail that class and jeopardize his future at Cornell.

"I will," he promises, "be in gym on time."

It's 9:33 p.m., and on the dance floor, boys start to lose their tuxedo straitjackets, while girls escape their stiletto prisons, the better to collide against each other like go-carts at an amusement park, unpracticed, wildly free. In the hallway, friends hug as if they haven't seen each other in ages, like long-lost relatives reuniting at the airport.

"Remember, this is only the beginning!" the DJ bellows.

For Katie, the senior who spurned the Ivies in favor of Haverford, it certainly doesn't seem like high school's over. As she stands at the perimeter of the darkened dance floor, at the edge of an endless ocean, taking it all in—the romantic melody of Barry White and the beauty of the sparkling people and the glorious place—she can't help but be transported back to the stark reality of Stuyvesant and next week's math test. "I don't know that it's hit me, that it's the end yet," she says wistfully. "When I'm on the dance floor, it's another dance."

Not for Jane. The senior, abdicating to her addiction, never showed.

Andrew, the managing editor of the school paper, did. The date of a senior, Andrew came prepared for the prom, not with the typical paraphernalia, a flask of whiskey, but with a heavy dose of facts. "I brought my history textbook," says the junior, upholding the Stuyvesant tradition of books before bacchanalia. He has an advanced placement exam in U.S. history on Monday, and between now and then, he plans to squeeze in a little studying while staying up as part of an extended prom party. "If I have less sleep," he says, "I function better the next day." He calls the phenomenon "hyperdrive."

By 12:37 a.m., the evening is winding down. A strange quietude overcomes the ballroom, giving it a mood of fin de siècle. The dance floor thins out. Bodies slump languidly at linen tables where the ruins of ice cream sundaes topple, reminiscent of the remnants of a lost civilization. At 1:04 a.m., the lights come up, and the magic dissipates, as for Cinderella after midnight, in the bright glare of smudged mascara, torn stockings, and the irresolute look of teenagers on their way into the night and into the rest of their lives. Mr. Teitel leans over the balcony railing, alone, scanning these final snapshots of another senior class on their way out the door. This year, to his great relief, there are no naked streakers.

On Monday, June 12, students make their way to the ballot box in what turns into a landslide victory in the election for the proverbial oval office of the Student Union. The white-Asian pairing prevails again. But the real drama unfolds in the election for senior class president, usually an afterthought. The election board discovers that fifty-five forged votes were stuffed in the ballot box. It turns out, someone had photocopied an authentic ballot and stamped on it BOE APPROVED, the board of election's imprimatur. But the fake contained a slight flaw in the first *P* in APPROVED. And if that wasn't a dead giveaway, the forged ballots were stuck together like a stack of pancakes. Fifty-two of the fake ballots cast votes for a candidate who lost by a wide margin. The other three forged ballots went for the winning candidate, who didn't need them to carry the day. The election skulduggery remains an unguarded secret lost in the vapor trail of the recently departed prom. Classes are almost over. A stretch of finals is about to begin. Mr. Polazzo, the coordinator of student affairs, shrugs off the forgeries. "The way I see it," he says, "it's like a hacker attack. We improve our defenses." Besides, the real scandal circulating through school is that in the wee hours of an after-prom party, an inebriated student had the audacity to vomit in the sink at the home of a friend's relative, a movie star of an earlier generation, Kathleen Turner.

> *Forever My Skool*
>
> —desktop graffiti, Stuyvesant High School

CHAPTER TWENTY-SIX

The Final Days

MONDAY, JUNE 12, THE SECOND-TO-LAST DAY OF classes, is almost over as the clock nears the end of tenth period in room 840, sophomore English, where Mariya sits by the teacher's desk, her right hand holding up her forehead in a pose of complete catatonia or undiluted concentration, such is her perfect equipoise. When the bell rings, Mariya heaves her blue backpack over her shoulders and approaches the teacher, girding herself for the devastating news about to befall her, that she earned a mere 90 on her last test. "I'm scared because my mother's going to freak out," she says, heading out the door, where the excuse is already forming. "I'll tell her the story that goes along with it," she says, "that everyone else did bad, et cetera." But Mariya's heart isn't in the excuse. She isn't selling it with verve. She doesn't really care. What she really cares about is four floors down, faithfully waiting for her by her locker, Jarek.

At six foot five, he towers over Mariya, looking like he just outgrew, Jack-and-the-Beanstalk style, the long denim shorts he's wearing. The front of his black T-shirt announces, GAME OVER. Most of his wardrobe, he says, is either black or blue, matching Mariya's getup gothic for gothic, including her own black T-shirt today, which portrays an abstract devil's skull.

Ah, young love.

They head down the escalator, which isn't working, as usual, while holding hands. Jarek wants to walk to nearby Chinatown. Mariya doesn't. So they resolve their differences the only way mature teenagers can: in a game of rock, paper, scissors. Jarek wins. Chinatown, it is. At the onset, Jarek bemoans the loss of his beloved Poland in the World Cup. It must be a terrible blow because Mariya, now all of sixteen, cups his broad face in her hands and gently kisses his cheek. "Don't worry," she coos. They've been dating for a month and six days but have the easy playfulness of lovers who've known each other for years. Already, they have their favorite places, like the little hole in the wall in Chinatown where Jarek likes to buy Mariya steaming hot sixty-cent pork buns. That's where they're heading now. Along the way, as they move up Worth Street, the conversation turns to their differences. "She studies too much," Jarek says. "I study too little."

Mariya, though, protests, as if studying is a badge of dishonor. "I don't study at all," she says. "I don't remember the last time I did my home-work." Then she immediately corrects herself. "Actually, last night," she says sheepishly, "I did my homework."

A left on Mulberry Street, and they're now in another world, where ancient Asian women hunch on stools on the sidewalk amid a series of fishmongers speaking in foreign tongues. Jarek and Mariya plunge into a little shop and order their pork buns, then make their way to a nearby park, where a couple of weeks ago they cut class and lay out on a bench during a downpour.

"I kind of feel like it's over," Jarek says of school, even though he still faces a few statewide exams.

"You've felt like it's over for a *month*," Mariya says.

"Sun's shining," Jarek says, offering a sunny smile by way of explana-tion.

The sun's been shining on Jarek since he began dating Mariya, which coincidentally started at about the same time that he felt school had effectively ended. Recently, when he met Mr. Jaye, the ubiquitous math chairman asked Jarek what was new. Mr. Jaye intended the question to elicit an answer that he could incorporate in a college report on Jarek's behalf, but the student could think of only one thing noteworthy in his life.

"Well," Jarek said, "I got a new girlfriend."

Mr. Jaye wasn't impressed. "I don't think colleges are interested in your sex life," he responded.

To Jarek and Mariya, school seems a fast-receding fact, about to be replaced by the coming summer, when he'll be traveling to a small village in Poland to train to be a camp counselor, while Mariya will be off to the Poconos resort area in search of a part-time job. He promises to e-mail her once a day and, being an old-fashioned romantic, to send a handwritten letter once a week too. She can't wait for the handwritten notes. It's so quaint in a twentieth-century way—and so authentic. But there is still time to enjoy before the note writing. They are holding hands as they rise, heading for the subway station. They haven't let go since leaving school nearly an hour ago. Making their way to the end of the platform, they hop on the local Q train. He can't take his eyes off her. "What?" she wants to know, blushing. "Don't look at me like that." But he says, unabashed, "I'm just looking." She lets him. It can't be helped. This is what happens. When the train jolts to a stop at Avenue J in Brooklyn, they step off together, walking against the gust of the train suddenly barreling away, the last bell at Stuyvesant long forgotten; they're still holding hands.

The last bell of the last period of the last day of class rings at 3:32 on Tuesday, June 13, signaling the end of an impossibly long semester, now a montage sequence of brutal nights of studying, a conveyor belt of tests, homework, expectations, pressure, and performance, and yet all that Romeo can muster the energy to do in this final moment is to rise from his desk chair and approach his notoriously tough history teacher. "Thank you a lot, Mr. Sandler," Romeo says. "I learned a lot."

Romeo reaches out to shake his hand, an offering that seems to catch the teacher off guard, so unusual is the little gesture of appreciation. The ambitious junior doesn't have to curry favor. His grade will be astronomically high. That, they both know. "There's not many kids like him,"

Mr. Sandler says, when Romeo isn't around to hear the compliment. At the moment, though, Mr. Sandler doesn't let on. Stoically, he recovers in time to shake Romeo's hand, the teacher's admiration left unsaid. Romeo heads out of room 339, maintaining his grim game face.

"I'm still in work mode," he explains.

The only thing that stops Romeo is the frenzied sound of hip-hop booming by the white senior bar, where, as if by spontaneous combustion, several girls are breaking out in a wild celebration of the semester's end, dancing, hugging, banging lockers, taking digital pictures. A circle of students forms around the revelers, while Romeo looks on, mesmerized but apart from the moment. He doesn't stay for long, moving toward the second-floor bridge exit when he's intercepted by Xevion, his lunchtime companion, his conscience. They lock arms around each other's shoulders and share a quick greeting; it seems like it's been ages since they last spoke, but it doesn't last. Romeo peels off, as if in a hurry to catch a cab, though he doesn't have anywhere particular to go. It could just be that he's tired. Last night, he managed only four hours of sleep, and with two statewide tests, in biology and U.S. history, and one final, in differential equations, on the immediate horizon, he knows there are more sleepless nights to come.

"I just tell myself I've done it before, I can do it again," he says.

For now, though, Romeo follows the strong undertow of students surging toward the riverside park behind school. When he arrives at the edge of the expansive lawn, he approaches no one, choosing instead to pick up his cell phone—school contraband if discovered. He calls his father in Harlem, his PR man who sends football tapes to Harvard recruiters, the voice in Romeo's head, telling him that there's no *can't*, only *how*, who wants his son to pay tribute to his black forefathers, the man whom Romeo feels he hardly sees anymore. Before long, his father will be moving to Boston. Romeo hopes to be heading up there soon too. Harvard. It's almost Father's Day. Romeo already bought him a teddy bear. He'll be buying him cologne too. The phone rings. No answer.

That leaves Romeo to contemplate the scene unfolding before him, boys and girls recklessly thumping a soccer ball, fecklessly flinging a Frisbee, carefree, unbound. "I should be more of a kid," he observes ruefully, as if it's too late for him. "I feel like I'm too serious." He spots a lanky blond boy on the playing field. They used to be the best of friends in eighth grade. They used to play chess. And now. That boy is a Hacky Sack–playing ladies' man. Romeo chose a different path. Which is okay. Romeo isn't big on best friends at the moment. Friends are fine, he notes, "as long as it's at a distance." And that distance is growing now that he's on the cusp of becoming, finally, a senior. "There's going to be no one to look up to," he says. "It's going to be strange." Students will be looking up to him. But then, they already do that. So do the adults. Romeo is the future, and he feels the burden of that responsibility. Which is why he's still pursuing his Intel science project at NYU. He isn't succeeding just for himself, his mother, or his father. There's a great, big world needing rescuing out there, and he calculates it doesn't need another writer, even if he's a gifted writer, and that's why he says his calling lies elsewhere. "There are too many humanities people. We need more scientists. I feel like I'd be betraying it if I leave it alone."

The phone rings. On the other end of the line comes the familiar sound of a father's reminder, a scolding. Romeo, the dutiful son, listens, promises not to do something, then mumbles, "Love you, bye." It's time now. Romeo lies down alone in the grass in this park behind this school on this glorious afternoon, under a pastel blue sky and a receding sun, and closes his eyes, if only for the briefest of moments, to rest.

Rest is the last thing on Milo's mind as he steps out of his apartment building on a gusty Thursday, June 15, heading for the last time this year to Stuyvesant, armed with a power bar, a calculator, three sharpened pencils, and a ruler—weapons of math destruction contained in a black backpack that reads PS 234 TRIBECA, now just a relic of his former fifth-grade life. The little man-child is on his way to take a statewide math final in algebra, geometry, and trigonometry intended for students who are generally older by about 50 percent, mathematically speaking. "There's nothing hard about the test," he notes. "You just have to focus."

Milo isn't sweating that today's test is weighted as *two* tests toward his final grade in his trig class. He's already done the math. Worst-case scenario, he bogeys the test with an 80, which would be, like, a total disgrace, not to mention a major improbability. But even with that unbearable eventuality, Milo calculates he'd still finish with a respectable 90 in the high school class. The grade, though, doesn't really mean anything. It doesn't count toward a real report card. It's just a number. Less than that. It's a game. Milo doesn't compile a high school transcript yet. He's not officially enrolled. Heck, he's years from puberty. But the grade is a symbolic representation of achievement, of a semester of homework, of hard work. Even more, if he aces the test, he figures it may represent something more tangible. "I hope my Dad gives me a pizza party," he says.

For Milo, it all happened so fast, the withdrawal from fifth grade, the homeschooling, the last semester at Stuyvesant. It's hard to believe the term is over. He's pretty sure he learned a lot about math. He thinks he may have grown an inch, topping out at about four and a half feet. But what he learned about high school, he says, "I don't know." There's little time to contemplate that conundrum now. The future is fast approaching, including this summer, when he plans to read about an eighteenth-century mathematical hero in *Euler: The Master of Us All*. Milo already has next semester mapped out at Stuyvesant, a course load probably including honors precalculus, math team, math research, advanced placement computer science, history, and a double period of chemistry.

Piece of cake. By then, he'll be the ripe old age of eleven.

But now, Milo's ten, and he has a pizza party to win. He enters Stuyvesant, where the escalator transports him to the fourth floor and a scene of anxious teenagers cramming last-minute for the test. Milo swiftly cuts through the crowd, like a child in a forest of towering redwoods, making his way to the front, where the hall proctor, a chiseled gym teacher wise to the ways of crowd control, stands at the mouth of the corridor, blocking the way until it's time. Marveling at the restive group, the gym teacher finally puts the students out of their misery, giving the word, a simple "Okay." With that, the test takers are unleashed, flooding into classrooms, scrambling to take position for the statewide math exam. Milo, a Zen master in the art of test taking, saunters into room 431 and calmly slips into a seat, front row center, where he removes his three pencils and calculator and neatly lines them up on his desk. The test starts promptly at 12:30 p.m. They have until 4 p.m.

to finish. The earliest they can leave is 2:30. At precisely 2:31, Milo moves to leave, making him the first to finish. He was done at 2:05 but bided his time, munching on his energy bar. Somehow, you get the feeling that if Milo can solve the riddles of algebra, geometry, and trigonometry with such ease, it's just a matter of time before the ten-year-old figures out this whole high school thing too. After all, it's just the beginning for Milo. On his way out of the exam, the little boy whispers, "It was really easy."

On Monday, June 26, seniors gather around the gushing fountain of the grand courtyard of Lincoln Center, site of world-class ballet, the genius of Mozart, and, in just a few moments, the end of the beginning of their lives.

It's the only place that the city would crown the jewel of its school system, the best digs in Manhattan, an epic monument to civilization, like the Roman Colosseum. And yet the mood is strangely subdued as seniors wait for their big moment, idling awkwardly, posing stiffly for pictures, and reluctantly embracing friends under a gray sky threatening a downpour. It's as if the end of high school is unfathomable. The tests are over, the all-nighters finished, the race to college done. Now what? A tuxedoed man finally offers purpose, waving them inside Lincoln Center's Avery Fisher Hall. "Let's go, graduates."

What lies beyond is almost an archetype, so familiar is the commencement tableau: A high school music teacher swings his arms like a metronome, conducting a student orchestra that is something less than an oiled machine, behind which hangs a banner in blue with red lettering: STUYVESANT HIGH SCHOOL. The principal, garbed in a black robe like a priest, takes the podium. "Ladies and gentlemen, good morning and welcome," Mr. Teitel begins. "Please rise and allow me to introduce you to Stuyvesant's spectacular class of 2006." Cheers erupt from the cavernous hall—except nothing follows. There is no class of 2006, spectacular or otherwise. Parents crane their necks, camcorders rolling, orchestra booming bombastically, all waiting for the star attraction, the graduates, to march down the aisles, but they are nowhere to be seen. Mr. Teitel nods his head with a rueful smile—this feels more like a high-school production than *La Traviata* at Lincoln Center—and gestures to his wristwatch, which has no effect. The principal stands alone on one of the world's great stages, performing nothing so much as a sheepish stance for about three full minutes before thousands of onlookers. He punctuates the performance snafu with histrionics more suitable for the theater of the absurd: a shrug, palms up. But then it happens: seniors begin to pour down the right aisle, then the left, an army draped in blue satin gowns, a processional that, from the balconies above, appears as identical square hats filling row after row of the orchestra seats to Verdi's "Triumphal March" from *Aida*.

Back on track, the principal reads from a set of notes, barely looking up, though a similar script echoes in high school graduation ceremonies in gymnasiums and auditoriums throughout the land. "Once again, as often in our history, the hope for mankind lies in our youth," Mr. Teitel intones, like Moses handing down the tablets to the masses, adding, "We at Stuyvesant are confident that you have been prepared to meet the challenge of keeping the United States ahead of the pack."

Apparently, Conan O'Brien didn't get the memo. The late-night television comic takes the podium as the keynote speaker—again, only the best for a gold-plated graduation—dismissing all semblance of gravity. "Just last year," he says, "I was offered fifty thousand dollars to speak at a graduation, but I said, 'You go to hell, Bronx Science.'" It's a smart opening strategy, launching right into a joke at the expense of Stuyvesant's rival to win over the partisan crowd, which roars in approval. "Then they said sixty thousand, and I took it, but I never showed up." Another roar. "Those guys are idiots." Referring to his own alma mater, Harvard, he informs the Stuyvesant students, "I'm a pompous, self-important jackass," and he's now completely won them over. Recalling his graduation from Brookline High, a public school outside Boston, he says, "Just like you, I sat in a large auditorium, daydreaming about experiences yet to come—college, my first job, puberty." Another eruption from the crowd. His father "put his hand on my shoulder, looked me right in the eye, and said, 'I'm not your father.' Then he wrapped me in his strong Samoan arms and said, 'Don't ever call me.'" It's a perfect salve for four painful, harrowing years of high school: the forgetfulness of laughter. The comedian is just loosening up.

"Your school is named after Peter Stuyvesant, head of the Dutch West Indian trading company, which explains, by the way, why your teachers are still paid in grain and salt." Now he's won over the adults too. "In 1950," he continues with his history lesson, "students at Stuyvesant tried to build a particle accelerator. By way of comparison, that's the same year my public high school discovered fire." By now, the students are doubled over. "In 1969," he moves on, "girls were admitted to Stuyvesant for the first time. This started a new trend among the boys called showering."

More jokes ensue, increasingly sophomoric, which is just the way the students want it, until Conan O'Brien has them just where he wants them—circling back to an unexpected moment of seriousness so he can impart a bit of advice from the heart. "I did a lot of things in high school not because I enjoyed them but because I thought they'd look good on an application, if you know what I'm talking about." They do. But on a lark in college, he wrote a piece for the *Harvard Lampoon*, the school's humor magazine, and he found joy. "I honestly didn't care where it took me, or what it paid." When he graduated from Harvard, he says, "I told my parents, thanks for the amazing Ivy League education, now I want to be a comedian." The laughter resumes. "Later, in the emergency room, after they woke up, they said they were fine with my decision, and I was on my way." And then the final punch line: "Don't get me wrong. I've worked extremely hard at being an ass, and yes, I make some sweet, sweet coin."

It might have been enough to end graduation right there, letting the seniors float off on a heliumlike high. But reality intrudes, and the ceremony is immediately grounded by a jarring pivot, when the schools chancellor takes center stage and presents symbolic diplomas to the relatives of April and Kevin, the two students who perished in the car accident. Around this time, the principal conveys more somber news, whispering on stage to Mr. Polazzo that he will not be reappointed coordinator of student affairs. True to his word, Mr. Teitel made a decision before the end of June, but he picked a time to deliver it when those who cared the most, the seniors at graduation, would care the least. The moment passes as anonymously as a shot fired in the dark, and the only one who feels its penetration is the target, Mr. Polazzo, who can do nothing but wince. "I lose all my superpowers," he says. Not that the decision was easy on Mr. Teitel. The principal has lost about ten pounds in the past two weeks, unable to sleep or eat as his mind constantly turns over the pressing issues in front of him, whether it's the fate of the coordinator of student affairs, budget cuts, or staff evaluations. "I sleep when I'm absolutely tired," he says at another time in the quiet of his office, "but as soon as I'm not, I wake up because there's too many things on my mind, you know, that I'm constantly thinking about." At least he hasn't had to deal with the cell phone ban. The school system has yet to install the metal detectors, sparing him that headache. Still, the prospect of retirement tugs at him. It's not long off. About five years ago, Mr. Teitel sat for a head shot photo, preparing for the day when his picture would be framed, perhaps in haste, along with the other dozen principals who came before him. In that snapshot, he possessed a full head of brown hair. Now it's streaked gray.

On this day, though, the strain doesn't show. One by one, seniors soberly step on stage to shake hands with the principal and accept their diplomas in this final rite of high school passage. There they go: Jamie and Olga and Barbara and Elizabeth and Reyna and Amanda and Namita and Deke and Becky and Daisy and Nathan and Sophia and Naomi and Molly and Jonathan and Erica and Rachel and Kristen and Elisa and all the rest. One name isn't called. Jane. She isn't here. She didn't graduate. The recovering drug addict didn't recover.

The following day, Ms. Lee, the student teacher, shuffles down the stairs after class at Columbia, a step closer to her own graduation, a step further away from Stuyvesant, the school already becoming a fond memory growing ever more distant. On her last day teaching there, several of her students lingered by her desk to present going-away gifts to her—a scented candle, a bag of chocolate truffles, a collection of unspoken admiration. When she returned to Stuyvesant one last time, the end came almost imperceptibly in the quotidian task of submitting grades in her history and Korean classes. The building was empty, except for a residue of teachers loitering in the fourth-floor faculty lounge. Ms. Lee said her good-byes. That was all. She had nothing to do. She had nothing to take, no belongings, not even a desk to call her own. But that's okay. Ms. Lee got the call.

The Syosset superintendent asked Ms. Lee to come in. The meeting took less time than the wait outside her office before the meeting, all of about five minutes. The superintendent asked how Ms. Lee was doing, how her classes were going at Columbia. And then she asked if Ms. Lee wanted to teach history at Syosset High School. The moment, so long in coming, so hard to come by, so dearly coveted, seemed surreal. Ms. Lee may have said thank you but can't be sure. All she is certain of is that, afterward, she picked up her cell phone right away and called her father.

"I got the job," she said, still seeking approval from the man who once told her she had failed part of her life when she was rejected by the Ivy League. She will have to wait for her father's approval yet. He was thrilled about her new job but gave all credit to God, not to his daughter. How else could he explain that such a good school as Syosset would hire a mere student teacher when there were so many more qualified candidates? Nor was Ms. Lee's mother's reaction terribly satisfying as she noted that being a high school teacher wasn't enough. Her daughter, she said, should now aspire to something greater, to become a *college professor*. It turns out, Ms. Lee isn't entirely satisfied herself. "I am entering a realm where I can be acknowledged and I can be part of that greater vision of an American Dream," she says. "But I can't say I've achieved it yet, not quite yet." Her parents have taught her well, perhaps all too well.

Mr. Jaye isn't satisfied either. That's because it's Thursday, June 29, and the fourth floor of Stuyvesant no longer belongs to him. The math chairman isn't the math chairman anymore, a fact underscored by the number of yellow stickies left on his desk: none. A multitude of cardboard boxes covers his office and spills out into the hallway, which is deathly still, bereft of the clamor of shrill student voices gone until next semester. How do you pack thirty-four years of history?

Quietly. A fan blows hot air from an open window, rustling the last remaining papers on his desk, accompanied by the muffled sound of a radio on low. Mr. Jaye rifles through folders, tosses out some detritus, files other stuff in cabinets in what feels like a pantomime act because it can't possibly be happening, because it doesn't seem right, what with Mr. Jaye not in a crisp button-down and tie but in a casual, flaming red shirt, opened two buttons at the collar, exposing a thick gold chain. And yet it's happening. It's happened. He still hasn't signed a contract with the New Jersey school, but it's all but a certainty. Yesterday he went for a physical and, more to the point, Mr. Teitel announced at a staff meeting that Mr. Jaye was retiring, making it official. And yet, it didn't feel right. After making the cursory announcement, the principal moved on, making Mr. Jaye feel as if his retirement were little more than a signpost noted and passed on the highway to other end-of-semester matters. "I never got a chance to stand up and thank all the people I worked with," Mr. Jaye says. "And you know what? I'm an interesting character in this building in that there's a lot of people who hate me, and they should, and there's a lot of people who love me, and they should." Earlier today, though, Mr. Jaye got in a last word, interjecting at the principal's kitchen cabinet meeting, fighting to make sure his replacement as math chairman is assured a seat at these private gatherings. The assistant principal for social studies rose to thank Mr. Jaye for always finding creative ways to solve any problem, which was a polite way of applauding him for being a productive troublemaker. That meant a lot to Mr. Jaye.

Now, surrounded by a cascade of lifted memories, like overturned rocks, he picks up a random slip of paper on his desk. Ah, yes. A student's math exam. Mr. Jaye immediately recalls the details. The girl had mis-bubbled her score sheet, giving answers to the wrong questions. When she received a low score, her incensed mother, a prominent New York journalist, called Mr. Jaye, threatening to use her considerable clout unless they regraded her child's test to accurately reflect her performance. Mr. Jaye didn't begrudge her. Here was a mother fighting for her child. It's what *he* does. "When you have kids, you've got to advocate for your kid," he says. But he wasn't sure what to do. That is, until he took the problem to another administrator, who simply told him to regrade the test; after all, it wasn't that the girl didn't know the answers to the test. She had just lost her way on the bubble sheet. With that, Mr. Jaye tosses the once-controversial exam into the classroom paper recycling bin.

"This is such a weird place," he says.

Mr. Jaye resumes packing, stacking boxes on a trolley. Inside them: Billy Joel's *The Nylon Curtain* CD; a pair of suede work gloves; *Higher Arithmetic*, an 1848 book preserved in a plastic sandwich bag. And he begins to free-associate, his mind leaping from his oldest daughter's visit today to his tutoring business, which helps to pay for her education at Yale, to the scolding from a wealthy New Yorker who once told him he should be ashamed of himself for letting his family down by forgoing what would have come naturally to him—a lucrative career on Wall Street—given his uncanny penchant for numbers and negotiations. Why, the wealthy woman asked, do you teach? "Because," he said, "I love it, and I'm good at it."

But now Mr. Jaye is worried. Not about himself but about Mr. Siwanowicz, who's joining him at the school in New Jersey next semester. Mr. Siwanowicz recently fell into a deep funk when he lost out on an application for an apartment that he intended to rent with his girlfriend. The problem: he doesn't have a credit card. Mr. Jaye told him to get one. Mr. Siwanowicz refused on principle, much as he had refused to take a college exam, saying he would not borrow from anyone. Mr. Jaye explained that he didn't need a credit card to borrow money; he needed it to obtain a rental. "You have to enter society." Mr. Jaye tried to reason with him. What else can he do?

Mr. Zamansky, the computer science coordinator, drops by. They won't be taking early-morning bike rides up to Harlem anymore. Mr. Zamansky refrains from saying that. Perhaps it's too sentimental. Instead, he looks in wonder at the packing in progress, taking note of the clutch of Stuyvesant math trophies collecting dust on top of a set of cabinets.

"You going to take all your trophies?" he asks.

Mr. Jaye wasn't planning to. "Yeah," he says.

Mr. Jaye ties a box closed. "It's amazing," he says. "I can't believe I'm doing this."

A custodial worker enters his office to empty a garbage bin. She can't believe Mr. Jaye is doing this, either. "You'll be back," she says, embracing him. "You'll miss us."

Moments later, Mr. Grossman pays a visit. Mr. Jaye continues to pack, removing tacks from a cabinet behind his desk. There isn't much to say that hasn't already been said. Mr. Grossman doesn't mention Jane, his heartbreak. He doesn't mention that she had recently left three voice mail messages for him at his office, that she said she hadn't meant to call him but proceeded to recite some of her writings into the recording. He doesn't mention that in her final voice mail, she read from a suicide note, and how he tried to call her but didn't get through, or how he saw her later in school, wearing a kimono and crying to him that she was scared, or how he told her to come back the next day to help him with some paperwork, but she didn't.

What Mr. Grossman says is "I see you're hard at work clearing your office."

Mr. Jaye doesn't mention his own heartbreak, that he's leaving behind a school he never wanted to leave. He doesn't mention how he worries about the department he built, the people whom he hired. He doesn't mention that he has no idea how he's going to pack thirty-four years of his life.

What Mr. Jaye says is this, that even with his departure, the end of an era at Stuyvesant, there's at least one thing about this school he will never worry about. "The kids," he says, "will remain great."

Epilogue: Back to the Future

Gone is the North Face backpack. Taking its place is the battered leather briefcase, which sat in a closet, awaiting my return to the *Washington Post* after studying that oddest of cultures, high school life, in that strangest of places, Stuyvesant High School. Lugging the briefcase to the office, leaning against the wind of a wintry day, I refuse to carry it by the handles. Not cool. Instead, I sling the briefcase strap over my shoulder, an unspoken nod to the cavalier attitude of the teenage world from which I have just emerged. Instantly, I think of a fourteen-year-old freshman who would have approved of the subtle gesture. *Mad*, she might have said with a goofy but golden smile that would have broken my heart. The stone-faced adults take no notice of my minor rebellion. Why should they? I look like one of them. No more clumpy, black combat boots, just civilized lace-up cordovan shoes. And dry-cleaned tailored slacks have replaced those trusty pockmarked jeans, which I've retired to a lower drawer of the dresser, the Florida of my wardrobe, brought out only on the occasional day off when it doesn't matter.

There's a stab of regret. My days back in high school more than two decades after my own graduation from Stuyvesant were a kind of Indian summer, a kaleidoscope of yearnings, aspirations, and hopes that recede in the ramble of time. So I pay the bills. I rake the leaves. And I miss the kids, the whole messy lot of them at Stuyvesant. How they didn't show up when we had an appointment. How I learned their class bell schedules so I knew where to intercept them in the hallway. How they wanted to make the world a better place, no matter how corny that sounds, because it was true and sincere and right.

They are gone, remnants in my mind, but Stuyvesant remains stubbornly immutable. The place is a fierce anachronism whose ideal dates back to a Jeffersonian notion. The founding father believed in the idea of making education available to every citizen as a way to ward off tyranny, but he also believed in fostering an aristocracy of talent. The great irony is that when Stuyvesant was founded a century ago, it wasn't intended to be a selective public school, merely a manual training school for boys, a reflection of the emerging industrialization then. As Mr. Mathews, the education expert, says of the introduction of the entrance exam, "Educators decided you could create an absolutely magic atmosphere if you bring together all the best kids."

That, however, isn't the prevailing sentiment today. Now, he says, "It goes against the mainstream movement that you should not segregate the great brains." Dr. Loveless, another education authority, describes the Stuyvesant mission bluntly: "It's politically incorrect and it's completely fallen out of favor."

The argument against schools like Stuyvesant is the same argument that civic activists have made in decades past, that it's an elitist institution, a leading objection being that such public exam schools deprive regular schools and regular students of a milieu in which academically driven students can serve as a spark to raise the collective performance of an entire school.

"The greatest force in American high schools is peer pressure," Mr. Mathews says. "If you don't have peers who are very academically oriented, if you cut back on that, you have fewer peers who admire these kids, and it reduces the amount of academic interest in the school. . . . Then it affects all the other students in the school."

Which brings educators and policy makers to today's overarching problem: "Based on students' performance, American education is generally flat, where it has been for the last thirty, thirty-five years in terms of [student] test results, graduation rates," says Chester E. Finn Jr., president of the Washington, D.C.–based Thomas B. Fordham Foundation, which supports research in education reform.

The debate in education circles has turned to the paucity of academic improvement, particularly among students in secondary schools. "Only one in three high school freshmen graduate on time with the academic preparation necessary to succeed in college," writes Craig D. Jerald in *A Report on the High School Reform Movement* for Education Sector, an education think tank in Washington, D.C. He notes that "today's 17-year-olds score no higher in reading and math than did teenagers in the early 1970s."

Says Mr. Toch, Education Sector's cofounder and codirector, "At the high school level, we haven't done much."

Educators and policy makers ascribe a dizzying array of causes to the intransigent problem: that teachers don't expect enough of students. That schools create a disruptive learning environment. That parents don't take their children's education seriously enough. That schools are too big and impersonal and bureaucratic. That schools are too small and balkanized and disorganized. That education standards are higher in Asia and Europe. That teachers are better trained in foreign nations. That we watch too much television. That we don't read enough. That we are a profligate, decadent, id-obsessed, Internet-surfing, consumer-driven, sports-crazed society.

This much they can agree on: there is no agreement.

In recent years, with good reason, educators and policy makers have paid particular attention to disadvantaged students who need the most help and resources, introducing such initiatives as the No Child Left Behind Act, which stresses, among other things, measuring progress through testing and standards, and charter schools, which operate independently of traditional school systems. Policy makers and education reformers have offered up other solutions, such as school vouchers, as a way to give students more choice about which school they can attend. Also on the rise are magnet schools that build around a theme, like the sciences or arts, but shy away from selective admissions policies like those at Stuyvesant. And lately, foundations have been pouring money into developing smaller schools. But often overlooked are gifted and talented students.

"They are the forgotten group today," says Dr. Ravitch, the noted education historian.

The sense among many educators and policy makers is that students at schools like Stuyvesant will succeed no matter what, that they are the exception to the rule, a thin layer at the top academic echelon whose experience doesn't apply to the rest of the student population in the United States. Mr. Teitel, Stuyvesant's principal, argues otherwise. The school isn't just the test, he asserts. What makes Stuyvesant great isn't merely its selective admissions policy. Mr. Teitel talks about the importance of maintaining a truly "rigorous curriculum," not just giving lip service to the idea, a policy which he says other schools could heed. "Some schools, what they've done, they've taken a one-year course and in order to get the kids through it, they've stretched it to either a year and a half or two years," he says. "Well, then, it's really not that rigorous. When you say 'rigor,' it means if a course is supposed to be taught in one year, it's taught in one year, that's it. You don't get any extras, folks, put it in there."

Implicit in what Mr. Teitel advocates is a powerful idea that can find a place at other schools: high expectations. They flourish at Stuyvesant. Teachers expect nothing but the best from their students. It's ingrained in the culture. High expectations, Stuyvesant hands like to say, create their own momentum. The school tells the students that they are the best, and then they work hard to make it so. Students at Stuyvesant push each other academically, sometimes to a fault. Indeed, the pressure is enormous, and some students—and parents—take it too far, becoming obsessed with grades to the extent that cheating is widespread, health sacrificed. Other students, recoiling from the pressure, defy school altogether, sometimes finding solace in drugs. But Stuyvesant veterans say there's no motivating force so effective as students who feel good about themselves. A school like Stuyvesant, to be sure, has the luxury of creating such lofty aspirations for its driven students. But for other schools, the attempt to raise expectations would cost nothing.

Stuyvesant benefits from another powerful idea: freedom. Students study on the hallway floors. They hang around school until late in the evening, practicing dances, rehearsing instruments, playing chess, building robots, strumming to their iPods. It's their home, and they are encouraged to make it so. It becomes something more than a forbidding citadel of learning. It becomes a place of exploration, a refuge. Again, at a school like Stuyvesant, creating such a freewheeling atmosphere is easier than for most, especially at a time when mounting concerns about safety and terrorism are making metal detectors a permanent feature at schools everywhere, including Stuyvesant. But for other schools, the attempt to foster a sense of freedom would cost nothing.

At Stuyvesant, there is one other great force, largely unseen but perhaps wielding the greatest influence: parents. They drive cabs. They run delis seven days a week. They are, for the most part, of modest means. And yet, they have spent years equipping their children with a wealth of experience—piano lessons, math camp, computer tutorials—so that by the time they arrive at Stuyvesant as freshmen, they are already ahead of the game. And the parents don't stop there. They get involved. They join various after-school committees. They bake cookies to raise school funds. They e-mail teachers. Their presence is always felt if not always seen, sometimes to an extreme, but they ensure the best for their children. Again, at a school like Stuyvesant, parental involvement is almost a given. But for other schools, the attempt to involve parents more would cost nothing.

The payoff is priceless. Today's Stuyvesant students, like generations before them, will make great breakthroughs in medicine. They will solve mysteries of science. They will travel in space. They will enact laws in the chambers of Congress, build new industries, create lasting literature. You can't see the future, though, at least not by walking the empty halls on a lonely summer day when school is out.

I miss Milo, the ten-year-old unofficial freshman. I miss playing chess with him. He beat me once. I miss playing foosball with him. He beat me every time. He did pretty well in school too, finishing the Stuyvesant term with a 95 in honors trigonometry, a 99 in math research, and a 100 in his speaker-building class for an even 98 overall grade point average. Not bad for a kid who isn't even enrolled in high school yet. (He also received credit for math team class.) As for that statewide math exam, Milo didn't just finish it before any of the other students in the class: he earned a 91. Meanwhile, he and his older sister, Willa, recently took the Stuy test. Reports Milo in an e-mail, "We both thought that it was easy." And they both got in.

I miss Mariya, the sophomore immigrant from Ukraine. I miss lunchtime, sitting on the Wall, talking with Mariya about life and parents and the miseries of chemistry, a class in which, incidentally, she ended up with a final grade of 88. She matched that in her other tough class, computer science, but fared better otherwise with a 92 in Japanese, a 94 in math, a 96 in both English and history, and a 99 in Spanish, finishing the term with a 93.29 average. More than respectable. But her overall average fell from 94.86 the previous semester. "My mom was pretty mad but calmed down when I swore to do better next year," Mariya says. She can comfort herself with this thought: Jarek is still the last living heir of the last Polish knight, and chivalry isn't dead.

I miss Romeo, the junior football captain. I miss our long talks about aspiring to greatness, about the challenges of being biracial, about the question of love and its possibilities. For Romeo, it's all possible. He completed the term with a 95 in biology, a 96 in French, a 97 in both English and differential equations, a 98 in both gym and U.S. history, a 99 in math research, and a 100 in precalculus. That's a cool 97.5 average. And the football team finished the season five and five—an amazing accomplishment for a motley crew of brainiacs. But Romeo didn't win the Intel science contest. It's okay, though. His partner on the project, the aged professor, marches on as of this writing. So does Romeo. On Friday, December 15, 2006, he received one particular e-mail from a certain university: "In making each admission decision, the Committee keeps in mind that the excellence of Harvard College depends most of all on the talent and promise of the people assembled here, particularly our students. In voting to offer you admission, the Committee has demonstrated its firm belief that you can make important contributions during your college years and beyond." Harvard decided early to admit Romeo. So he'll be joining his father in moving to Massachusetts after all. Romeo, though, won't be joining his conscience, Xevion. "As for prom," she writes in an e-mail, "I'll be going with my boyfriend—

and sorry, it's not who you're probably hoping." Romeo is taking his first real girlfriend, Jenny, whom he's been dating for months. Love, after all, is possible.

I miss Jane, the senior struggling with a demon of a drug addiction. She essentially stopped speaking to me after one evening late in the semester when she called my cell phone while I was waiting to board a plane. In a frenzied, nearly incoherent state, she asked to borrow a hundred dollars to pay her drug dealer. I said no. She hung up on me. I tried calling her back. I wanted to explain why, that as a journalist writing about her and the school, I couldn't give her money because it could have potentially cast doubt on the veracity of her story. That as an adult, I couldn't in good conscience lend her money, knowing that it was going to be used for illicit drugs. That as someone who cared, I couldn't give her money that would have contributed to her destructive path. But I never got to tell her any of that. I couldn't get through. When I tried to talk to her in school, she skulked away. When I e-mailed her, she didn't respond. When I called, she didn't return my messages, except once, when she left a happy yet scrambled message for me, the din of loud music and partying in the background. It was difficult to hear what she was saying in the recording. She sounded euphoric. She sounded surrounded by friends. Perhaps it was a sign of change. After the term ended, Jane began attending night school in Maryland to finish her high school diploma. She's even planning to apply to college.

I miss the adults too. Mr. Polazzo is a mere mortal again, sheared of his duties as coordinator of student affairs, even though no one may have been better suited for the job. So dearly did he love the students that he seemed a student himself. But maybe that was the problem. Mr. Teitel had trouble finding a replacement. He said he sought out one candidate, who declined the offer. He then offered the position to another teacher who didn't apply for the job. That teacher agreed but had second thoughts and tried to resign before assuming the job. His resignation wasn't accepted. Two teachers now share the student coordinator duties. So goes high school politics. Mr. Polazzo, meanwhile, holds court from his classroom, where he continues to delight students as a government teacher. For her part, Ms. Lee, the gifted student teacher, is now a full-time teacher at Syosset High, dazzling students there just as she did at Stuyvesant. Mr. Siwanowicz is now substitute-teaching and training teachers to use technology at Bergen County, along with his protector and advocate, Mr. Jaye, who's now director of academy programs there, causing his usual trouble and loving every minute of it. Meanwhile, Ms. Damesek, the assistant principal of organization, remains at Stuyvesant. Some notice a change in her. "She's even got a posse of students who she's adopted and who hang out in her office all the time now," Mr. Grossman, the English chairman, says in an e-mail. "And even though it doesn't often show, she is very sensitive."

It's a funny thing. Stuyvesant, like all high schools, possesses a short, merciless memory. Every year, a senior class departs, and with it goes four years of shared history. It's as if what came before doesn't exist anymore as another class enters, and the cycle begins anew. "It's like you've never been there before," says a wistful senior, Emily Hoffman, on the last day of school before heading off to Yale. "It's the nature of the school. It's a student factory. Everything seemed so monumental. All the drama seemed so important, and no one's going to remember it."

There is only what lies ahead.

Appendix: Notable Alumni

Leo Roon, 1908
Chemist; chief, chemical division, Squibb & Sons; chairman, board of trustees, Columbia College of Pharmacy

Lewis Mumford, 1912
Urban planner; architecture and social critic; author; awarded U.S. Medal of Freedom; made Knight Commander of the British Empire

Charles W. Taussig, 1914 June
Industrialist; member of FDR's New Deal brain trust

Jack Kriendler, 1917 January
Restaurateur; founder and owner of "21" Club

Ray Arcel, 1917
Inducted into International Boxing Hall of Fame; trained twenty world boxing champions including Larry Holmes

James Cagney, 1917 or 1918
Won Academy Award, best actor; awarded American Film Institute's Life Achievement Award; founding member of Screen Actors Guild; named "14th greatest movie star of all time" by *Entertainment Weekly*

Ted Husing, 1919
Sportscaster; largely responsible for play-by-play broadcasting

Marcus Kogel, MD, 1921 June
Founding dean, Albert Einstein College of Medicine

Peter Sammartino, PhD, 1921
Chancellor, Fairleigh Dickinson University; member, President's Commission on Higher Education

Irving Saypol, 1923 January
Attorney and judge; prosecutor in espionage case against Julius and Ethel Rosenberg and Morton Sobell

Sidney Sugarman, 1922
U.S. District Court judge

Herbert Zelenko, 1922
U.S. congressman

Norman C. Armitage (Cohn), PhD, 1923 June
Fencer; member of six U.S. Olympic teams; won Olympic bronze medal

Lt. General Garrison H. Davidson, 1923
Coach, Army football team; superintendent, U.S. Military Academy; commanding general, U.S. Seventh Army and First Army; U.S. military representative to the United Nations

Herbert Tenzer, 1923 June
U.S. congressman; philanthropist

Frank Hussey, believed to have graduated in 1924
Won Olympic gold medal, 400-meter relay—record-setting

Joseph Mankiewicz, 1924
Won four Academy Awards for writing and directing

Sheldon Leonard, 1925
Won Emmy Awards for producing and directing; film and TV actor, director, and producer

John R. Ragazzini, 1927 June
Dean of engineering and science, New York University; participated in Manhattan Project during World War II

Robert Alda, 1930
Actor and entertainer; father of Alan Alda

Gustave J. Dammin, MD, 1930
Professor of pathology, Harvard Medical School; awarded Legion of Merit for research on dysentery in India and Burma; part of team that performed first kidney transplant; conducted important research on Lyme disease; the tick *Ixodes dammini* named after him

Edward V. Kolman, 1931 January
NFL player, Chicago Bears, and coach, New York Giants

Irving V. Glick, MD, 1933 January
Orthopedist and sports medicine pioneer; inducted into International Tennis Hall of Fame

Bernard Meltzer, 1934 June
Radio show host; chairman, Philadelphia Planning Commision

Thomas Macioce, 1935 June
Chief executive officer, Allied Stores; member of the board of trustees, Columbia University

Thelonious Monk, 1935 (did not graduate)
Jazz musician

Albert "Albie" Axelrod, 1938 June
Fencing great; member of five U.S. Olympic teams; Won Olympic bronze medal

Charles W. Dryden, 1938
Commanded the first group of Tuskegee Airmen to engage in aerial combat against Germany; author, *A-Train: Memoirs of a Tuskegee Airman*

Eugene Garfield, 1938
Founder and chairman emeritus, Thompson Scientific

John L. Tatta, 1938
President of Cablevision

Benjamin Rosenthal, 1940 June
U.S. congressman

Joshua Lederberg, PhD, 1941 January
Awarded Nobel Prize for medicine (1958); awarded National Medal of Science (1989); president, Rockefeller University

Marshall Rosenbluth, PhD, 1942 June (year he graduated)
Nuclear scientist; worked on hydrogen bomb project

Jan Merlin, 1942
Won Emmy Award for writing

Art Baer, 1943 June
Won Emmy Award for writing

Rolf W. Landauer, PhD, 1943
Pioneer in computer theory

Samuel P. Huntington, PhD, 1943 June
Political theorist

Robert W. Fogel, PhD, 1944 June
Awarded Nobel Prize in economics (1993)

Howard Cane (Cohen), 1944 January
Actor; played Major Hochstetter on *Hogan's Heroes*

William Greaves, 1944 January
Won Emmy Award for executive producing

Mace Neufeld, 1945 June
Film and TV producer

Otto Eckstein, PhD, 1946
Economist; member, Council of Economic Advisers; economic consultant to President Lyndon Johnson

Albert Shanker, 1946 June
President of the American Federation of Teachers; awarded Presidential Medal of Freedom

David Margolis, 1947
Chairman and chief executive officer, Coltec Industries; board member of NYU Stern School of Business

Hans Mark, PhD, 1947
Chancellor, University of Texas

Ben Gazzara, 1948 (did not graduate)
Actor; Won Emmy Award for acting

Sidney I. Lirtzman, PhD, 1948
President, Baruch College

Sherwood M. Schwarz, 1948
Owner, Toronto Argonauts football team

Elias Stein, 1949 January
Awarded Wolf Prize in mathematics (1999)

Paul J. Cohen, 1950
Mathematician; awarded Fields Medal (1966)

Kenneth H. Keller, PhD, 1952
President, University of Minnesota

Robert Moses, 1952

Civil rights leader; codirector of the Council of Federated Organizations during the Mississippi Freedom Summer in 1964; awarded MacArthur Foundation "genius" grant

Alvin Poussaint, MD, 1952 June

Consultant to Bill Cosby television programs; associate dean of Harvard Medical School

Frank Conroy, 1953

Author, *Body and Soul* and *Stop-Time*

David Durk, 1953

New York police officer; worked with Frank Serpico to reform police department

Neil Grabois, 1953

President, Colgate University

Alan Heim, 1954

Won Academy Award and Emmy Award for film editing

Bernard Nussbaum, 1954

Special counsel to President Bill Clinton

Joe Paletta, 1954

Fencer; member, U.S. Olympic team

Herbert J. Stern, 1954

U.S. District Court judge

Roald Hoffman, PhD, 1955

Awarded Nobel Prize in chemistry (1981)

Edmar Mednis, 1955

Chess grandmaster; first player to beat Bobby Fischer in a U.S. Chess Championship tournament

Saul Katz, 1956
President, New York Mets

Jeffrey Loria, 1957
Florida Marlins owner

Peter Biskind, 1958
Author, *Easy Riders, Raging Bulls*

Richard Ben-Veniste, 1960
Task force leader for Watergate prosecutions; member of 9/11 Commission

Arthur Blank, 1960
Founder of Home Depot; Atlanta Falcons owner

Harvey Pitt, 1961
President of the SEC

Bobby Colomby, 1962
Musician and producer; drummer, Blood, Sweat & Tears

Col. Ron Grabe, 1962
Lead astronaut for development of the International Space Station

Michael Silverstein, PhD, 1962
Professor of anthropology, linguistics, and psychology, University of Chicago; awarded MacArthur Foundation "genius" grant

Richard Axel, 1963
Awarded Nobel Prize in physiology/medicine (2004)

Ron Silver, 1963
Actor, director, producer

Dick Morris, 1964
Political consultant

Robert Siegel, 1964
Host, National Public Radio's *All Things Considered*

Charles Scott, 1964 (did not graduate; left after spring 1963)
Won Olympic gold medal, basketball; NBA guard

Jerrold Nadler, 1965
U.S. Congressman

Walter Becker, 1967
Half of the band Steely Dan; won three Grammys in 2000; inducted into Rock and Roll Hall of Fame (2001)

Chris Albrecht, 1969
Chairman and chief executive officer, HBO

Martin Brest, 1969
Director, *Scent of a Woman*, won Golden Globe for Best Picture; directed *Meet Joe Black*, *Midnight Run*, and *Beverly Hills Cop*

Joseph A. Grundfest, 1969
Professor, Stanford Law School; SEC commissioner and presidential economic adviser

Denny Chin, 1971
U.S. District Court judge

Paul Levitz, 1973
President, DC Comics and *Mad* magazine

Paul Reiser, 1973
Television actor, *Mad About You*

Eric S. Lander, PhD, 1974
Leader, Human Genome Project; Rhodes Scholar

Tim Robbins, 1976
Won Academy Award, best supporting actor

Brian Greene, 1980
Rhodes Scholar; best-selling author, *The Elegant Universe*

Helen Reale, 1980 (née Rochlitzer)
Professional beach volleyball player

Noam Elkies, PhD, 1982
Youngest full-tenured professor at Harvard at the age of 27; won Math Olympiad gold medal

Kate Schellenbach, 1983
Drummer, Beastie Boys

Lucy Liu, 1986
Actor

Gary Shteyngart, 1991
Author, *The Russian Debutante's Handbook*

Source: *Stuyvesant High School: The First 100 Years*; Stuyvesant High School Alumni Association; other historical resources.

Notes

Prologue

2 *How many other high schools:* Stan Teitel, interview with author.

2 Life *magazine once posed:* "Is This the Best High School in America?" *Life,* October 1994.

2 *on the eve of:* Stuyvesant High School, *Indicator,* 1908 yearbook, p. 10.

2 *the nation's estimated 25 percent dropout rate:* U.S. Department of Education, 2006 report.

2 *"We have to sweep them":* Eric Grossman, interview with author.

2 *there are no official class rankings:* Susan E. Meyer, *Stuyvesant High School: The First 100 Years* (New York: The Campaign for Stuyvesant/Alumni[ae] & Friends Endowment Fund Inc., 2005), p. 37.

3 *aristocracy of talent:* Thomas Jefferson, *Autobiography* (1821), reprinted with preface by Philip S. Foner, ed., *Basic Writings of Thomas Jefferson* (Garden City, NY: Halcyon House, 1950), p. 430.

3 *Any eighth- or ninth-grade student:* New York City Department of Education, *The Specialized High Schools Student Handbook,* p. 4.

3 *about 3 percent:* Stuyvesant High School.

4 *loving ode:* Frank McCourt, *Teacher Man* (New York: Scribner, 2005), pp. 183–257.

4 *"it was nerd, nerd, nerd":* Jonathan Lethem, *The Fortress of Solitude* (New York: Vintage Books, 2004), p. 218.

4 *Nearly nine out of ten students:* Nancy Kober, *A Public Education Primer* (Washington, DC: Center on Education Policy, 2006), p. 5.

5 *a century ago:* Meyer, p. 10.

5 *three thousand students:* New York City Department of Education, 2004–2005 Annual School Report, p. 1.

5   *more than half:* Ibid., p. 2.
8   *"The greatness of the school":* Danny Jaye, interview with author.
8   *"Enjoy being a kid again":* Julie Gaynin, yearbook note to author.
8   *"You've continuously asked":* Becky Cooper, yearbook note to author.
9   *"We're a diverse":* Kristen Ng, yearbook note to author.

PART 1: DELANEY CARDS

1. Romeo

13   *It's 7:38 a.m.:* Author observations.
14   *"I do a lot of math":* Romeo Alexander, interview with author.
14   *"Almost nobody on the team":* "Coach Burnett Gets Sacked," *Spectator*, March 9, 2006.
14   *"Nobody really cares":* Romeo Alexander, interview with author.
14   *"We don't really":* Stuyvesant defensive tackle, interview with author.
14   *The moniker comes from:* Russell Shorto, *The Island at the Center of the World* (New York: Doubleday, 2004), p. 147.
15   *His mother, Catherine:* Catherine Wideman, interview with author.
15   *"I was always":* Romeo Alexander, interview with author.
16   *At the age of:* "The Astonishing John Wideman," *Look*, May 21, 1963.
17   *It was at Romeo's age:* "Writer's Son Given Life Term in Death of New York Youth," *New York Times*, October 16, 1988.
17   *"My dad wanted me":* Romeo Alexander, unpublished autobiography, Stuyvesant High School English class assignment, printed with permission.
17   *His father, speaking to:* Charles Alexander, interview with author.
18   *"I was on his case":* Catherine Wideman, interview with author.
18   *"There is a life of the mind":* John Edgar Wideman, interview with author.
18   *"I think a lot about that":* Romeo Alexander, interview with author.
20   *"I'm always telling him":* Xevion Baptiste, interview with author.
20   *"You know as well":* Romeo Alexander, story, Stuyvesant High School English class, printed with permission.
20   *"someone who has a disorder":* Romeo Alexander, interview with author.
20   *It's 8:23 a.m.:* Author observations.

2. The Gauntlet

21   *250 feet:* Meyer, p. 182.
21   *$10 million:* "Feds Probe School Span Pacts," *Newsday*, February 5, 1993.
21   *$150 million edifice:* "Building Flaws Tarnish Stuyvesant's Showcase," *New York Times*, January 28, 1993.
22   *September 9, 1992:* "Finally, a Façade to Fit Stuyvesant," *New York Times*, September 8, 1992.
22   *on a landfill packed:* Meyer, p. 175.

22 *emergency shelter:* "Stuy Reinvented," *Spectator,* Special Stuyvesant Edition, Fall 2001.

22 *twice the height:* "On the Hudson, Launching Minds Instead of Ships," *New York Times,* June 6, 1993.

22 For Knowledge and Wisdom: Stuyvesant High School Alumni Association, www.shsaa.org.

22 *four-minute break:* www.stuy.edu.

23 *450 computers:* Ibid.

23 *"The superintendent":* Stan Teitel, interview with author.

23 *"It's like going to":* Ned Vizzini, *Teen Angst? Naaah* . . . (Minneapolis, MN: Free Spirit Publishing, 2000), pp. 36–37.

23 *"Its architecture":* Karen Cooper, interview with author.

23 *"Pie a Teacher!!!":* School fund-raising flyer.

23 *"pathetic loser":* Student flyer.

24 *"Life has a higher end":* School flyer.

25 *more than two hundred clubs:* Stuyvesant High School, *Comprehensive Educational Plan 2006–2007,* p. 6.

25 *Bookworm:* Stuyvesant High School, *Indicator,* 2006 yearbook, pp. 209–10.

25 *thirty-some student publications:* Stuyvesant High School, *Comprehensive Educational Plan 2006–2007,* p. 6.

25 *existentialism:* Stuyvesant High School.

25 *"The students make":* Namita Biala, interview with author.

25 *about five hundred:* Danny Jaye, interview with author.

25 *two hundred members:* Stuyvesant High School students and faculty, interviews with author.

25 *Stuyvesant produces among:* Stuyvesant High School, *Comprehensive Educational Plan 2006–2007,* p. 6.

25 *on the Preliminary:* http://www.nationalmerit.org.

25 *ninety-nine Stuyvesant students:* 2006 Stuyvesant commencement program.

25 *By comparison:* http://www.nationalmerit.org and "The Hundred Best High Schools in America," *Newsweek,* May 16, 2005.

25 *more than seven hundred:* Meyer, p. 58.

25 *2,800 advanced placement:* Stan Teitel, interview with author.

25 *"qualified" to receive:* The College Board, www.collegeboard.com.

25 *97 percent:* New York City Department of Education, 2004–2005 Annual School Report, p. 9.

26 *only 75 percent:* U.S. Department of Education, 2006 report.

26 *average SAT score is a 691:* Stuyvesant High School, *Comprehensive Educational Plan 2006–2007,* p. 10.

26 *95th percentile:* The College Board, www.collegeboard.com.

26 *average U.S. test scores:* The College Board, press release, August 30, 2005.

26 *enroll in four-year colleges:* Stuyvesant High School, *Comprehensive Educational Plan 2006–2007,* p. 10.

26 *only 67 percent:* U.S. Department of Education, 2006 report.

26 *one in four:* Stan Teitel, interview with author.

26 *Harvard accepts more:* "Putting Dreams to the Test: A Special Report; Elite High School Is a Grueling Exam Away," *New York Times,* April 2, 1998.

26 *to win the Nobel Prize:* http://nobelprize.org.

27 *Eric S. Lander:* "Eric Lander: Unraveling the Threads of Life," *Time,* April 26, 2004.

27 *lead astronaut:* Orbital Sciences Corp, www.orbital.com.

27 *Stuyvesant pennant:* "New York's Stuyvesant High School, a Young Achiever's Dream," *Los Angeles Times,* December 30, 1990. .

27 *For a school:* Stuyvesant High School Alumni Association; Meyer, pp. 200–18.

27 *"I embrace being":* Becky Cooper, interview with author.

27 *"Today, Stuyvesant has":* Conan O'Brien, commencement speech, Stuyvesant High School, 2006.

28 *twenty-six thousand:* Stan Teitel, interview with author.

28 *9 percent:* America's Best Colleges 2007, http://www.usnews.com.

28 *"You could theoretically":* Stan Teitel, interview with author.

28 *150-minute:* New York City Department of Education, *2005–2006 Specialized High Schools Student Handbook,* p. 10.

28 *"There are five bookshelves":* Ibid., p. 17.

29 *"What is the smallest positive":* Ibid., p. 23.

29 *"I don't think":* Alexa Solimano, interview with author.

30 *"I'm going to fail":* Susan Levinson, interview with author.

30 *"Everyone wants to":* Brittany DiSanto, interview with author.

30 *"I like to think":* Andrew Saviano, interview with author.

31 *"It's very competitive":* Kristen Chambers, interview with author.

31 *"Higher score":* advertisement, *Spectator,* June 9, 2006.

31 *"Classes are just taken":* "Religion at Stuy?" *Stuyvesant Standard,* May 24, 2006.

31 *"Stopping Stress":* "Stopping Stress at Stuyvesant," *Stuy Health,* 2006.

31 *"the pressure is crazy":* Student panel member, Parents' Association meeting.

31 *He says that:* Michael Waxman, interview with author.

32 *Her first student:* Eleanor Archie, interview with author.

32 *"It is tempting":* Eric Grossman, graduation speech transcript, 2004.

32 *"I have spoken":* Eleanor Archie, interview with author.

32 *One parent called:* Michael Waxman, interview with author.

33 *"free free free":* Copy of parent letter to teacher, January 9, 2006.

33 *"You can't make":* Michael Waxman, interview with author.

33 *"Being a Stuyvesant Parent":* School Tone Committee meeting handout.

33 *"have a nervous breakdown":* Eleanor Archie, interview with author.

34 *"Methamphetamine is becoming":* Angel Colon, interview with author.

34 *Adderall, a prescription drug:* Stuyvesant students, interviews with author.

34 *According to a recent survey:* "A Survey on Sleep Habits of Students," *Spectator*, January 19, 2006.

34 *recommended for teenagers:* "Adolescent Sleep Needs and Patterns," National Sleep Foundation, 2000.

34 *"students often complain":* "Lack of Sleep," *Stuy Health*, 2006.

3. The Wizard of Oz

35 *Dead of night:* Author observations.

35 *"When you work":* Danny Jaye, interview with author.

36 *It's 4:52:* Author observations.

36 *looms ahead:* Danny Jaye, interview with author.

37 *Tucked in a corner:* Author observations.

37 *He puts it more:* Danny Jaye, interview with author.

37 *largest public education system:* "Bucking School Reform, a Leader Gets Results," *New York Times*, December 4, 2006.

37 *If a student:* Danny Jaye, interview with author.

39 *Edward C. Delaney:* "The Cards That Put Students in Their Place," *New York Times*, September 14, 2003.

39 *The attendance and grade:* Danny Jaye, interview with author.

40 *The book now sits:* Author observations.

40 *"Danny's like a":* Mike Zamansky, interview with author.

40 *garbed more appropriately:* Author observations.

41 *Mr. Jaye is sitting:* Ibid.

42 *lack of a teacher's license:* New York State Education Department, www.highered.nysed.gov.

43 *Putnam Fellowship:* Mathematical Association of America, math.scu.edu.

43 *"He's the smartest":* Author observations.

4. Cuddle Puddle Muddle

45 *Behind closed doors:* Author observations.

45 *"Love and the Ambisexual":* New York, February 6, 2006.

46 *He reads aloud:* Author observations.

46 *A Brooklyn boy:* Stan Teitel, interview with author.

47 *spreads like a virus:* Author observations.

48 *room 640, where:* Ibid.

48 *The author, Alex:* Alex Morris, interview with author.

48 *In class, the journalism:* Author observations.

48 *"it used sensationalism":* Alair, interview with author.

48 *Ms. Morris disputes:* Alex Morris, interview with author.

48 *"It's not soft porn":* Alair, interview with author.

48 *"I know some of them":* Alex Morris, interview with author.

49   *story has legs:* Author observations.

49   *serious tack, dissecting:* "Cuddle Puddle Muddle," *Spectator*, February 16, 2006.

49   *None of which stops:* "Sex, Drugs, and Enticing Jew-Fros," *New York*, April 10, 2006.

49   *chock-full of teenage:* Julia Baskin, Lindsey Newman, Sophie Pollitt-Cohen, and Courtney Toombs, *The Notebook Girls* (New York: Warner Books, 2006).

49   *The topic, for instance:* Author observations.

50   *"check that out":* Honors student, interview with author.

50   *"The Hudson staircase is":* "The Hudson Staircase," *Spectator*, February 2, 2006.

50   *Someone edited out:* Faculty member, interview with author.

50   *as he enters room 615:* Author observations.

51   *97 percent attendance:* Stuyvesant High School, *Comprehensive Educational Plan 2006–2007*, p. 8.

51   *"We don't need":* Author observations.

51   *The Student Union government:* Student Union representatives, interviews with author.

51   *weighed in as well:* "Why Make Us Beg?" *Spectator*, January 19, 2006.

51   *"kind of like prison":* Andrew Saviano, interview with author.

51   *believe a strict:* Students and teachers, interviews with author.

51   *Believed to be forty-one:* public records, Lexis-Nexis database.

52   *Grinch-like:* "Party Policy Challenged," *Spectator*, December 22, 2005.

52   *ripping down a star-studded:* "Not So Welcome: Second Term Senior Signs Removed," *Spectator*, February 2, 2006.

52   *subsequent student editorial:* "Ms. Damesek, Talk to Us," *Spectator*, February 16, 2006.

52   *It hasn't been an easy:* "Stuyvesant Sprouts Six New Heads," *Spectator* Online, http://www.stuyspectator.com, September 10, 2002. See also Clara Hemphill with Pamela Wheaton and Jacqueline Wayans, *New York City's Best Public High Schools* (New York: Teachers College, Columbia University, 2003), p. 92.

52   *From the beginning:* "Students and Assistant Principal Must Work to Mend the Fences," *Spectator* Online, http://www.stuyspectator.com, May 15, 2003.

52   *Her father:* Eric Grossman and Stan Teitel, interviews with author.

52   *clashes with Mr. Jaye:* Eric Grossman and other school faculty, interviews with author.

52   *And even Mr. Teitel:* Stan Teitel, interview with author.

53   *the best intentions:* Eric Grossman, interview with author.

53   *guards her privacy:* Ibid.

53   *Mr. Teitel adds:* Stan Teitel, interview with author.

53   *Arms akimbo:* Author observations and interviews with students.

53 *a discussion of:* Author observations.

53 *Some students will tap:* Stuyvesant students and faculty, interviews with author.

53 *A front-page article:* "Students Cheat on Math Final, Sun Continues to Rise and Set," *The Broken Elevator,* June 2003.

54 *mainstream reading:* School Leadership Team committee meeting handout.

54 *"I was told":* Author observations.

54 *"It's more acute":* Ibid.

54 *at a subsequent:* Student panel members, Parents' Association meeting.

54 *Usually, teachers:* Stuyvesant teachers, interviews with author.

55 *sing the contract:* Matt Polazzo, interview with author.

55 *A service that's gaining:* "The Twists and Turns of Turnitin," *Spectator,* February 16, 2006; "High Tech War against Plagiarism Is Coming to New York Schools," *New York Sun,* March 2, 2006.

55 *hawkers pass out:* business card advertisements.

55 *A recent Stuyvesant graduate:* "Confessions of SAT Test Faker," *New York Post,* May 14, 2006.

55 *The intricacies of cheating:* Author observations.

5. Jane's Addiction

57 *"My hobby is":* Jane, a Stuyvesant senior, interview with author.

60 *Violence of any:* New York City Department of Education, 2004–2005 Annual School Report, p. 2.

60 *Suspensions are:* Ibid.

60 *"silly things":* Eleanor Archie, interview with author.

60 *a couple of years:* "Easy Buy at Stuy 'High': Top Kids Running an Open Drug Mart," *New York Post,* December 12, 2004.

60 *"If you have a calc":* Johnathan Khusid, interview with author.

60 *Demonstrating.pot's:* Sixteen-year-old Stuyvesant student, interview with author.

61 *"the amount of":* Jane, interview with author.

61 *"I didn't want":* Eric Grossman, interview with author.

61 *They met in:* Jane, interview with author.

62 *calls that elusive:* Eric Grossman, interview with author.

62 *"I wish to bestow":* Jane's unpublished poetry, printed with permission.

63 *"The only thing":* Jane, interview with author.

6. Open House

65 *stalks the escalators:* Author observations.

65 *Last Saturday:* Romeo Alexander, interview with author.

66 *Nearly thirty years:* "Cortines Has Plan to Coach Minorities into Top Schools," *New York Times,* March 18, 1995.

66 *even though nearly:* "More Minority Students Enter Elite Schools," *New York Times*, May 8, 1997.

66 *"The racial demographics":* Jonathan Kozol, *The Shame of the Nation* (New York: Crown Publishers, 2005), p. 140.

66 *"As educators":* "Cortines Has Plan to Coach Minorities Into Top Schools."

66 *"I see that":* Romeo Alexander, interview with author.

67 *"I wanted to prove":* Catherine Wideman, interview with author.

67 *5.5 percent by 1997:* "More Minority Students Enter Elite Schools," *New York Times*, May 8, 1997.

67 *more than 70 percent:* Kozol, p. 140.

67 *only 2.2 percent:* "In Elite Schools, a Dip in Blacks and Hispanics," *New York Times*, August 18, 2006.

67 *down from 4.3 percent:* "Cortines Has Plan to Coach Minorities into Top Schools."

67 *to 3 percent:* New York City Department of Education, 2004–2005 Annual School Report, p. 2.

67 *dipped from 40 percent:* "Cortines Has Plan to Coach Minorities into Top Schools."

67 *to about 39 percent:* New York City Department of Education, 2004–2005 Annual School Report, p. 2.

67 *half of Stuyvesant:* "Cortines Has Plan to Coach Minorities into Top Schools."

67 *about 55 percent:* New York City Department of Education, 2004–2005 Annual School Report, p. 2.

67 *Specialized High Schools Institute:* Eleanor Archie, interview with author.

68 *"disadvantaged" students:* New York City Department of Education, *The Specialized High Schools Student Handbook*, p. 14.

68 *As many as:* Eleanor Archie, interview with author.

68 *"more proactive outreach":* School Leadership Team committee meeting handout.

68 *the author writes:* "In Elite Schools, a Dip in Blacks and Hispanics."

68 *Policy makers and others:* Policy makers, educators, and others, interviews with author.

69 *"There's so much more":* Eleanor Archie, interview with author.

69 *glaringly obvious:* Author observations.

69 *"Race is part of":* Matt Polazzo, interview with author.

69 *Predominantly white seniors:* Stuyvesant students, author interviews, and author observations.

69 *"We were told":* "Outcast by Design," *Stuyvesant Standard*, May 24, 2006.

69 *About ten feet away:* Stuyvesant students, author interviews, and author observations.

70 *"it's cool":* Samantha Whitmore, interview with author.

70 *The others who:* Stuyvesant students, author interviews, and author observations.

70 *"The school is":* Kieren James-Lubin, interview with author.
70 *When an Eastern:* Stuyvesant student, interview with author.
70 *A Korean girl:* Stuyvesant student, interview with author.
70 *An Indian freshman:* Eleanor Archie, interview with author.
70 *"I think we self-segregate":* Liana-Marie Lien, interview with author.
70 *"At Stuy, it seems":* "Diversity Week," *Spectator,* March 9, 2006.
71 *"Get your diversity on":* School flyer.
71 *"I try not to":* Stuyvesant junior, interview with author.
71 *"Have you ever":* Black Students League flyer.
71 *One out of five:* Stuyvesant High School, *The Case for Stuyvesant High School,* 2003. See also "Seeking the American Dream," *Spectator,* May 24, 2006.
71 *That explains why:* Stuyvesant students, interviews with author, and Stuyvesant High School, *Indicator,* 2005.
71 *"They came here":* Katherine Kim, interview with author.
72 *At the threshold:* Author observations.
72 *"They're all crazy":* Michael Son, interview with author.
73 *"When I saw the view":* Daniel Alzugaray, interview with author.
73 *fifty-nine languages:* " 'Do You Speak Stuyvesantian?' " *Spectator,* April 12, 2006.
73 *The staccato:* Stuyvesant students, interviews with author, and author observations.
73 *17 percent:* New York City Department of Education, 2004–2005 Annual School Report, p. 2.
73 *visible signs:* Author observations.
73 *"Please understand my":* Student handout.
74 *an event in:* Author observations.
74 *"Only in New York":* Stuyvesant teacher, interview with author.
74 *packing the auditorium:* Author observations.
74 *"I've never seen":* Stan Teitel, Stuyvesant Open House address.

7. Like a Polaroid

75 *the telltale signs:* Author observations.
75 *Named after a:* Milo Beckman and Emily Shapiro, interviews with author.
76 *"I remember feeling":* Milo Beckman, interview with author.
76 *"It's not like":* Emily Shapiro, interview with author.
76 *"Dad said I":* Milo Beckman, interview with author.
76 *"I couldn't get":* Eric Beckman, interview with author.
77 *"A four-year-old":* Tim Novikoff, interview with author.
77 *"I used to drag":* Emily Shapiro, interview with author.
77 *the next level:* Tim Novikoff, interview with author.
77 *started taking classes:* Milo Beckman and Emily Shapiro, interviews with author.

78   *"Only when she":* Milo Beckman, interview with author.

78   *"It's a mixed":* Emily Shapiro, interview with author.

78   *"like name-calling":* Milo Beckman, interview with author.

78   *"He didn't ask":* Emily Shapiro, interview with author.

79   *was heartbroken when:* Tim Novikoff, interview with author.

79   *"with kids my age":* Milo Beckman, interview with author.

80   *"I stopped caring":* Jan Siwanowicz, interview with author.

80   *which requires a:* New York State Education Department, www.highered.nysed.gov.

80   *He only has:* Jan Siwanowicz, interview with author.

81   *"saving his life":* Danny Jaye, interview with author.

81   *once remarked:* Tim Novikoff, interview with author.

8. Sing!

83   *Problems are escalating:* Author observations.

83   *"When you're dealing":* Xevion Baptiste, interview with author.

84   *biggest events:* Stuyvesant High School faculty and students, interviews with author.

84   *generating a whopping:* Matt Polazzo, interview with author.

84   *"The perfect school":* Danny Jaye, interview with author.

85   *with a budget of:* Stan Teitel, interview with author.

85   *"scary skinny":* Eric Grossman, interview with author.

86   *"If the seniors":* Liz London, interview with author.

86   *According to school:* Meyer, p. 87.

86   *Seniors have never taken:* Stuyvesant students, interviews with author.

87   *"We're definitely":* Liam Ahern, interview with author.

87   *"I caved":* Xevion Baptiste, interview with author.

87   *Confidence is at:* Stuyvesant students, interviews with author, and author observations.

87   *"We have some":* Taylor Shung, interview with author.

9. The Natural

89   *Outside, it's:* Author observations.

90   *"I never saw":* Jennifer Lee, interview with author.

90   *"You come to a point":* Jim Cocoros, interview with author.

91   *Some parents and:* Stuyvesant parents and teachers, interviews with author.

91   *Teachers looking to:* Sol Stern, *Breaking Free: Public School Lessons and the Imperative of School Choice* (San Francisco: Encounter Books, 2003), p. 68.

91   *"I'll be honest":* Stan Teitel, interview with author.

91   *"teachers told me":* Matt Polazzo, interview with author.

91   *"dirty little secret":* Stern, p. 68.

91 *"Incompetence was"*: Ibid., p. 81.

91 *"With a few notable"*: The Teaching Commission, *Teaching at Risk: Progress & Potholes*, Spring 2006, p. 16.

91 *In the mid-1990s:* Stern, p. 77.

92 *"Integration transfers frequently"*: Ibid., p. 74.

92 *Recent changes in:* "The UFT Agreement," *New York Sun*, October 4, 2005. See also "Bloomy & UFT: It's a Deal! 15% Pay Hike, Longer Hours for Teachers," *New York Daily News*, October 4, 2005; "Guide to UFT Contract Changes," New York City Board of Education memo, November 29, 2006.

92 *"We're still dealing"*: Danny Jaye, interview with author.

92 *"The most difficult"*: Eric Grossman, interview with author.

92 *about $72,000:* Stan Teitel, interview with author.

92 *the best include:* Stuyvesant students and faculty, interviews with author.

93 *longest-tenured:* Stan Teitel, interview with author.

93 *"Why are we"*: Author observations.

93 *"She'll probably forget"*: Sammy Sussman, interview with author.

94 *"He was lured"*: Jennifer Lee, interview with author.

PART 2: DETENTION

10. Lost in Gatsby

99 *"All these people"*: Romeo Alexander, interview with author.

100 *"Gatsby is incredibly"*: Author observations.

101 *"I have my"*: Romeo Alexander, interview with author.

101 *she wanders into:* Author observations.

102 *"I just wanted:* Xevion Baptiste, interview with author.

102 *on his hands:* Author observations.

102 *"What were they"*: Jan Siwanowicz, interview with author.

103 *In a meeting:* Danny Jaye, interview with author.

104 *full battle mode:* Author observations.

104 *But after her latest:* Jane, interview with author.

105 *A day later:* Author observations.

105 *"This is huge"*: David A. Stein Riverdale/Kingsbridge Academy sophomore, interview with author.

105 *"Stuyvesant kids are"*: David A. Stein Riverdale/Kingsbridge Academy senior, interview with author.

105 *Many other schools:* School officials, educators, and others, interviews with author.

106 *annual list:* "2006 America's Best High Schools: The Top 100 and the 'Public Elites,'" *Newsweek*, May 8, 2006. p. 54.

106 *impressive 1344:* Gretchen Whitney High School, School Accountability Report Card Reported for School Year 2002–2003, p. 13.

106 *"We make no"*: Patricia Hager, interview with author.

106 *averaged 1270:* New Trier High School New Trier High School 2006–2007 Profile, pamphlet, p. 2.

107 *Long after the last:* Author observations.

107 *With a strong:* New Trier High School teachers, and administrators, interviews with author.

107 *"We do an excellent":* Debra L. Stacey, interview with author.

107 *"This is New Trier's":* Jan Borja, interview with author.

107 *"It's so smart":* Cara Harshman, interview with author.

107 *solid 1236 average:* Lowell High School 2002–2003 Profile, fact sheet, p. 2.

107 *"critical not only":* Paul Cheng, interview with author.

108 *score well exceeded:* http://www.prepreview.com.

108 *"the kids are there":* Evan M. Glazer, interview with author.

108 *She attended a:* Lisa Ha, interview with author.

108 *a strong 1290:* Hemphill, p. 119.

108 *seven Nobel Prize:* http://bxscience.edu.

108 *"We make do":* Lisa Ha, interview with author.

109 *For one, the freshman:* Jerry Wang, interview with author.

109 *overriding feature:* Author observations.

109 *"It's so stressful":* Gui Bessa, interview with author.

109 *"You put it":* Alexa Solimano, interview with author.

110 *"Terrible":* Gui Bessa, interview with author.

11. Great Expectations

111 *who broods:* Author observations.

111 *"It's sort of dead":* Mariya Goldman, interview with author.

112 *"It has come to":* Copy of Mariya's petition.

113 *"It's sort of ridiculous":* Mariya Goldman, interview with author.

113 *"I dream about":* Yelena Goldman, interview with author.

114 *part of a growing:* Stuyvesant High School faculty members, interviews with author.

114 *"If you don't help":* Author observations.

114 *Down the hall:* Ibid.

114 *"It was kind of a drag":* Milo Beckman, interview with author.

115 *only about 70 percent:* "Public High School Graduation and College-Readiness Rates: 1991–2002," Manhattan Institute for Policy Research, February 2005.

115 *In an April:* "Dropout Nation," *Time,* April 17, 2006.

115 *At about the same:* *The Silent Epidemic: Perspectives on High School Dropouts,* Bill & Melinda Gates Foundation, March 2006.

116 *or technical training:* U.S. Department of Education, 2006 fact sheet.

116 *For instance, in science:* U.S. Department of Education, 2006 report.

116 *U.S. eighth graders:* Trends in International Mathematics and Science study, 2003.

116 *"Our superiority was":* "Is America Flunking Science?" *Time,* February 13, 2006.

116 *"no measurable":* Trends in International Mathematics and Science study, 2003.

116 *Things don't improve:* U.S. Department of Education, 2006 report.

117 *"No one really":* Tom Loveless, interview with author.

117 *Other experts:* Educators, policy makers, and others, interviews with author.

117 *"The problem we":* Stan Teitel, interview with author.

117 *"Unless we start":* The Teaching Commission, p. 11.

118 *on the third floor:* Author observations.

118 *"Sing! is in":* Liz Livingstone, interview with author.

118 *"It's not good":* Alexa Solimano, interview with author.

118 *"We might have":* Erica Sands, interview with author.

119 *The question puts:* Author observations.

119 *It's no accident:* Ibid.

12. The Real World

121 *students are discussing:* Author observations.

122 *He's all business:* Eric Grossman, interview with author.

122 *in which the last-hired:* The United Federation of Teachers contract.

122 *"Fair?":* Eric Grossman, interview with author.

123 *"I get a sense":* Jane, interview with author.

123 *"aromatic amnesia":* Jane's unpublished poetry, printed with permission.

124 *"I've seen this":* Eric Grossman, interview with author.

124 *Its relationship with:* Stuyvesant senior, interview with author.

124 *"Instead of being":* Copy of students' letter to the New York City Department of Education.

125 *The object of the:* Author observations.

125 *Mr. Teitel proved his:* Stan Teitel, interview with author.

126 *pair of handcuffs:* Ibid.

126 *assistant principal of biology:* "Two Teachers at Stuyvesant Suspended after Accusations by Students of Misconduct," *New York Times,* September 23, 1999.

126 *After a newly initiated:* Stan Teitel, interview with author.

126 *always on the go:* Jennifer Lee, interview with author.

129 *Sitting at his cluttered:* Danny Jaye, interview with author.

130 *"Why do people":* Author observations.

130 *at a round:* Ibid.

131 *"Several times":* Jan Siwanowicz, interview with author.

131   *"It's a horrible":* Alexa Solimano, interview with author.
131   *"It's pretty hectic":* Ben Alter, interview with author.
131   *"You never know":* Liam Ahern, interview with author.
132   *"If we don't win":* Molly Ruben-Long, interview with author.
132   *"I'm worried about":* Author observations.
133   *"I think he needs":* Xevion Baptiste, interview with author.

13. Protests and Demands

135   *Thursday night:* Author observations.
135   *"My thing was":* Marty Davis, interview with author.
135   *"Oh, that worked":* Author observations.
136   *"Everybody has":* Marty Davis, interview with author.
136   *"I've gained so":* Katie Johnston-Davis, interview with author.
136   *"There's never been":* Marty Davis, interview with author.
136   *"You're so cheesy":* Author observations.
136   *"The Stuyvesant she":* Marty Davis, interview with author.
136   *In the beginning:* Landmarks Preservation Commission records, May 20, 1997,
        p. 1. See also http://www.stuy.edu; Stuyvesant High School, *Indicator*, 1905
        yearbook, pp. 11–19.
136   *Peter Stuyvesant:* Henry H. Kessler and Eugene Rachlis, *Peter Stuyvesant and
        His New York* (New York: Random House, 1959), p. 37.
136   *college dropout:* Shorto, p. 149.
137   *a tremendous swamp:* Philip M. Scandura, interview with author.
137   *A five-story:* Landmarks Preservation Commission records, May 20, 1997.
137   *In a ceremony:* Meyer, p. 10.
137   *fewer than 7 percent:* Education Week staff, *Lessons of a Century: A Nation's
        Schools Come of Age* (Bethesda, MD: Editorial Projects in Education, 2000),
        p. 12.
137   *Most people with:* Diane Ravitch, interview with author.
137   *"Now we are a nation":* Stuyvesant High School, *Indicator*, 1905 yearbook,
        p. 12.
138   *more than 70:* Diane Ravitch, *Left Back: A Century of Battles over School
        Reform* (New York: Touchstone, 2000), p. 56.
138   *"The island was just":* Philip M. Scandura, interview with author.
138   *Manhattan also teemed:* Ibid. See also Jacob A. Riis, *How the Other Half Lives*
        (New York: Charles Scribner's Sons, 1890; repr., New York: Penguin Books,
        1997); Luc Sante, *Low Life: Lures and Snares of Old New York* (New York:
        Farrar, Straus and Giroux, 1991).
138   *where traditional academics:* Stuyvesant High School, *Indicator*, 1905 year-
        book, p. 18.
138   *"The city boy":* Ibid., p. 17.

139 *With rising enrollment:* Landmarks Preservation Commission records, May 20, 1997, p. 5.

139 *exam in 1934:* Meyer, pp. 25–26.

139 *The first entrance: Stuyvesant High School Parent Handbook* (New York: Stuyvesant Parents' Association), p. 28.

139 *Not until the:* Meyer, p. 27.

139 *"It was a period":* Diane Ravitch, interview with author.

139 *In response, Stuyvesant:* "How Gotham's Elite High Schools Escaped the Leveller's Ax," *City Journal,* Spring 1999.

140 *As a compromise:* Abstract, *New York Times,* May 20, 1971.

140 *The controversy flared:* Meyer, p. 27. See also "HS Admission Biased—Study Sez Many Denied Key Prep Course," *New York Daily News,* May 8, 1997.

140 *The activists, known:* "Secret Apartheid II," Association of Community Organizations for Reform Now, 1997.

140 *In a statement:* "HS Admission Biased—Study Sez Many Denied Key Prep Course."

140 *"There's a difference":* Stan Teitel, interview with author.

141 *"Gifted children":* Danny Jaye, interview with author.

142 *"Where they came":* Eleanor Archie, interview with author.

142 *"being at Stuy":* Matt Polazzo, interview with author.

142 *"With less pressure":* Mariya Goldman, interview with author.

142 *Unlike Stuyvesant:* Natasha Borchakovskaia, interview with author.

142 *"Everyone here is":* Xevion Baptiste, interview with author.

142 *"Stuy kids":* Elaine Liu, interview with author.

143 *"I guess it's not":* Rosabella Magat, interview with author.

143 *"In the back":* Francisco Bencosme, interview with author.

144 *"the yeast that":* Diane Ravitch, interview with author.

144 *"It's elitist":* Thomas Toch, interview with author.

144 *"I've crossed them":* Katie Johnston-Davis, interview with author.

144 *"In the end":* Marty Davis, interview with author.

14. Grief Virus

145 *gifted piano:* "Thruway Horror—Tanker Crash Kills 4 in QNS. Kids' 'Y' Van," *New York Post,* March 18, 2006.

145 *"Good-bye, Daddy":* "Van in Twist of Fate; Thruway Trucker Missed CB Alarm for Swim Moms' Vehicle," *New York Post,* March 19, 2006.

145 *At about 7 a.m.:* "Thruway Tragedy Kills 4, 3 Kids & Woman Die in Crash on Way to YMCA Meet," *New York Daily News,* March 18, 2006.

146 *"Get over!":* "His Warning Came Too Late," *New York Daily News,* March 19, 2006.

146 *about sixty feet:* "Thruway Tragedy Kills 4, 3 Kids & Woman Die in Crash on Way to YMCA Meet."

146 *In the sudden:* "A Dad's Agonizing News; Father Tells Injured Son His Sister Was Killed in Crash That Also Left 3 Others Dead and His Mom Hospitalized," *Newsday*, March 19, 2006.

146 *Kevin dies there:* "His Warning Came Too Late."

146 *"I have lost":* "Thruway Tragedy Kills 4, 3 Kids & Woman Die in Crash on Way to YMCA Meet."

146 *Police do not:* "His Warning Came Too Late"; "Thruway Tragedy Kills 4, 3 Kids & Woman Die in Crash on Way to YMCA Meet."

146 *Word of the tragedy:* Stuyvesant students, interviews with author, and author observations. See also "Two Stuy Students Killed in Tragic Car Accident," *Spectator*, March 29, 2006; "Students Cope with Loss," *Spectator*, March 29, 2006.

146 *Namita can't stop:* Namita Biala, interview with author.

146 *"That could've been":* Alex Larson, interview with author.

147 *the principal cannot:* Stan Teitel, interview with author.

147 *In the chaos:* "An Administration in Crisis," *Spectator*, Special Stuyvesant Edition, Fall 2001.

147 *"They saw this":* Stan Teitel, interview with author.

148 *many students returned:* "Anxieties over Toxins Rise at Ground Zero," *USA Today*, February 7, 2002.

148 *The last class:* "Dread of the Class, 9-11 Casts Shadow on Seniors at Elite Stuyvesant High School Then Now," *New York Daily News*, March 7, 2005.

148 *a big gaping:* Author observations. See also "Attack Location Remains an Open Wound," *Weekend Australian,* September 9, 2006; "The Long and Winding Road to Rebuilding Ground Zero," *Agence France-Presse*, September 3, 2006.

148 *American spectacle:* "Discord Delays Ground Zero Rebirth; After Half a Decade, the Site Remains Largely a Hole in the Ground," *USA Today*, September 6, 2006.

148 *"This was different":* Stan Teitel, interview with author.

148 *Several students straggle:* Author observations.

149 *during seventh period:* Ibid.

150 *The principal consulted:* Stan Teitel, interview with author.

150 *By eighth period:* Matt Polazzo, interview with author.

150 *"We're not as ready":* Olga Safronova, interview with author.

150 *mayhem on the:* Author observations.

151 *"Our Sing! is about":* Sophomore singer, interview with author.

151 *changed some of the:* Taylor Shung, interview with author.

151 *"It didn't seem":* Alexa Solimano, interview with author.

151 *At 5:41, the thirty-fourth:* Author observations.

152 *"Pretty smooth":* Richard Geller, interview with author.

152 *juniors take the stage:* Author observations.

153 *"The juniors are going":* Matt Polazzo, interview with author.

153 *no hard feelings:* Author observations.

153 *Chelsea Piers:* Author observations.

154 *"Here, he's a kid":* Gil Rubin, interview with author.

154 *During a break, Milo:* Author observations.

155 *"That'll keep me":* Milo Beckman, interview with author.

155 *In Queens the following day:* "Family's Goodbye for Crash Victims Is Rooted in Ritual," *New York Times,* March 25, 2006.

155 *attendance scanners arrive:* "Long-Anticipated ID Scanners Installed," *Spectator,* March 29, 2006.

155 *Sing! reaches a crescendo:* Author observations.

156 *Later, it comes out:* "Sing! Scores," *Spectator,* March 29, 2006.

156 *at Sing! drunk:* "Sing! Judges Inebriated," *Spectator,* March 29, 2006.

156 *By the following:* Students, interviews with author, and author observations.

15. Polazzo's Time

157 *In a cluttered cubbyhole:* Author observations.

157 *"He's a kid":* a Stuyvesant junior, interview with author.

158 *"I'm trying to convince":* Matt Polazzo, interview with author.

158 *Student Union office:* Author observations.

158 *"The kids are really":* Matt Polazzo, interview with author.

158 *Not all of them:* Author observations.

159 *The principal has indicated:* Stan Teitel, interview with author.

159 *The thought of being:* Matt Polazzo, interview with author.

159 *"I'm freaking":* Xevion Baptiste, interview with author.

160 *"I bet Xevion":* Romeo Alexander, interview with author.

160 *"I'm going to win":* Author observations.

160 *"He's playing":* Xevion Baptiste, interview with author.

160 *Romeo plans a:* Romeo Alexander, interview with author.

160 *Xevion, rising from:* Xevion Baptiste, interview with author.

160 *Romeo calmly explains:* Romeo Alexander, interview with author.

161 *"It's all about":* Reyna Ramirez, interview with author.

161 *"I wasn't going":* Danielle Fernandes, interview with author.

161 *is animated:* Author observations.

162 *He's ranting about:* Danny Jaye, interview with author.

162 *producing a copy:* Copy of student letter to principal.

162 *"We're looking to":* Copy of Eddie Wong letter.

163 *Mr. Jaye suspects:* Danny Jaye, interview with author and author observations.

163 *Milo's mother:* Emily Shapiro, interview with author.

164 *"copping out":* Danny Jaye, interview with author.

164   *a Buddhist monk:* "Teenager Killed in Thruway Accident Is Buried," *Associated Press*, March 31, 2006. See also "Last Teary Farewell to Swim Team Teen, 'A 15-Year-Old Shouldn't Be Burying Her Friends,'" *New York Daily News*, April 1, 2006.

16. Hell's Kitchen

165   *On the first:* Author observations.
165   *But Jane isn't:* Jane, interview with author.
166   *"simple reduction":* Jane's unpublished poetry, printed with permission.
167   *"No one can":* Jane, interview with author.
167   *intervened about a:* Eric Grossman, interview with author.
168   *Parents have called:* Stan Teitel, interview with author.
168   *In the meantime:* Eric Grossman, interview with author.
168   *begin agitating:* Students, interview with author. See also http://www.stuycom.net.
169   *gets the message:* Ibid.; Stan Teitel, interview with author; also "Scanners Here to Stay," *Spectator*, April 12, 2006.
169   *"It seems like":* Nathan Buch, http://www.stuycom.net.
169   *"All in all":* "What's Up with Those Scanners?," *S.U. Newsletter!*, April 11, 2006.
169   *own nightmare:* Mariya Goldman, interview with author.
170   *There they grab:* Author observations.
170   *Mariya wonders:* Mariya Goldman, interview with author.
171   *After school:* Author observations.
171   *A block away:* Ibid.
171   *great consternation:* Milo Beckman, interview with author.
171   *"Global warming may":* "What's With the Weather?," *234 Latte*, issue 3.
172   *A ponytailed girl:* Author observations.
172   *"That's how old":* Milo Beckman, interview with author.
172   *Against a muslin-draped:* Author observations.
172   *unconsciously rotates:* Milo Beckman, interview with author.
172   *When he returns:* Author observations.

17. The Contest

175   *On a drizzling:* Author observations.
175   *"I don't normally":* Danny Zhu, interview with author.
176   *Minutes before:* Author observations.
176   *"I already have":* Stan Teitel, interview with author.
176   *"This is football":* Danny Jaye, interview with author.
176   *He entered his:* Jie Zhang, interview with author.
177   *Danny can't explain:* Danny Zhu, interview with author.

177 *"He came in"*: Danny Jaye, interview with author.

177 *11:19 a.m.*: Author observations.

178 *"In its own"*: Danny Jaye, interview with author.

178 *retire to the:* Author observations.

179 *"Tired"*: Danny Zhu, interview with author.

179 *It happens with:* Milo Beckman, interview with author.

179 *That night:* Stan Teitel, interview with author. See also "Susan Biering, Biology Teacher, Passes Away," *Spectator,* April 12, 2006.

180 *Ms. Biering is buried:* "Susan Biering, Biology Teacher, Passes Away."

180 *state of sorrow:* Author observations.

181 *Ms. Lee feels:* Jennifer Lee, interview with author.

182 *is surrendering:* Romeo Alexander, interview with author.

183 *her eyes lift:* Catherine Wideman, interview with author.

183 *"I've always felt"*: Romeo Alexander, interview with author.

PART 3: SENIORITIS

18. Zero Tolerance

187 *At one end:* Author observations.

188 *particularly daft:* Kristen Ng, interview with author.

188 *"Only in school"*: Matt Polazzo, interview with author.

188 *while student leaders:* Students, interviews with author. See also "COSA Up for Reappointment," *Spectator,* May 4, 2006.

188 *"It's all a war"*: Matt Polazzo, interview with author.

188 *The mayor introduced:* New York City government, press release, April 13, 2006. See also "Students to Get No Warning Before Searches," *New York Times,* April 14, 2006.

188 *About 20 percent:* "Students to Get No Warning Before Searches."

188 *illegal weapons:* New York City government, press release, April 13, 2006.

188 *violent crime has dropped:* Ibid.

189 *The rate of violent:* U.S. Department of Justice, press release, November 20, 2005.

189 *students are more likely:* National Education Association, www.nea.org.

189 *The school reported:* New York City Department of Education, 2004–2005 Annual School Report, p. 2.

189 *"We don't have"*: Matt Polazzo, interview with author.

189 *"They all know"*: Eric Grossman, interview with author.

189 *In a follow-up letter:* Copy of principal's letter to parents.

189 *"I resisted"*: Stan Teitel, interview with author.

190 *students are posting:* Student flyer.

190 *a formal warning:* School notice.

191 *"You're going to stab"*: Nathan Buch, interview with author.

191 *"Of all the schools"*: Molly Ruben-Long, interview with author.

191	*"It's the questing"*: Author observations.

193	*Upstairs, in room 401:* Ibid.

194	*To recall the last:* Jan Siwanowicz, interview with author.

195	*almost on tiptoes:* Author observations.

19. College Night

197	*perched alone atop:* Author observations.

197	*John F. Kennedy:* Edward Klein, *The Kennedy Curse* (New York: St. Martin's Press, 2003), p. 148.

197	*"Competition":* Romeo Alexander, interview with author.

198	*Senior Deke Hill:* Author observations.

198	*"This is not your":* Deke Hill, interview with author.

199	*They're all here:* Author observations.

199	*"Throughout the night":* "College Acceptance, The Other Way Around," *Spectator,* May 4, 2006.

200	*A boy who:* Author observations.

200	*The average tuition:* The College Board, press release, October 24, 2006.

200	*Between 1984 and 1994:* National Center for Education Statistics.

200	*about a quarter:* Stan Teitel, Interview with author.

200	*room 511 is virtually:* Author observations.

200	*"You know you're":* Babson College pamphlet.

201	*"We'd love to get":* Babson College recruiter, interview with author.

201	*Harvard isn't giving:* Author observations.

202	*"The pursuit of excellence":* Harvard College pamphlet.

202	*"We know Stuyvesant":* Author observations.

202	*"It was nothing":* Romeo Alexander, interview with author.

202	*Deke, the senior, leaves:* Deke Hill, interview with author.

20. Peter Pan Tilts

205	*the little man-child:* Author observations.

205	*"It's not usually":* Milo Beckman, interview with author.

205	*his desk, over which:* Author observations.

206	*"I always have trouble":* Milo Beckman, interview with author.

206	*wanders over to:* Author observations.

206	*"Milo knows everything":* Willa Beckman, interview with author.

207	*By now, Milo:* Author observations.

207	*The following morning:* Danny Jaye, interview with author.

208	*The principal knows:* Stan Teitel, interview with author.

208	*"His inability to control":* Danny Jaye, interview with author.

209	*When the phone rings:* Author observations.

209	*That afternoon, Mariya:* Ibid.

210 *"really cool":* Mariya Goldman, interview with author.
210 *As is the sign:* Author observations.
210 *"I haven't been telling":* Mariya Goldman, interview with author.
210 *marveling at her daughter:* Yelena Goldman, interview with author.
210 *"My mother always":* Mariya Goldman, interview with author.
210 *Mrs. Goldman corrects:* Yelena Goldman, interview with author.
210 *"I wanted to be like":* Mariya Goldman, interview with author.
211 *At parent-teacher conferences:* Yelena Goldman, interview with author.
211 *discounted her own:* Mariya Goldman, interview with author.
211 *"I was happy":* Yelena Goldman, interview with author.
211 *"If I can be similar":* Mariya Goldman, interview with author.
211 *The next day, Thursday:* "COSA Up for Reappointment," *Spectator,* May 4, 2006.
211 *accompanying editorial:* "A Fight for the Crusader," *Spectator,* May 4, 2006.
211 *around the corner:* Author observations.

21. Neutral Ground

213 *seems to float:* Author observations.
213 *"I wouldn't trade":* Jan Siwanowicz, interview with author.
215 *a warm Saturday:* Author observations.
215 *He did a month:* Mike, interview with author.
215 *pounding pavement:* Author observations.
216 *he's scared:* Eric Grossman, interview with author.
216 *she can't shake:* Jane, interview with author.
216 *with a lesson:* Eric Grossman, interview with author.
216 *Tony Montana flavor:* Author observations.
216 *particular vantage point:* Jane, interview with author.
217 *Until now:* Author observations.
218 *"I think life is so":* Jane, interview with author.
218 *his own fate:* Author observations.
218 *"I kind of took":* Matt Polazzo, interview with author.
218 *"Like when the":* Author observations.
218 *"Ever since I arrived":* Copy of Matt Polazzo's application.
218 *"This is the worst":* Author observations.
218 *"Whenever a student":* Matt Polazzo, interview with author.
219 *Teitel barges:* Author observations.
219 *Friday, May 12:* Jennifer Lee, interview with author.

22. Love Notes

221 *on a quiet patch:* Author observations.
221 *harried few days:* Matt Polazzo, interview with author.
222 *A gaggle of girls:* Author observations.

222 *primitive state:* Author observations.
223 *the mother hen:* Matt Polazzo, interview with author.
223 *When it's dark:* Author observations.
223 *"I can't wait until":* Taylor Shung, interview with author.
223 *growing up faster:* Author observations.
224 *another transmutation:* Ibid.
224 *"Ultimately, what it's":* Eric Grossman, interview with author.
224 *the dreaded affliction:* http://en.wikipedia.org.
224 *a cautionary note:* Stuyvesant and college postings.
225 *Around the corner:* Author observations.
225 *School lore has it:* Students and teachers, author interviews.
225 *over-the-top crush:* Author observations.
225 *"There's no accounting":* Matt Polazzo, interview with author.
225 *here at the wall:* Author observations.
226 *"It's a cause":* Jonathan Edelman, interview with author.
226 *after school today:* Students, interviews with author. See also "Student Leaders Oppose New COSA Applicants," *Spectator*, May 24, 2006.
226 *just finished performing:* Elisa Lee, interview with author.
226 *pull of narcotics:* Elisa Lee's unpublished monologue, printed with permission.
227 *But Jane hasn't stopped:* Jane, interview with author.

23. The Players

229 *No one can stop:* Author observations.
230 *climbs into a harness:* Author observations.
230 *"They're bigger, blacker":* Stuyvesant running back, interview with author.
230 *Romeo says nothing:* Author observations.
230 *He's used to:* Romeo Alexander, interview with author.
231 *"He likes to see":* Ibid.
232 *hunched in his:* Author observations.
232 *"profanity, defamation":* Stuyvesant High School Board of Elections, *Official Rules and Regulations for the Spring 2006 Student Union Elections*.
232 *"It's to level":* Jamie Paul, interview with author.
232 *"The Asians are":* Matt Polazzo, interview with author.
233 *"Asian-white pair":* Amanda Wallace, interview with author.
233 *"definitely a factor":* Matt Polazzo, interview with author.
233 *"We're two white kids":* Marta Bralic, interview with author.
233 *going against the grain:* Matt Polazzo, interview with author.
233 *half Thai and half Filipino:* Student e-mail to author.
233 *who is half Asian:* Ibid.
233 *"IN THE PAST":* Campaign pamphlet.
234 *Not even a third:* "The Ideal Democracy," *Spectator*, May 24, 2006.

234 *"arguably the best"*: Suh Films, letter to Stuyvesant students and parents, May 1, 2006.

234 *his own accounts*: Dick Morris, *Behind the Oval Office: Winning the Presidency in the Nineties* (New York: Random House, 1997), p. 44.

234 *"struggle endures"*: Campaign poster.

234 *world-weariness*: Author observations.

234 *Mariya met a boy*: Mariya Goldman, interview with author.

235 *"Dear Mariya, Mount Holyoke"*: Mount Holyoke College e-mail.

236 *From Marist College*: Marist College e-mail.

236 *And another*: Oxford College of Emory University e-mail.

236 *"Every week, I throw"*: Mariya Goldman, interview with author.

24. The Human Element

237 *It's 8:58 a.m.*: Author observations.

237 *his mind racing*: Romeo Alexander, interview with author.

238 *"Of course, I have to"*: Paul Garabedian, interview with author.

238 *seems to become aware*: Author observations.

239 *"The point is to keep"*: Paul Garabedian, interview with author.

239 *"I'm going to go"*: Milo Beckman, interview with author.

239 *undulating dock*: Author observations.

240 *"was really stupid"*: Milo Beckman, interview with author.

241 *On Tuesday*: Author observations.

241 *"I have all these"*: Eric Grossman, interview with author.

242 *her own heartbreak*: Jennifer Lee, interview with author.

25. The Last Dance

247 *It's a strange*: Author observations.

248 *"They're attached by"*: Harvey Blumm, interview with author.

248 *That includes two*: Author observations.

248 *"Some of them"*: Michael Zaytsev, interview with author.

248 *One of the smaller*: Author observations.

248 *Upstairs in his office*: Ibid.

248 *School officials have*: Danny Jaye, interview with author.

249 *pokes his head*: Author observations.

249 *"The fourth floor"*: Danny Jaye, interview with author.

249 *most telling sign*: Author observations.

249 *"I've spent a little"*: Danny Jaye, interview with author.

250 *familiar pose*: Author observations.

250 *It started off*: Stuyvesant student leaders, interviews with author. See also "Stuyvesant Leaders Oppose New COSA Applicants."

250 *In a subsequent*: "A Mishandled Controversy," *Spectator*, June 9, 2006.

250 *prompting Mr. Teitel:* Andrew Saviano, interview with author.

250 *"I am sorry":* Stan Teitel, letter to Stuyvesant community, June 9, 2006.

251 *"I formally and":* Junior class president, letter.

251 *growing perception:* School administrators, interviews with author.

251 *decide his fate:* Author observations.

251 *"It was pretty":* Matt Polazzo, interview with author.

252 *barges back into:* Author observations.

252 *"It's so gorgeous":* Siyu "Daisy" Duan, interview with author.

252 *Upstairs, in the:* Author observations.

252 *"There'll be a lot":* James Lonardo, interview with author.

252 *Momentum builds:* Author observations.

253 *"My mom forbid":* Nameeta Kamath, interview with author.

253 *cleans up well:* Author observations.

253 *"I don't understand":* Stan Teitel, interview with author.

253 *Deke, for his:* Deke Hill, interview with author.

254 *It's 9:33 p.m.:* Author observations.

254 *"I don't know":* Katie Johnston-Davis, interview with author.

254 *Not for Jane:* Author observations.

254 *"I brought my":* Andrew Saviano, interview with author.

255 *By 12:37 a.m.:* Author observations.

255 *The election board:* Matt Polazzo, interview with author.

26. The Final Days

257 *Monday, June 12:* Author observations.

257 *"I'm scared because":* Mariya Goldman, interview with author.

257 *At six foot five:* Author observations.

258 *"She studies too":* Jarek Lupinski, interview with author.

258 *"I don't study":* Mariya Goldman, interview with author.

258 *A left on:* Author observations.

258 *when he met:* Jarek Lupinski, interview with author.

259 *Mariya will be:* Mariya Goldman, interview with author.

259 *holding hands as they rise:* Author observations.

259 *The last bell:* Ibid.

259 *"There's not many":* Robert Sandler, interview with author.

260 *At the moment:* Author observations.

260 *"I'm still in":* Romeo Alexander, interview with author.

260 *frenzied sound of:* Author observations.

260 *"I just tell":* Romeo Alexander, interview with author.

260 *strong undertow of:* Author observations.

260 *"I should be":* Romeo Alexander, interview with author.

261 *The phone rings:* Author observations.

261 *steps out of:* Ibid.
261 *"There's nothing hard":* Milo Beckman, interview with author.
262 *He enters Stuyvesant:* Author observations.
263 *"It was really easy":* Milo Beckman, interview with author.
263 *On Monday, June 26:* Author observations.
265 *Around this time:* Matt Polazzo, interview with author.
266 *Not that the decision:* Stan Teitel, interview with author.
266 *One by one:* Author observations.
266 *The following day:* Ibid.
266 *On her last day:* Jennifer Lee, interview with author.
267 *Mr. Jaye isn't:* Author observations.
268 *Yesterday he went:* Danny Jaye, interview with author.
269 *drops by:* Author observations.
270 *doesn't mention Jane:* Eric Grossman, interview with author.
270 *What Mr. Grossman:* Author observations.
270 *his own heartbreak:* Danny Jaye, interview with author.
270 *What Mr. Jaye says:* Author observations.

Epilogue

272 *Jeffersonian notion:* Jefferson, p. 430.
272 *"Educators decided":* Jay Mathews, interview with author.
272 *"It's politically incorrect":* Tom Loveless, interview with author.
272 *"The greatest force":* Jay Mathews, interview with author.
272 *"Based on students'":* Chester E. Finn Jr., interview with author.
273 *"Only one in three":* "A Report on the High School Reform Movement," Education Sector, March 2006.
273 *"At the high school":* Thomas Toch, interview with author.
273 *a dizzying array:* Educators and policy makers, interviews with author.
274 *"They are the forgotten":* Diane Ravitch, interview with author.
274 *The sense among:* Educators and policy makers, interviews with author.
274 *argues otherwise:* Stan Teitel, interview with author.
274 *They flourish:* Stuyvesant administrators, parents, and students, interviews with author.
275 *I miss Milo:* Milo Beckman and Emily Shapiro, interviews with author.
276 *I miss Mariya:* Mariya Goldman, interview with author.
276 *I miss Romeo:* Romeo Alexander, interview with author.
276 *"In making each":* Copy of Harvard College letter to Romeo Alexander, December 15, 2006.
276 *joining his conscience:* Xevion Baptiste e-mail to author.
277 *After the term ended:* Stuyvesant teacher, interview with author.
277 *trouble finding a replacement:* Stan Teitel, interview with author.

277 *That teacher agreed:* Copy of resignation letter to Stan Teitel and interviews with school faculty.

277 *For her part:* Jennifer Lee, interview with author.

278 *director of academy programs:* Danny Jaye, interview with author.

278 *"She's even got":* Eric Grossman e-mail to author.

278 *"It's like you've":* Emily Hoffman, interview with author.

Selected Bibliography

Arak, Jonathan. *Cracking the New York City Specialized High Schools Admissions Test*. New York: Random House, 2003.

Baskin, Julia, Lindsey Newman, Sophie Pollitt-Cohen, and Courtney Toombs. *The Notebook Girls*. New York: Warner Books, 2006.

Bissinger, H. G. *Friday Night Lights: A Town, a Team, and a Dream*. Cambridge, MA: Da Capo Press, 2004.

Boynton, Robert S. *The New New Journalism: Conversations with America's Best Nonfiction Writers on Their Craft*. New York: Vintage Books, 2005.

Bridgeland, John M., John J. Dilulio Jr., and Karen Burke Morison. *The Silent Epidemic: Perspectives of High School Dropouts*. Bill & Melinda Gates Foundation, March 2006.

Cagney, James. *Cagney by Cagney*. Garden City, NY: Doubleday, 1976.

Dostoyevsky, Fyodor. *Crime and Punishment*. Trans. David McDuff. London: Penguin Books, 1991.

Education Week staff. *Lessons of a Century: A Nation's Schools Come of Age*. Bethesda, MD: Editorial Projects in Education, 2000.

Fitzgerald, F. Scott. *The Great Gatsby*. New York: Scribner, 1925.

Freedman, Samuel G. *Small Victories: The Real World of a Teacher, Her Students, and Their High School*. New York: Harper Perennial, 1990.

Golden, Daniel. *The Price of Admission: How America's Ruling Class Buys Its Way into Elite Colleges—and Who Gets Left Outside the Gates*. New York: Crown Publishers, 2006.

Hemphill, Clara, with Pamela Wheaton and Jacqueline Wayans. *New York City's Best Public High Schools*. New York: Teachers College, Columbia University, 2003.

Humes, Edward. *School of Dreams: Making the Grade at a Top American High School*. New York: A Harvest Book, 2003.

Jefferson, Thomas. *Thomas Jefferson: Autobiography*. 1821. In *Basic Writings of Thomas Jefferson*, edited by Philip S. Foner. Garden City, NY: Halcyon House, 1950.

Jerald, Craig D. *Measured Progress: A Report on the High School Reform Movement*. Washington, DC: Education Sector, 2006.

Kessler, Henry H., and Eugene Rachlis. *Peter Stuyvesant and His New York*. New York: Random House, 1959.

Klein, Edward. *The Kennedy Curse*. New York: St. Martin's Press, 2003.

Kober, Nancy. *A Public Education Primer*. Washington, DC: Center on Education Policy, 2006.

Kouwenhoven, John A. *The Columbia Historical Portrait of New York*. New York: Icon Editions, Harper & Row, 1972.

Kozol, Jonathan. *The Shame of the Nation: The Restoration of Apartheid Schooling in America*. New York: Crown Publishers, 2005.

Landmarks Preservation Commission. Archival records, Designation list 20, LP-1958. May 20, 1997.

Lethem, Jonathan. *The Fortress of Solitude*. New York: Vintage Books, 2004.

Maran, Meredith. *Class Dismissed: A Year in the Life of an American High School, a Glimpse into the Heart of a Nation*. New York: St. Martin's Griffin, 2000.

McCabe, John. *Cagney*. New York: Alfred A. Knopf, 1997.

McCourt, Frank. *Teacher Man*. New York: Scribner, 2005.

Meyer, Susan E. *Stuyvesant High School: The First 100 Years*. New York: Campaign for Stuyvesant/Alumni(ae) & Friends Endowment Fund, 2005.

Miller, Donald L. *Lewis Mumford: A Life*. New York: Weidenfeld & Nicolson, 1989.

Morris, Dick. *Behind the Oval Office: Winning the Presidency in the Nineties*. New York: Random House, 1997.

Mumford, Lewis. *Sketches from Life*. New York: Dial Press, 1982.

———. *My Works and Days: A Personal Chronicle*. New York: Harcourt Brace Jovanovich, 1979.

New York City Board of Education. *Stuyvesant High School Course Guide.* 2002–2003.

New York City Department of Education. *The Specialized High Schools Student Handbook.* 2005–2006.

———. 2004–2005 Annual School Report. 2006.

Ravitch, Diane. *The Great School Wars: A History of the New York City Public Schools.* Baltimore: Johns Hopkins University Press, 2000.

———. *Left Back: A Century of Battles over School Reform.* New York: Touchstone, 2000.

Riis, Jacob A. *How the Other Half Lives: Studies among the Tenements of New York.* New York: Charles Scribner's Sons, 1890. Repr., New York: Penguin Books, 1997.

Robbins, Alexandra. *The Overachievers: The Secret Lives of Driven Kids.* New York: Hyperion, 2006.

Sante, Luc. *Low Life: Lures and Snares of Old New York.* New York: Farrar, Straus and Giroux, 1991.

Shorto, Russell. *The Island at the Center of the World.* New York: Doubleday, 2004.

Sittenfeld, Curtis. *Prep.* New York: Random House, 2005.

Stern, Sol. *Breaking Free: Public School Lessons and the Imperative of School Choice.* San Francisco: Encounter Books, 2003.

Stuyvesant High School. *The Case for Stuyvesant High School.* 2003.

———. *Indicator.* 1905 yearbook.

———. *Indicator.* 1908 yearbook.

———. *Indicator.* 1985 yearbook.

———. *Indicator.* 2005 yearbook.

———. *Indicator.* 2006 yearbook.

———. *The Spectator,* Special Stuyvesant Edition. Fall 2001.

Teaching Commission. *Teaching at Risk: Progress & Potholes.* New York: The Teaching Commission, Spring 2006.

Vizzini, Ned. *Teen Angst? Naaah.* . . . Minneapolis, MN: Free Spirit Publishing, 2000.

Acknowledgments

Thank you, Stuyvesant High School. Once upon a time, you gave me my first kiss. You gave me my first heartbreak. You gave me the inspiration to write. And you welcomed me back, as if I'd never left, more than twenty years later, so that I could take one last test: to write this book. Now I want to give back. I am donating a portion of my royalties from this book to Stuyvesant, designating the money for the school newspaper, the *Spectator*, which helped give me my start in journalism way back when. I will also donate copies of this book for school fund-raising purposes. It's the least I can do. I received a free high school education at Stuyvesant—twice.

I want to thank Stan Teitel, Stuyvesant's principal, a good and kind man who had the wisdom and foresight to give students and teachers— and this writer—the freedom to grow and learn.

I want to thank Romeo Alexander, for his dreams of greatness and sense of great responsibility; Milo Beckman, for his sublime ability to retain the purity of his childhood even while he surpasses adults in intellect; Mariya Goldman, for choosing love over grades; Jane, for trying to overcome her addiction and recognizing the beauty in poetry; Danny Jaye, for being an expert troublemaker in the name of helping students; Jennifer Lee, for her uncommon grace under great expectations; Matt

Polazzo, for being an overgrown kid because that's what the kids needed; and Jan Siwanowicz, for finding daily sustenance in the undiluted world of teenagers.

For sharing their lives, hopes, and fears, I want to thank all of the other Stuyvesant students, an incredible array of talent, including Liam Ahern; Karim Ahmed; Alair; Ben Alter; Daniel Alzugaray; Atrish Bagchi; Xevion Baptiste; Lucy Baranyuk; Eleonora Bershadskaya; Gui Bessa; Namita Biala; Nikki Bogopolskaya; Guergana Borissova; Marta Bralic; Nathan Buch; Allie Caccamo; Kristen Chambers; Lauren Chan; Vanessa Charubhumi; Abraham Chien; Yun-ke Chin-Lee; Becky Cooper; Brittany DiSanto; Siyu "Daisy" Duan; Jonathan Edelman; Cat Emil; Rachel Ensign; Danielle Fernandes; Zach Frankel; Hannah Freiman; Julie Gaynin; Lauren Gonzalez; Emma Gorin; Deke Hill; Emily Hoffman; Lingji Hon; Jackie Hsieh; Kieren James-Lubin; Katie Johnston-Davis; Talia Kagan; Nameeta Kamath; Tina Khiani; Johnathan Khusid; Katherine Kim; Samantha Krug; Fadi Laham; Alex Larsen; Elisa Lee; Stacey Lee; Eileen LeGuillou; Susan Levinson; Amy Li; Sandy Liang; Liana-Marie Lien; Liz Livingstone; Richard Lo; Liz London; Jarek Lupinski; Yasha Magarik; Wyndam Makowsky; Eli Mlyn; Mariana Muravitsky; Ada Ng; Kristen Ng; Jamie Paul; Reyna Ramirez; Molly Ruben-Long; Anna Rubin; Olga Safronova; Erica Sands; Maria Santos; Stella Savarimuthu; Andrew Saviano; Alex Schleider; Alix Schneider; Taylor Shung; Paul Silverman; Alexa Solimano; Suman Som; Naomi Sosner; Sammy Sussman; John Taylor; Dylan Tramontin; Rukshan Uddin; Amanda Wallace; Anna Weissman; Samantha Whitmore; Barbara Yang; Michael Zaytsev; and Danny Zhu.

For making this a better book, I am also grateful to the quiet heroes of Stuyvesant—a remarkable collection of teachers, administrators, and staff—as well as Stuyvesant friends and family members, educational and other authorities, and students, teachers, and administrators from other schools, including Charles Alexander; Eleanor Archie; Christopher Asch; Eric Beckman; Willa Beckman; Francisco Bencosme; Laura Blair Bertani; Roz Bierig; Harvey Blumm; Vito Bonsignore; Natasha Borchakovskaia; Jan Borja; Paul Cheng; Robert Y. R. Chung; Jim Cocoros; Angel Colon; Karen Cooper; Michael Cooper; Randi Damesek; Marty Davis; Warren Donin; Lynne Evans; Maryann Ferrara; Chester E. Finn Jr.; Donna

Fiscina; Paul Flaig; Katherine Fletcher; Erika Frankel; Paul Garabedian; Richard Geller; Evan M. Glazer; Yelena Goldman; Eric Grossman; Lisa Ha; Patricia Hager; Holly Hall; Cara Harshman; Ashvin Jaishankar; Gary Jaye; Barbara Johnston; Susan Kalish; Wendy Keyes; Elaine Liu; James Lonardo; Marie Lorenzo; Tom Loveless; Rosabella Magat; Melissa McDermott; Kelly McMahon; Susan E. Meyer; Emily Moore; Alex Morris; Philip Mott; Tim Novikoff; Oana Pascu; Mary Patchell; Bonnie Pizzarelli; Diane Ravitch; Gil Rubin; Brian Sacks; Deno Saclarides; Robert Sandler; Philip M. Scandura; Joy Schimmel; Emily Shapiro; Julie Sheinman; Lisa Shuman; Michael Son; Debra L. Stacey; Caroline Suh; Jennifer Suri; Annie Thoms; Thomas Toch; Jerry Wang; Michael Waxman; Jonathan Weil; Raymond Wheeler; Catherine and John Edgar Wideman; Bruce Winokur; Eddie Wong; Mike Zamansky; and Jie Zhang.

For their support from beginning to end, a special thanks goes to the Stuyvesant High School Alumni Association, including Henry Grossberg, Sari Halper Dickson, and Tara Regist-Tomlinson.

I am thankful to my gifted research assistants for all of their contributions to the book: Ellen Herman, a Georgetown University undergraduate; Jean Hwang, an English master's degree student, also at Georgetown; and Danielle Ulman, who is earning a master's degree in journalism from the University of Maryland.

To my former Georgetown University students, I appreciate all the advice during my time last year at Stuyvesant. Thank you, Lizette Baghdadi; Nicholas Barnicle; Brittany Bassett; Michael Birrer; Katherine Boyle; Geoffrey Greene; Catherine Kelley; Amy Koizim; Elizabeth Lee; Margaret Lenahan; Christina Livadiotis; Kurt McLeod; Regina Moore; Matthew Nemeth; Alison Noelker; Jessica Rettig; Leila Sidawy; and Christine Strait. I would also like to thank my Georgetown students from last semester, who always reminded me of the compassion needed in a project like this, including Jessica Bachman; John Burke; Esha Chhabra; Luann Dallojacono; Erin Delmore; Ben Fierberg; Chantal Grinderslev; David Loebsack; Kate Moody; Claudia Naim; Meghan Orie; Michael Schlembach; Rebecca Sinderbrand; Mary Katherine Stump; and Jane Yu.

Esther Newberg is simply the best literary agent in the business. Thank you, Esther, for truly understanding an author's passion.

Bob Bender, my editor at Simon & Schuster, is a writer's dream. Thank you, Bob, for bringing great wisdom, a gentle but clear vision, and perfect understanding to the project. Thanks also to Peg Haller, Amber L. Husbands, Johanna Li, David Rosenthal, and Brian Ulicky. I want to acknowledge the Smith Richardson Foundation for its generous support and Mark Steinmeyer in particular for helping to identify several important issues of education and public policy relevant to this project. Thanks also to the Education Writers Association, especially Lisa Walker, and the Reporters Committee for Freedom of the Press for their assistance.

At the *Washington Post*, the best of all newspapers, I want to thank the leadership of Phil Bennett, Len Downie, Jill Dutt, Don Graham, Greg Schneider, and Sandy Sugawara for supporting me in the pursuit of this project. Thanks also to Alice Crites, Eric Lieberman, Jay Mathews, Larry Roberts, and Griff Witte for their keen insights. And to Andrea Caumont and Henry Wytko for helping to point me in the right direction.

Thanks also to Dan Golden of the *Wall Street Journal*, Cindy Hanson, and Doris and Sorin Iarovici for their sage suggestions to improve the manuscript. And to Barbara Feinman Todd of Georgetown University for her wise counsel throughout. Additional thanks to Kathy Temple, also of Georgetown, American University's Rose Ann Robertson, and Penny Bender Fuchs and Steve Crane, both of the University of Maryland, for their help.

I will always cherish my old Stuyvesant friends who made high school a magical time, so much so that I wanted to return to the place more than two decades later: Sorin and Laura and James and James and Jeff and Jeff and Stephen and Bram and Jessica and David and David and Sam and Lenny and Jason and all the rest of the motley crew. Thanks also to my old Stuyvesant teachers, whom I never got to thank, especially Dr. Bindman and Mr. McCourt for encouraging me to get into this cockamamie business of writing. And to Ron Cancemi, not just a school counselor but a true friend even now in memory.

Special gratitude goes to my family for their unconditional support, especially my sister Kathy Goodnough, a great roommate and sounding board during my time in New York while I was researching Stuyvesant into the small hours of the morning. Also to my father, Edward Klein, for teaching me the eternal lessons of good and right journalism. To my mother, Emiko Goodnough, sister Karen Hirsch, and brother-in-law, Steven Hirsch, for listening to my rants as I tried to swim through a sea of information and find my way to the heart of the story. And to Dolores Barrett, Bob Goodnough, and the rest of the extended family. Thanks also to the wonderful Chicago clan for their unwavering support: Eileen Graziano; Frida and Jim Graziano; Alexis, Mia, Nicholas, Paul, and Julie Graziano; J. P. Graziano; and Ann-Marie, Joe, J. P., and Reilly Hayes.

The greatest thanks of all belongs to my wife, Julie-Ann, and to my daughter, Ryan Isabella, in whose names and for whom I do everything.

About the Author

Alec Klein is an award-winning journalist and author. His first book, *Stealing Time: Steve Case, Jerry Levin, and the Collapse of AOL Time Warner*, was an acclaimed national bestseller that was translated into Japanese and Chinese, excerpted in Great Britain, and hailed by the *New York Times* as "vivid and harrowing" and a "compelling parable of greed and power and hubris."

For nearly twenty years, Klein has worked as a newspaper reporter, starting at the *Virginian-Pilot* covering education before moving on to the *Baltimore Sun*, the *Wall Street Journal*, and the *Washington Post*, where for the past seven years he has been a staff writer. Klein's investigations have led to significant reforms, congressional hearings, federal law, millions in government fines, and criminal convictions. He has won numerous national journalism awards.

Klein, a frequent guest speaker on various writing, media, education, and business issues, teaches journalism at Georgetown University and conducts workshops throughout the country on investigative reporting.

Klein is also a playwright, novelist, and Phi Beta Kappa graduate of Brown University. Born in Sleepy Hollow, New York, and raised in New York City, he is the son of an American journalist and a Japanese artist. He lives in Washington, D.C., with his wife, Julie-Ann, and their daughter, Ryan Isabella.